Entrepreneurship and Innovation Policy and the Economy 2

Entrepreneurship and Innovation Policy and the Economy 2

Edited by
Benjamin Jones and Josh Lerner

The University of Chicago Press
Chicago and London

NBER Entrepreneurship and Innovation Policy and the Economy, Number 2, 2023

Published annually by The University of Chicago Press.
www.journals.uchicago.edu/EIPE

Subscriptions: For individual and institutional subscription rates, visit www.journals .uchicago.edu, email subscriptions@press.uchicago.edu, or call (877) 705-1878 (US) or (773) 753-3347 (international). Free or deeply discounted institutional access is available in most developing nations through the Chicago Emerging Nations Initiative www.journals .uchicago.edu/inst/ceni).

Please direct subscription inquiries to Subscription Fulfillment, 1427 E. 60th Street, Chicago, IL 60637-2902. Telephone: (773) 753-3347 or toll free in the United States and Canada (877) 705-1878. Fax: (773) 753-0811 or toll-free (877) 705-1879. E-mail: subscriptions @press.uchicago.edu.

Standing orders: To place a standing order for this book series, please address your request to The University of Chicago Press, Chicago Distribution Center, Attn. Standing Orders/Customer Service, 11030 S. Langley Avenue, Chicago, IL 60628. Telephone toll free in the U.S. and Canada: 1-800-621-2736; or 1-773-702-7000. Fax toll free in the U.S. and Canada: 1-800-621-8476; or 1-773-702-7212.

Single-copy orders: In the U.S., Canada, and the rest of the world, order from your local bookseller or direct from The University of Chicago Press, Chicago Distribution Center, 11030 S. Langley Avenue, Chicago, IL 60628. Telephone toll free in the U.S. and Canada: 1-800-621-2736; or 1-773-702-7000. Fax toll free in the U.S. and Canada: 1-800-621-8476; or 1-773-702-7212. In the U.K. and Europe, order from your local bookseller or direct from The University of Chicago Press, c/o John Wiley Ltd. Distribution Center, 1 Oldlands Way, Bognor Regis, West Sussex PO22 9SA, UK. Telephone 01243 779777 or Fax 01243 820250. E-mail: cs-books@wiley.co.uk.

The University of Chicago Press offers bulk discounts on individual titles to Corporate, Premium and Gift accounts. For information, please write to Sales Department—Special Sales, The University of Chicago Press, 1427 E. 60th Street, Chicago, IL 60637 USA or telephone 1-773-702-7723.

This book was printed and bound in the United States of America.

ISSN: 2771-1668
E-ISSN: 2771-1676
ISBN-13: 978-0-226-82829-9 (pb.:alk.paper)
ISBN-13: 978-0-226-82830-5 (e-book)

Relation of the Directors to the Work and Publications of the NBER

1. The object of the NBER is to ascertain and present to the economics profession, and to the public more generally, important economic facts and their interpretation in a scientific manner without policy recommendations. The Board of Directors is charged with the responsibility of ensuring that the work of the NBER is carried on in strict conformity with this object.

2. The President shall establish an internal review process to ensure that book manuscripts proposed for publication DO NOT contain policy recommendations. This shall apply both to the proceedings of conferences and to manuscripts by a single author or by one or more coauthors but shall not apply to authors of comments at NBER conferences who are not NBER affiliates.

3. No book manuscript reporting research shall be published by the NBER until the President has sent to each member of the Board a notice that a manuscript is recommended for publication and that in the President's opinion it is suitable for publication in accordance with the above principles of the NBER. Such notification will include a table of contents and an abstract or summary of the manuscript's content, a list of contributors if applicable, and a response form for use by Directors who desire a copy of the manuscript for review. Each manuscript shall contain a summary drawing attention to the nature and treatment of the problem studied and the main conclusions reached.

4. No volume shall be published until forty-five days have elapsed from the above notification of intention to publish it. During this period a copy shall be sent to any Director requesting it, and if any Director objects to publication on the grounds that the manuscript contains policy recommendations, the objection will be presented to the author(s) or editor(s). In case of dispute, all members of the Board shall be notified,

and the President shall appoint an ad hoc committee of the Board to decide the matter; thirty days additional shall be granted for this purpose.

5. The President shall present annually to the Board a report describing the internal manuscript review process, any objections made by Directors before publication or by anyone after publication, any disputes about such matters, and how they were handled.

6. Publications of the NBER issued for informational purposes concerning the work of the Bureau, or issued to inform the public of the activities at the Bureau, including but not limited to the NBER Digest and Reporter, shall be consistent with the object stated in paragraph 1. They shall contain a specific disclaimer noting that they have not passed through the review procedures required in this resolution. The Executive Committee of the Board is charged with the review of all such publications from time to time.

7. NBER working papers and manuscripts distributed on the Bureau's web site are not deemed to be publications for the purpose of this resolution, but they shall be consistent with the object stated in paragraph 1. Working papers shall contain a specific disclaimer noting that they have not passed through the review procedures required in this resolution. The NBER's web site shall contain a similar disclaimer. The President shall establish an internal review process to ensure that the working papers and the web site do not contain policy recommendations, and shall report annually to the Board on this process and any concerns raised in connection with it.

8. Unless otherwise determined by the Board or exempted by the terms of paragraphs 6 and 7, a copy of this resolution shall be printed in each NBER publication as described in paragraph 2 above.

Contents

Acknowledgments

This volume was made possible by a generous grant from the Ewing Marion Kauffman Foundation. The foundation has been a critical source of support for the NBER's research activities on entrepreneurship and innovation for nearly 2 decades, and it has played a key part in advancing research on these issues. We would also like to thank Helena Fitz-Patrick for assistance in the editorial process and for her key role in shepherding the papers toward final publication, Jim Poterba for his ongoing support for this conference series, and Rob Shannon for his usual expertise and organizational acumen in overseeing the logistical details, invitations, and operational aspects of the Washington meeting.

Entrepreneurship and Innovation Policy and the Economy, volume 2, 2023.

Introduction

Benjamin Jones, *Northwestern University and NBER,* United States of America
Josh Lerner, *Harvard University and NBER,* United States of America

This volume is the second installment in the National Bureau of Economic Research (NBER) *Entrepreneurship and Innovation Policy and the Economy* (EIPE) series. Entrepreneurship and innovation are widely recognized as key drivers of economic dynamics and long-term prosperity, including rising wages and improved human health. The EIPE series draws together leading researchers to review, synthesize, and communicate key findings about the drivers and implications of entrepreneurial and innovative activity across the economy. The EIPE meeting and volume acts as a bridge between public policy and research. In addition to communicating key research insights into the policy sphere and public square, our goal is to further stimulate research by exposing researchers to the issues, goals, and constraints that policy makers face.

This year's meeting was held in a hybrid format in May 2022, with the in-person meeting in Washington, DC. The six contributions, collected in this volume, all address critical innovation issues. The first two chapters focus on special challenges associated with pharmaceuticals, including vaccine innovation and generic drugs. The second pair of chapters focuses on climate change and clean technologies, including the role of venture capital and start-ups in driving green technological advance and the role of corporate governance in incentivizing clean innovation in public firms. The final chapters address equity issues in innovation, focusing on regional inequality in innovation investment in the United States and the constraints in accessing financial markets for Black-owned businesses.

Entrepreneurship and Innovation Policy and the Economy, volume 2, 2023.

Collectively, these chapters draw out lessons from recent research in economics and related fields that can help shape key policy questions and direct future research into entrepreneurship and innovation.

In "Accelerating Vaccine Innovation for Emerging Infectious Diseases via Parallel Discovery," Joseph Barberio and coauthors explore substantial incentive challenges associated with developing vaccines against future pandemics. They highlight that pharmaceutical firms have relatively weak incentives to develop vaccines against prospective diseases. Vaccines are expensive to develop, the investments are risky, and the expected returns are frequently modest because, unlike medicines for regular and high-incidence health challenges such as cancer or heart disease, the potential pandemic often does not materialize and the revenues from vaccine sales may be limited.

The authors consider whether a portfolio approach could be a powerful way to finance vaccine research. In particular, a number of promising drug candidates could be financed through a vehicle that pays off if any (or multiple) of the candidates yield profits. This kind of "megafund" has been applied to diseases outside the vaccine space. The paper applies this investment idea to mRNA vaccines and undertakes a variety of simulations, using plausible assumptions. The simulations suggest that although pooling investments is more attractive than financing each vaccine project individually, the pooled financing vehicle in the vaccine context will still not be sufficiently attractive to financially motivated investors. The authors thus conclude that without government support, these projects will not be undertaken.

In "The Generic Drug Trilemma," Daniel Hemel and Lisa Ouellette focus on generic pharmaceuticals. Traditional economic reasoning suggests that the expiration of a patent—entrance to the "patent afterlife," in the authors' evocative phrase—should result in a competitive market, with businesses providing the formerly patented product at prices close to costs and the market being served in an efficient manner. As the authors point out, however, the patent afterlife often does not run smoothly in the context of generic drugs. For example, there are numerous instances of enormous price increases appearing among generic products. In addition, there can be shortages of key medicines, which can be surprisingly persistent.

The authors locate these challenges in a "trilemma" based on trade-offs between quality, price, and access that appear in this postpatent phase. The authors' framework elucidates key tensions that can help explain outcomes we observe. A core insight concerns quality. Because the public is concerned about quality (i.e., the safety and efficacy of the drugs), regulatory requirements are implemented that help ensure quality but raise barriers to entry, limiting the number of producers. The resulting decrease in competition raises prices and also raises the risk of disruptions and shortages. On the other hand, failing to address quality can result in problematic safety lapses.

Meanwhile, regulatory instincts often push toward lowering prices to provide greater access, and more equitable access, for key medicines. But capping prices also makes entry less profitable. Thus, price constraints can ultimately limit access and further raise risks of shortages as the number of producers shrinks. Hemel and Ouellette elucidate numerous trade-offs along these lines, indicating that it is difficult in a regulatory context to achieve distinct goals around price, access, and quality simultaneously. They then consider how various public interventions—including antitrust policy and supply-chain initiatives—might help limit these trade-offs.

The next two chapters consider the advance of green technologies. In "Innovating to Net Zero: Can Venture Capital and Start-Ups Play a Meaningful Role?" Ramana Nanda and Silvia Dalla Fontana examine the transition to a carbon-free world. To get a handle on these complex issues, they examine a primary means through which new ideas are protected in this arena: patents. The authors highlight several provocative findings. First, relative to other technological areas, "net-zero patents" (as they term them) are close to the scientific frontier. This is particularly true when it comes to the subset of these awards to firms backed by venture investors. This subset of awards is particularly influential to future innovators, as seen in the citations in subsequent patent documents. Second, they find that the share of net-zero patents that are venture-backed is quite modest. Moreover, patenting by venture-backed firms has been increasingly directed to areas outside clean tech and other "deep" technologies in recent years. The authors suggest that this shift is a consequence of the difficulties of successfully commercializing these inventions. They offer a variety of suggestions that may help address these barriers.

In "To Starve or to Stoke? Understanding Whether Divestment versus Investment Can Steer (Green) Innovation," Jacquelyn Pless examines investor behavior as a means to meet clean innovation goals. Specifically, investors may consider divestment from firms in dirty industries. A primary economic aim in such divestment is to raise the cost of capital for these firms and thus slow their growth. However, drawing on extant literature, this chapter points out that divestment even by large numbers of investors will have negligible effects on the costs of capital for these industries, so long as other investors are willing to own these companies. Moreover, by departing these investments, green-oriented investors lose their vote and voice to help shape practices from within the firm. Indeed, the "clean-oriented" investors end up leaving the corporate boards under the control of those who care less about green innovation.

In light of the potentially limited effectiveness of divestment, the chapter goes on to consider how staying "in" the firm and addressing specific management practices and priorities may help shift firms toward cleaner solutions. Performing a deep dive into environmental, social, and governance (ESG) metrics, Pless further shows that certain management practices predict substantially better carbon-mitigation performance for firms. Although ESG scores overall come in many forms and have limitations that Pless elucidates, this chapter's investigations suggest that specific submetrics may have real value for management behavior. This conclusion reinforces the hypothesis that staying invested and engaging with green corporate governance practices may be a far more effective approach than divestment.

The final pair of papers turns to a different challenge: the uneven distribution of entrepreneurship and innovation across the economy. These chapters focus on differences in access to investment across race and geography in the United States.

In "Racial Inequality in Capital Access for Innovative Firms," Rob Fairlie and David Robinson examine the ability of innovative firms to access capital. This analysis builds on an abundant literature showing that business ownership appears to be a key avenue for wealth accumulation. The chapter further builds on the authors' earlier work demonstrating large disparities between start-ups begun by founders of different races in the use of financial capital in the first few years of operations.

Turning specifically to the subset of innovative-intensive new businesses, which can have especially broad and substantial economic impact, the authors find that Black-owned businesses start smaller than their peers and do not converge in size over time. Exploring the drivers of this difference, the chapter highlights that differential access to bank financing is a major factor. In many cases, the Black-owned businesses do not even approach banks, anticipating that their applications will be rejected. These differences persist among incorporated business with intellectual property, and the differences are more severe in areas where bank lending to small businesses is commonplace. The authors highlight how the reliance on "soft information," which is often thought to help new businesses that do not have established track records, can instead exacerbate bias in lending, increasing barriers for Black founders and limiting entrepreneurial pathways to prosperity.

Finally, in "Place-Based Productivity and Costs in Science," Jonathan Gruber, Simon Johnson, and Enrico Moretti consider the regional concentration of innovative activity in the United States. The chapter starts by noting that innovative activity is extremely geographically concentrated, and increasingly so. This concentration may have several benefits, such as the leveraging of local knowledge spillovers, which make researchers more productive when colocating in dense areas. However, innovation clusters often coincide with expensive urban areas, where real estate, labor, and other costs are substantially higher—especially in "superstar" locations such as New York City and the San Francisco Bay Area.

This paper empirically weighs the local agglomeration advantages against the local production costs to see whether innovative activity would be more or less efficient were it to spread to less-dense areas. The analysis finds the concentration of activity has net advantages today: the productivity gain from colocating researchers exceeds the additional costs it imposes. The findings are thus consistent with the tendency toward increased spatial concentration.

However, it also appears that the concentration of innovation may have hit its limit. The net advantages appear small to nonexistent in the (very expensive) highest-density research locations. These findings are informative in light of recent policy steps (and proposals) to diversify innovative activity across more regions of the United States. Although the short-run assessment of costs and benefits favors concentration, it is also critical to understand the longer-run benefits (including equity, industrial diversification, and talent development) of seeding innovation clusters elsewhere. Both these sets of considerations are key to assessing the ultimate welfare implications of greater regional diversification.

Together, these six contributions tackle substantive and timely dimensions of entrepreneurship and innovation policy—regarding pharmaceuticals and vaccines, clean technologies and climate change, and issues of regional and racial inequality. The conceptual frameworks and empirical evidence synthesize recent research literature and push beyond its boundaries, providing important insights on contemporary issues and helping delimit the bounds of current knowledge. These chapters can both inform contemporary policy opportunities and highlight open issues for future research to undertake.

Endnote

Author email addresses: Jones (bjones@kellogg.northwestern.edu), Lerner (jlerner@
hbs.edu). For acknowledgments, sources of research support, and disclosure of the authors' material financial relationships, if any, please see https://www.nber.org/books
-and-chapters/entrepreneurship-and-innovation-policy-and-economy-volume-2/introduction
-entrepreneurship-and-innovation-policy-and-economy-volume-2.

Accelerating Vaccine Innovation for Emerging Infectious Diseases via Parallel Discovery

Joseph Barberio, *Strand Therapeutics Inc.,* United States of America

Jacob Becraft, *Strand Therapeutics Inc.,* United States of America

Zied Ben Chaouch, *MIT Laboratory for Financial Engineering and MIT Department of Electrical Engineering and Computer Science,* United States of America

Dimitris Bertsimas, *MIT Laboratory for Financial Engineering, MIT Operations Research Center, and MIT Sloan School of Management,* United States of America

Tasuku Kitada, *Strand Therapeutics Inc.,* United States of America

Michael L. Li, *MIT Operations Research Center,* United States of America

Andrew W. Lo, *MIT Laboratory for Financial Engineering, MIT Operations Research Center, MIT Computer Science and Artificial Intelligence Laboratory, MIT Sloan School of Management, Santa Fe Institute, and NBER,* United States of America

Kevin Shi, *Strand Therapeutics Inc.,* United States of America

Qingyang Xu, *MIT Laboratory for Financial Engineering and MIT Operations Research Center,* United States of America

Abstract

The COVID-19 pandemic has raised awareness about the global imperative to develop and stockpile vaccines against future outbreaks of emerging infectious diseases (EIDs). Prior to the pandemic, vaccine development for EIDs was stagnant, largely due to the lack of financial incentives for pharmaceutical firms to invest in vaccine research and development (R&D). This R&D requires significant capital investment, most notably in conducting clinical trials, but vaccines generate much less profit for pharmaceutical firms compared with other therapeutics in disease areas such as oncology. The portfolio approach of financing drug development has been proposed as a financial innovation to improve the risk/return trade-off of investment in drug development projects through the use of diversification and securitization. By investing in a sizable and well-diversified portfolio of novel drug candidates, and issuing equity and securitized debt based on this portfolio, the financial performance of such a biomedical "megafund" can attract a wider group of private-sector investors. To analyze the viability of the portfolio approach in expediting vaccine development against EIDs, we simulate the

Entrepreneurship and Innovation Policy and the Economy, volume 2, 2023.

financial performance of a hypothetical vaccine megafund consisting of 120 messenger RNA (mRNA) vaccine candidates in the preclinical stage, which target 11 EIDs, including a hypothetical "disease X" that may be responsible for the next pandemic. We calibrate the simulation parameters with input from domain experts in mRNA technology and an extensive literature review and find that this vaccine portfolio will generate an average annualized return on investment of –6.0% per annum and a negative net present value of –$9.5 billion, despite the scientific advantages of mRNA technology and the financial benefits of diversification. We also show that clinical trial costs account for 94% of the total investment; vaccine manufacturing costs account for only 6%. The most important factor of the megafund's financial performance is the price per vaccine dose. Other factors, such as the increased probability of success due to mRNA technology, the size of the megafund portfolio, and the possibility of conducting human challenge trials, do not significantly improve its financial performance. Our analysis indicates that continued collaboration between government agencies and the private sector will be necessary if the goal is to create a sustainable business model and robust vaccine ecosystem for addressing future pandemics.

JEL Codes: I10, I11, I18, L32, L65, G11, G24

Keywords: vaccines, pandemics, biotechnology, pharmaceuticals, impact investing, healthcare finance, public/private partnerships

I.   Introduction

The extraordinary human, social, and economic losses caused by the COVID-19 pandemic have heightened the global imperative to prepare for the next pandemic by proactively developing novel vaccines against emerging infectious diseases (EIDs). EIDs are a broad class of infectious agents that have either recently appeared for the first time or whose incidence has rapidly increased in terms of size of the affected population or geographic area (WHO 2014; NIAID 2018). A closely related threat is the reemergence of new variants of a previously identified EID, which may have become more transmissive or pathogenic through genetic mutation or shifting environmental conditions (Morens and Fauci 2020).

Given the dynamic and stochastic nature of EID outbreaks, the most effective strategy to prevent a future pandemic is to develop and stockpile vaccines before an outbreak occurs (Jarrett et al. 2021). A notable example of proactive vaccine development is the Coalition for Epidemic Preparedness Innovations (CEPI), which has a portfolio of 32 vaccine candidates. As of April 14, 2022, these vaccine candidates target COVID-19 and six other priority EIDs (CEPI 2022). Currently, the CEPI portfolio is diversified across 13 different therapeutic mechanisms (e.g., nucleic acid, recombinant protein) and five stages of clinical development, from pre-clinical research to Emergency Use Listing by the World Health Organization (WHO). A similar example of proactive response was the International Coordinating Group (ICG) on Vaccine Provision's stockpiling of 2 million doses of yellow fever vaccines during a global shortage in 2000 (Nathan et al. 2001). In 2019, members of ICG renewed their pledge to maintain a stockpile of 6 million yellow fever vaccine doses (WHO 2020). Stockpiling vaccines well before an epidemic outbreak enables local governments and public health agencies to quickly address the sharp increase in vaccine demand following the outbreak and facilitates more efficient vaccine allocation (Jarrett, Yang, and Pagliusi 2020).

These considerations—and the remarkable effectiveness of messenger RNA (mRNA) vaccine technology against COVID-19—naturally lead to the question of the financial feasibility of a portfolio of mRNA vaccine candidates diversified across target EIDs, including both local EIDs and pathogens that may cause the next global pandemic.

We address this question in this article by evaluating the financial performance of a hypothetical portfolio of 120 mRNA vaccine candidates targeting 11 EIDs and determining whether the risk/return profile of such a portfolio might be attractive to private-sector investors. We do this by performing Monte Carlo simulations of the outcomes of hypothetical vaccine development programs that conform to a prespecified set of parameters and examining the statistical distribution of these outcomes. We calibrate the parameters of these simulations using input from domain experts in mRNA technology and an extensive literature review.

We find that this vaccine portfolio yields an average annualized return on investment of −6.0% per annum, and a negative net present value of −$9.5 billion, despite the scientific advantages of mRNA technology and the financial benefits of diversification. We also show that the clinical trial costs of this vaccine portfolio account for 94% of the total investment, and vaccine manufacturing costs account for only 6%. The most important factor of the portfolio's financial performance is the price per vaccine dose. Other factors, such as the increased probability of success due to mRNA technology, the size of the portfolio, and the possibility of conducting human challenge trials (HCTs)—in which healthy subjects are vaccinated and then deliberately infected with the virus to test vaccine efficacy—do not significantly improve its financial performance.

If the goal is to create a sustainable business model for addressing EIDs effectively, our results suggest that a likely prerequisite will be continued collaboration between the public and private sector.

II. Brief Overview of Vaccine Development

A. *The Past: A Decline in Vaccine R&D*
Prior to the COVID-19 Pandemic

Before the COVID-19 pandemic, pharmaceutical firms had pivoted away from vaccine research and development (R&D) for EIDs, especially for small-scale but highly lethal agents such as the Ebola and Marburg viruses (Kelland 2019). Several important factors were involved in this exodus, including high R&D costs (Gouglas et al. 2018), a low probability of success (PoS) in developing a vaccine candidate from preclinical studies to regulatory approval (estimated to be between 6% and 25% by Davis et al. 2011; Pronker et al. 2013; Project ALPHA 2022; Vu et al. 2022), the low list prices of vaccines (CDC 2022), the uncertainty in vaccine demand and revenues (Glennerster and Kremer 2000; Plotkin, Mahmoud, and Farrar 2015), and the lack of sustainable funding from public and private sectors in the absence of an imminent epidemic outbreak. Pharmaceutical firms have a greater financial incentive to develop and manufacture vaccines for common seasonal epidemics such as influenza compared with EIDs because there is much less uncertainty in the estimated demand of these vaccines (Douglas and Samant 2018).

To illustrate the financial disincentives of vaccine R&D for EIDs more concretely, consider the following simplified model. Assume that the cost of developing a single vaccine candidate, from preclinical studies to regulatory approval or emergency use authorization (EUA), is $200 million, the probability of receiving regulatory approval is 25%, and the target EID occurs with probability 10% in any given year. If an outbreak does occur, we assume 10 million doses are manufactured, with a list price of $20 per dose. Under these assumptions, the total expected revenues over the next 20 years (which is the duration of a vaccine patent) are

$$25\% \times \$20 \times 10 \text{ million} \times 10\% \times 20 = \$100 \text{ million},$$

which is only half of the R&D costs, despite rather optimistic assumptions about these costs and the PoS compared with more realistic estimates found in the literature (Pronker et al. 2013; Project ALPHA 2022; Vu et al. 2022). This simple example also shows that the financial returns of vaccine R&D can be increased if the PoS can be improved due to scientific innovation (e.g., mRNA technology) or financial innovation (e.g., a portfolio approach to parallel vaccine development), or a combination of both.

B. The Present: A Revolution in mRNA Vaccines

Vaccine R&D has gone through a scientific revolution during the pandemic, exemplified by mRNA technology, which has demonstrated robust levels of safety, high efficacy, and unprecedented speed in clinical vaccine development (Chaudhary, Weissman, and Whitehead 2021). Once the genetic sequence of a pathogen is known, mRNA vaccine candidates can be designed more quickly than traditional vaccines. In addition, because mRNA vaccines do not require the production of inactivated or attenuated pathogens, they can be manufactured at large scale at higher efficiency, lower cost, and with more robust safety guarantees (Pardi et al. 2018). This technology has the potential to significantly reduce both the cost and the duration of vaccine R&D, enabling a much more rapid response to future EIDs. It is also particularly suited for the development of multiple mRNA vaccines in parallel, as in the portfolio approach taken by CEPI, because different mRNA vaccines may be able to share the same resources and facilities for preclinical studies, clinical testing, and post-approval manufacturing and delivery (Szabó, Mahiny, and Vlatkovic 2021).

As an illustration of the success of mRNA vaccine development, consider the mRNA-1273 vaccine developed by Moderna for COVID-19, which was designed in 2 days, tested on the first human volunteer in 63 days, and received an EUA from the US Food and Drug Administration (FDA) a little more than 11 months after the genetic sequence of the original viral strain was first released (Harbert 2020; Neilson, Dunn, and Bendix 2020). The R&D period of mRNA vaccines is significantly shorter than the usual 5–10 years for traditional vaccine development that were required before the COVID-19 pandemic.

We should note that the stunning successes of mRNA vaccine R&D against the COVID-19 virus was a result not only of technological advances but also due to the close partnership between the public and private sectors in developing a mature mRNA technology well over a decade before the pandemic (Dolgin 2021), as well as a product of the unprecedented collaboration between the government, regulatory agencies, scientists and clinicians around the world, and the pharmaceutical industry to expedite vaccine development in the midst of the COVID-19 outbreak. As we illustrate in subsequent sections, continued collaboration and funding support from the public sector are critical to ensuring that vaccine R&D for EIDs can be financially sustainable.

C.   The Future: Parallel R&D for mRNA Vaccines

mRNA technology brings a novel perspective to vaccine R&D in the portfolio approach used by CEPI by lowering the R&D and manufacturing costs through sharing resources on a common R&D platform, which improves the PoS of vaccine development by the "multiple-shots-on-goal" parallel strategy of discovery. However, a serious challenge to vaccine R&D remains in the lack of sufficient and sustainable funding to support the vaccine R&D pipeline over an extended period, typically multiple years from preclinical research to the regulatory approval of a vaccine, an issue known as the "valley of death" in translational medicine (Butler 2008).

Governments, international agencies, and nongovernmental organizations such as the Gates Foundation, Wellcome Trust, and CEPI have made significant contributions to the development of a portfolio of vaccine candidates, but these efforts are not sufficient due to the scale of the challenge (see Section 2 of Vu et al. 2022 for a detailed discussion). The private sector does have sufficient resources to bridge this funding gap but will do so only if the portfolio can generate sufficiently attractive financial returns for its investors.

To illustrate the benefits and challenges of applying the portfolio approach to vaccine R&D, we return to our earlier back-of-the-envelope calculation. Suppose we invest in a portfolio of 10 mRNA vaccines candidates targeting local epidemics. The total cost increases to 10 × $200 million = $2 billion, and the probability that at least one vaccine candidate receives regulatory approval (assuming statistically independent outcomes) increases substantially to $1 - (1 - 25\%)^{10} = 94.4\%$. The expected revenues over the next 2 decades become

$$94.4\% \times \$20 \times 10 \, \text{million} \times 10\% \times 20 = \$378 \, \text{million},$$

a financial loss of $1.6 billion. However, if the vaccine targets an EID that causes a global pandemic with an annual probability of 1%, and 1 billion vaccine doses are produced if a pandemic occurs, the expected revenues of the vaccine portfolio increase to

$$94.4\% \times \$20 \times 1 \, \text{billion} \times 1\% \times 20 = \$3.8 \, \text{billion},$$

a profit of $1.8 billion, whereas the expected revenues of investing in one vaccine are only

$$25\% \times \$20 \times 1 \text{ billion} \times 1\% \times 20 = \$1.0 \text{ billion,}$$

which implies a deficit of $1 billion.

These numbers highlight both the advantages of and the bottlenecks to applying a portfolio approach to funding vaccine R&D. First, the parallel discovery strategy improves the PoS of vaccine R&D. Even if vaccine development outcomes are correlated to each other, the probability of having an approved vaccine in a portfolio is still higher than the PoS of investing in a single vaccine program (assuming that the pairwise correlations are not equal to 1). An increased PoS can make vaccine R&D profitable for those EIDs capable of causing global pandemics. However, it is insufficient to generate financial value for vaccines against local EIDs, because the revenues of local vaccine sales are limited. In addition, because the mRNA vaccines share the same therapeutic mechanism, it is reasonable to assume that there will be no significant difference in efficacy between different approved mRNA vaccines for the same EID (as in the case of COVID-19). As a result, there will be considerable cannibalization of demand for vaccines targeting the same EID, because the demand for vaccines will not increase with the number of approved vaccines. Finally, the stochastic nature of EID outbreaks induces large variance in the revenues of vaccine sales. For vaccine R&D aimed at preventing a global pandemic, even though the expected financial return is positive, there is still a significant probability in our illustrative model of $(1 - 1\%)^{20} = 81.8\%$ that a global pandemic will not occur in the next 20 years, leading to a financial loss of $2 billion.

III.   Portfolio Approach to Financing Drug Development

A.   Challenges of the Drug Development Process

To develop a novel therapeutic candidate from laboratory discovery to regulatory approval, a drug developer needs to conduct multiple clinical trials to test the safety and efficacy of the therapeutic candidate on the target patient population. These clinical trials are conducted in sequence through four stages (preclinical, phase 1, phase 2, and phase 3).[1] Trials in a more advanced phase typically require a larger patient enrollment and a longer time to complete and are correspondingly more expensive. If the phase 3 clinical trial shows clear safety and efficacy, the drug developer files a new drug application (NDA) to the FDA for regulatory approval. If the FDA approves the NDA, the drug developer may manufacture the drug and collect revenues from drug sales. Sometimes, the FDA may require an additional phase 4 clinical trial after regulatory approval to test the long-term benefits and side effects of the drug on a large patient population.

Despite the tremendous breakthroughs in biomedicine over the past decades, new drug development has become slower, more expensive, and less likely to succeed, causing a significant funding gap for early-stage drug development programs. The lack of sufficient funding for translational biomedical R&D is due to several institutional features of drug development, including a low PoS, a long investment horizon, high clinical trial costs, and a high cost of capital, especially for small biotechnology companies, which typically do not have marketed drugs that generate revenues and must rely on external financing to sustain an R&D pipeline.[2] The declining efficiency of translating scientific discoveries in research laboratories into novel products has also been observed in other industries in the United States (Arora et al. 2020).

B.   Advantages of Financing Vaccine R&D via the "Vaccine Megafund"

To address the challenge of funding translational medicine, Fernandez, Stein, and Lo (2012) proposed a novel financing vehicle, the biomedical "megafund," which invests in a sizable portfolio of drug candidates diversified across different clinical stages and therapeutic areas. Using financial engineering techniques such as securitization, the authors show that the risk/return profile of the megafund is attractive to a wide group of investors. Originally proposed to finance oncology drug development, the megafund model was subsequently applied to other disease areas, including orphan diseases (Fagnan et al. 2014), Alzheimer's disease (Lo et al. 2014), pediatric cancer (Das et al. 2018), ovarian cancer (Chaudhuri et al. 2019), glioblastoma (Siah et al. 2021), and vaccines against EIDs (Vu et al. 2022). It is currently being applied by the National Brain Tumor Society to finance novel drug candidates to treat glioblastoma (NBTS 2021).

The key idea behind the megafund is to reduce the financial risks of its assets and improve its expected returns by raising capital to acquire a portfolio of vaccine candidates, issuing equity and securitized debt with different risk/return profiles that appeal to a wide range of private-sector investors. The vaccine candidates are used as collateral, and the revenues generated by future vaccine sales are used to service its debt and interest payments. The residual equity is then distributed among its equity holders. If the future cash flows are insufficient to service the debt, the megafund declares bankruptcy and the collateral is transferred to its bondholders.

The main advantage of portfolio diversification is that by increasing the probability of having at least one approved drug candidate, the megafund is able to lower the financial risks and attract large amounts of capital from the bond market, whose size is much larger than the venture capital, public equity, or private equity market (SIFMA 2021). In 2020, a total of $12.2 trillion worth of fixed income securities were issued in the United States, compared with $390 billion of equity. In the same year, the total private placement was $330.1 billion in the United States, of which $314.4 billion was in the form of debt and $15.8 billion in the form of equity (SIFMA 2021).

C.   Evaluating the Financial Performance of the Vaccine Megafund

In the vaccine megafund simulation analysis of Vu et al. (2022), the financial performance of a vaccine-focused portfolio is extremely unattractive to for-profit investors, with an expected annualized return of −61% and a standard deviation (SD) of 4%. Multiple factors lead to this negative financial return, including a low PoS of vaccine trials, high clinical trial costs, and limited revenues from vaccine sales. Based on these findings, the authors propose several strategies to finance the vaccine megafund, including higher vaccine prices, public sector funding, and a novel subscription model in which subscribers would pay annual fees for priority access to the vaccines in case of future outbreaks.

In this article, we extend the work of Vu et al. (2022) in several important ways. First, Vu et al. simulated vaccine trial outcomes stochastically but used a single fixed expected value to estimate the annual profit for approved vaccines. We implement a more realistic simulation framework in which the entire value chain of vaccine development, manufacturing, and sales is simulated under the stochastic occurrence of EID outbreaks. The uncertainty in future EID outbreaks increases the variance of megafund cash flows, which directly affects its risk/return profile. In addition, we use improved PoS estimates of mRNA vaccines to adjust the cash flows of the megafund and calibrate the cost structure of mRNA vaccine manufacturing with input from domain experts and an extensive literature review. Finally, although Vu et al. (2022) mainly focused on the annualized return of the vaccine megafund, we systematically investigate a wide spectrum of metrics to gauge its financial and social impact, such as the net present value and the number of EID outbreaks prevented. We also provide a detailed breakdown of the cost structure for the vaccine megafund to identify the main drivers of its financial performance.

The risk/reward profile of the vaccine megafund hinges on the scientific and business expertise of fund managers to select promising drug candidates and diversify the portfolio (Siah et al. 2021). For a real-world vaccine portfolio such as CEPI's, active portfolio management is critical, given budget constraints, to select a limited number of vaccine candidates. Gouglas and Marsh (2019) apply multicriteria decision analysis to select promising vaccine candidates for the CEPI portfolio in the context of multiple trade-offs and heterogeneous stakeholder preferences. In a subsequent study (Gouglas and Marsh 2021), the authors apply portfolio decision analysis to optimize the investment of CEPI in 16 vaccine technology platforms. Ahuja et al. (2021) analyzed the optimal investment strategy of vaccine manufacturing capacity for countries with different socioeconomic characteristics.

Although we fully recognize the importance of active portfolio management in improving the financial performance of a vaccine megafund, we do not impose exogenous budget constraints or perform any portfolio optimization in our simulation analysis, because our goal is to understand the relationships between the investment and revenues of the vaccine megafund and its endogenous factors such as the improvement in the PoS of mRNA vaccine development, the cost structure of mRNA vaccine manufacturing, the size of the megafund portfolio, and the possibility of conducting HCTs to expedite vaccine clinical trials.

IV. Simulation Methods

A. Vaccine Megafund Portfolio

We simulate the financial performance of a large portfolio of mRNA vaccine candidates using an adaptation of Vu et al.'s (2022) portfolio structure and probability of outbreak, P_a, of each EID, as shown in table 1. We also include 10 vaccine candidates that target "disease X," the unknown pathogen that may cause the next pandemic, in accordance with the updated CEPI portfolio (CEPI 2022). We assume that disease X has a

Table 1
Portfolio for Simulated mRNA Vaccine Megafund (CEPI 2022; Vu et al. 2022)

Targeted Emerging Infectious Disease (EID)	Number of Vaccine Candidates (N_{vac})	Annual Probability of Outbreak (P_a, in %)	Average Number of Infections (n_l)
Disease X	10	1.0	400,000,000
Chikungunya	16	10.8	523,600
Zika virus	18	4.3	500,062
Lassa fever	7	100.0	300,000
Rift Valley fever	3	10.5	79,414
SARS-CoV-1	2	7.1	8,098
West Nile virus	23	10.0	500
MERS-CoV	8	40.0	436
Crimean-Congo haemorrhagic fever	7	12.5	320
Nipah virus	20	15.8	136
Marburg virus	6	12.0	75

low annual probability of outbreak, $P_a = 1\%$, and the number of infected cases will be 400 million, close to that of COVID-19.

B. Vaccine Clinical Trials

We use the simulation framework in Siah et al. (2021) to model the correlated outcomes of vaccine clinical trials. The assumed values of the simulation parameters of a vaccine clinical trial are summarized in table 2. The simulated trial outcomes depend on two critical sets of parameters. First, the PoS in reaching each stage in the clinical development process is estimated using historical industry average values (Project ALPHA 2022; Vu et al. 2022). In addition, because the mRNA vaccine for COVID-19 is known to induce humoral immune protection by producing neutralizing antibodies (Jain et al. 2021), we assume that mRNA vaccines will have a higher PoS for the six EIDs in the portfolio whose correlates of protection are also neutralizing antibodies (Chikungunya virus, SARS-CoV-1, Marburg virus, Rift Valley fever, Nipah virus, and Zika virus). To reflect the increased PoS due to mRNA technology for these diseases, we multiply the historical PoS by a technology factor, α_{tech}. We set α_{tech} to 1.2 in the baseline model, which reflects a 20% increase in the PoS above the industry average. We do not increase the PoS for the other five diseases with cellular or unknown immune responses, including disease X. We vary α_{tech} in the sensitivity analysis to gauge the effect of increased PoS on financial performance.

Table 2
Simulation Parameters for Vaccine Clinical Trials

Parameter	PRE to P1	P1 to P2	P2 to P3	P3 to EUA	Source
Probability of success (PoS, in %)	60.0	83.6	65.8	80.9	Vu et al. (2022) Project ALPHA (2022) Wong et al. (2019)
Duration (months) standard clinical trial	18.0	24.0	18.0	14.0	Vu et al. (2022) Berry et al. (2020)
Development cost ($M) standard clinical trial	26.0	14.0	28.0	150.0	Gouglas et al. (2018)
Duration (months) human challenge trial	. . .	. . .	. . .	8.0	Berry et al. (2020)
Development cost ($M) human challenge trial	. . .	. . .	. . .	12.5	Berry et al. (2020)

Note: We assume that a vaccine receives emergency use authorization (EUA) once it successfully completes phase 3 of the clinical trial process. Furthermore, we assume human challenge trials are only applicable to phase 3. PRE = preclinical phase; P1 = Phase 1; P2 = Phase 2; P3 = Phase 3.

In addition, the correlations between vaccine trial outcomes play a major role in the simulation outcomes. If two vaccine trial outcomes are highly correlated (e.g., due to the same target pathogen or therapeutic mechanism), they are more likely to simultaneously succeed or fail, which leads to lower diversification benefits from the portfolio, greater variance in the cash flows of the megafund, and thus greater overall financial risk. Using the input of domain experts in mRNA technology, we construct a biologically motivated metric to estimate these correlations.

Specifically, we propose a novel distance metric, d_{ij}, between pathogens i and j, defined as the average of similarity scores based on four biological factors: taxonomy, qualitative features (e.g., type of disease vector, strand direction, nucleic acid topology), quantitative features (e.g., number of strands, total genome size), and the edit distance of protein sequences. Simply put, the more similar two pathogens are to each other, the more correlated we assume their trial outcomes will be. This value of d_{ij} is normalized between 0 and 1, with d_{ij} closer to 0 if pathogens i and j are more biologically similar, and $d_{ij} = 0$ if they are identical. Given the values of d_{ij}, a natural way to define the correlation, ρ_{ij}, between the outcomes of vaccine trials targeting pathogens i and j is $\rho_{ij} = 1 - d_{ij}$; that is, the vaccine trial outcomes have a higher correlation if their target EIDs are more biologically similar, and vice versa.

Figure 1 shows the heat map of ρ_{ij} between each pair of pathogens, excluding disease X (which we assume to be independent of the other pathogens, to reflect its a priori unknown biological properties). The correlation matrix ρ_{ij} defined this way is positive definite (PD) in our calibration, although it is not guaranteed to be PD in general and may need to be transformed into a PD matrix by an appropriate method (Qi and Sun 2006).[3] Because this metric does not specify the correlation between two vaccine trials targeting the same pathogen, we assume this correlation to be 0.8, which is higher than the maximum correlation of 0.64 across different pathogens (fig. 1). To gauge the impact of correlation on financial performance, we vary the assumed values of correlation in the sensitivity analysis.

C. Human Challenge Trials

Given the demonstrated safety and efficacy of mRNA vaccines for COVID-19, it is conceivable that HCTs may be ethically justified for

	Chikun.	SARS	MERS	Marburg	RVF	Lassa	Nipah	CCHF	WNV	Zika
Chikun.	1.00	0.30	0.30	0.37	0.27	0.39	0.38	0.29	0.38	0.33
SARS	0.30	1.00	0.58	0.32	0.21	0.25	0.28	0.26	0.29	0.28
MERS	0.30	0.58	1.00	0.33	0.20	0.25	0.28	0.26	0.29	0.28
Marburg	0.37	0.32	0.33	1.00	0.27	0.37	0.46	0.37	0.36	0.35
RVF	0.27	0.21	0.20	0.27	1.00	0.48	0.29	0.52	0.27	0.26
Lassa	0.39	0.25	0.25	0.37	0.48	1.00	0.36	0.35	0.40	0.40
Nipah	0.38	0.28	0.28	0.46	0.29	0.36	1.00	0.32	0.39	0.39
CCHF	0.29	0.26	0.26	0.37	0.52	0.35	0.32	1.00	0.29	0.28
WNV	0.38	0.29	0.29	0.36	0.27	0.40	0.39	0.29	1.00	0.64
Zika	0.33	0.28	0.28	0.35	0.26	0.40	0.39	0.28	0.64	1.00

Fig. 1. Estimated correlations between vaccine candidates. We assume that vaccine candidates for disease X are uncorrelated with vaccines for the other diseases and that vaccine candidates targeting the same disease have a 0.8 correlation. Color version available as an online enhancement.

mRNA vaccine candidates in our portfolio. The HCT is an efficient yet highly controversial clinical trial design, in which healthy participants with no previous exposure to a disease are deliberately infected with the live pathogen in a controlled clinical environment (e.g., an isolated ward in a hospital). The controlled setting of an HCT allows much more precise and rapid testing of the safety and efficacy of vaccines with a smaller number of trial participants than standard vaccine trials. As a result, an HCT may significantly reduce the cost and duration of clinical trials and lead to expedited regulatory approval of effective vaccines. In a simulation analysis, Berry et al. (2020) showed that conducting an HCT for COVID-19 vaccines may significantly reduce the number of infected and deceased patients in the United States compared with other clinical trial designs, provided that the vaccine is effective and the HCT is initiated in a timely manner.

Although conducting an HCT is in principle more efficient in time and cost than traditional vaccine trials, in practice it still faces multiple challenges. First and foremost, the ethical justification of deliberately injecting healthy participants with a live EID agent is highly controversial due to the absence of well-established ethical guidelines to specify the conditions under which an HCT may be deemed ethical. In addition, HCTs require more time and resources during their initial preparation stage (e.g., identifying and manufacturing low-risk virus strains, identifying low-risk populations, and establishing an acceptable HCT protocol with regulators). As a result, the first HCTs for COVID-19 were initiated after the mRNA vaccine candidates had already received EUA in the United States and Europe (Callaway 2020; Rapeport et al. 2021).

Although we recognize the ethical and practical challenges of HCTs, we model an idealized scenario in which an HCT is authorized for mRNA vaccine R&D and may be conducted in an ethical and timely manner. We use the binary variable HCT_i to denote whether an HCT is authorized by the FDA during an outbreak of disease i (i.e., $HCT_i = 1$ with probability p_{HCT} if the HCT is authorized by the FDA, and $HCT_i = 0$ with probability $1 - p_{HCT}$ otherwise). If $HCT_i = 1$, we use the reduced cost and duration of HCTs (rows 4 and 5 of table 2) instead of the corresponding values of standard trials. We assume $p_{HCT} = 0$ in the baseline model (i.e., no HCT is conducted) and gauge the effect of p_{HCT} in the sensitivity analysis.

D.   Vaccine Manufacturing and Supply Chain

The cost structures of mRNA vaccine manufacturing and its supply chain are key to simulating the cash flows of the megafund. Because mRNA vaccine manufacturers do not disclose this information, we use publicly available estimates in the literature (Kis and Rizvi 2021; Kis et al. 2021) to calibrate these cost structures. The line-item budget of mRNA vaccine manufacturing is summarized in table 3. The main factor driving the manufacturing costs is the amount of mRNA raw material needed to produce the target number of vaccines. We assume that each production line consists of a bioreactor with a 30-liter working volume and mRNA titer 5 g/L (Kis and Rizvi 2021). We also assume that each vaccine dose contains 65 μg of mRNA, the average of the Pfizer/BioNTech and Moderna vaccines for COVID-19.

Using the estimates in table 3, the variable cost of producing each mRNA vaccine dose is $1.60. We assume that each local EID outbreak requires 10 million vaccine doses. It takes 8.1 days to produce the mRNA needed with one production line, and an additional 4–5 weeks to perform quality control for each batch produced. The total manufacturing cost is $16 million if one uses the existing production line, and $75 million if one builds a new production line. Similarly, we assume that a disease X pandemic requires 1 billion vaccine doses. It takes 81.4 days to produce the mRNA needed with 10 production lines. The total cost is $1.6 billion with existing production lines, and $2.2 billion with new ones. Furthermore, we assume that the variable cost of delivering each vaccine dose in the supply chain is $1.00 (of the same order of magnitude as the manufacturing cost). We make a conservative assumption about the supply chain cost due to the lack of publicly available estimates in the literature. Our simulation results show that the supply chain costs

Table 3
Cost Structure of mRNA Vaccine Production (Kis and Rizvi 2021; Kis et al. 2021)

Category	Item	Unit Cost (US$)	Quantity
Fixed cost	Production line	58 million	1 Bioreactor of 30 L working volume
	Raw materials	456.6 million per year per production line	29,162 g of mRNA per production line per year
	Consumables	150 million per year per production line	
Variable costs	Labor	20 per hour	113,186 labor hours per production line per year
	Quality control	10 per hour	
	Fill-and-finish	.27 per dose	10-dose vials
	Lab, utility, waste management, etc.	<1% total cost	Not modeled here

constitute only 2% of total costs (fig. 2), so the financial performance is not sensitive to the detailed structure of supply chain costs, as long as it does not exceed $1.00 per dose by an order of magnitude.

To estimate the revenues generated by vaccine sales, we use the list prices of mRNA vaccines for COVID-19. As of October 26, 2021, the Pfizer/BioNTech vaccine is priced at $24.00 per dose in the United States and the Moderna vaccine at $15.00 per dose (Jimenez 2021). We assume that the price per vaccine dose is $20.00. This is likely to be an underestimate because it is below the prices of all adult vaccines listed in the vaccine price list of Centers for Disease Control and Prevention except for influenza vaccines (CDC 2022). To gauge the impact of the list price of vaccines, we vary the price in the sensitivity analysis.

E. Simulating Correlated Clinical Trial Outcomes

The key to simulating the financial performance of the vaccine megafund is to simulate the correlated binary outcomes of vaccine clinical trials. Vaccine clinical trials have five development phases (preclinical, phase 1, phase 2, phase 3, and EUA) and need to successfully complete the first four phases in sequence before receiving the EUA. As in previous biomedical megafund studies (e.g., Siah et al. 2021), we use the technique proposed by Emrich and Piedmonte (1991) to simulate the

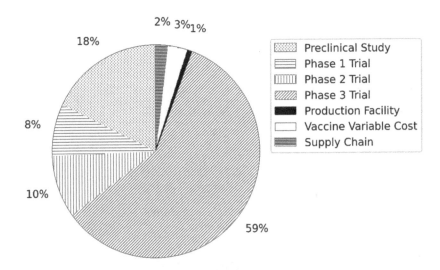

Fig. 2. Breakdown of cost structure of the vaccine megafund. Clinical trial costs constitute 94% of all costs and manufacturing costs constitute only 6%. Color version available as an online enhancement.

correlated outcomes of vaccine clinical trials in each phase. A detailed description of our method is provided in Section I of the Appendix.

F.   Overview of the Simulation Framework

At the initial time $t = 0$, all vaccine candidates enter the preclinical stage. For simplicity, we assume that the development costs of each phase are incurred at the start of the phase. In each subsequent year from $t = 1$ to $t = T$, we simulate whether any EID outbreaks (including the disease X pandemic) occur in year t. In the absence of any outbreaks, we develop each vaccine candidate (except the ones for disease X) from the pre-clinical stage to the completion of phase 2, assuming the cost and time-line of a standard clinical trial (rows 2 and 3 of table 2). We do not ini-tiate a large-scale phase 3 clinical trial unless an outbreak has occurred, because there will not be enough infected subjects with whom to test vaccine efficacy until then. From a financial perspective, this also reduces the significant late-stage clinical trial costs compared with the simula-tion analysis of Vu et al. (2022).

    If an EID outbreak occurs in year t, we assume that one of the four sce-narios below will occur (fig. 3):

1. At least one vaccine candidate targeting the disease has successfully completed a phase 3 trial during a previous outbreak of the same disease and received approval or an EUA from the FDA. We manufacture the vac-cines, supply them to the point of distribution, and collect the revenues from the vaccine sales.

2. At least one vaccine candidate targeting the disease has success-fully completed a phase 2 trial. We initiate the phase 3 clinical trial. If the phase 3 trial is successful, the vaccine receives an EUA from the FDA. We manufacture and supply the vaccines, and collect the revenues from the vaccine sales.

3. At least one vaccine candidate for the epidemic is in the preclinical or phase 1 stage. We initiate an accelerated phase 1/2 trial, which costs $28 million (the same as a standard phase 2 trial) and completes in 3 months, followed by a standard phase 3 trial, which completes in 14 months. If the phase 3 trial is successful, the vaccine receives an EUA. We manufacture and supply the vaccines, and collect the revenues.

4. No vaccine candidates for the disease have previously completed a phase 3 trial or remain in the R&D pipeline. In this case, no cash flows are generated because all vaccine candidates have failed in the clinical trial process.

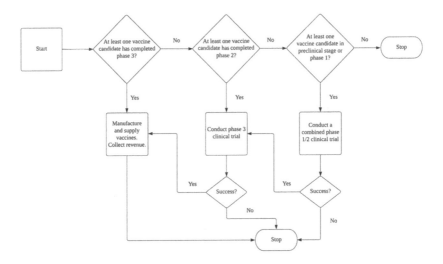

Fig. 3. Overview of the simulation framework in the event of an epidemic outbreak

We simulate an investment horizon of $T = 20$ years, which includes 5 years for standard clinical trial development from the preclinical phase to the completion of phase 2, and 15 years for the remaining duration of the vaccine patent. We compute the financial performance and social impact of the vaccine megafund at the end of the 20-year horizon.

V.   Results

There are four key observations and insights from the results of the simulation analysis:

- Despite the improved PoS of mRNA vaccines, the vaccine megafund does not generate financial value for the investors and is not a financially self-sustainable business model for the pharmaceutical industry.
- From the perspective of public policy, the vaccine megafund will require $9.5 billion in funding from the public sector at its initiation to generate positive financial value for investors.
- The main bottlenecks of the financial performance are the limited and uncertain revenues generated by vaccine sales and the significant costs of clinical trials, which account for 94% of the total investments in the megafund.
- The vaccine megafund generates significant social benefits by preventing, on average, 31 epidemic outbreaks out of 45 over the next

2 decades. In addition, there is a 66% probability that the next "disease X pandemic" will be prevented by vaccines developed from the megafund portfolio.

The performance of the baseline portfolio is summarized in table 4. We find that this portfolio has a negative expected annualized return, $E[R_a] = -6.0\%$ (SD$[R_a] = 6.7\%$), and a negative expected net present value (NPV) of –$9.5 billion (SE $13 million). The vaccine megafund does not generate positive financial value for its investors because the revenues generated by the vaccine sales ($7.5 billion on average) are insufficient to recover the investment in clinical trial development and vaccine manufacturing ($17.7 billion on average). However, the financial value to private-sector investors does not capture the benefits to society generated by the megafund. On average, 45 infectious disease outbreaks will occur in the simulation period, 31 of which will be prevented or contained by vaccines developed from the portfolio. In addition, there is a 66% probability that vaccines in the portfolio will prevent the next "disease X pandemic," should one occur. Using even the most conservative "quality-adjusted life year" estimate (e.g., Neumann, Cohen, and Weinstein 2014), the lives saved and socioeconomic losses avoided by the vaccines far exceed the negative financial value of the megafund.

The distribution of key performance metrics of the megafund is displayed in the histograms of figure 4. We find that, although R_a and NPV are negative in most simulations, there is a 9.8% probability that $R_a > 0$, and a 3.1% probability that NPV > 0. In addition, the distribution of megafund investments is smooth with a single peak (i.e., this is a

Table 4
Performance of the Baseline Portfolio Computed with 100K Monte Carlo Simulations

Metric	Mean	Standard Error	Standard Deviation	Median	25% Qt.	75% Qt.
Annualized return (R_a, %)	−6.0	.021	6.7	−5.7	−7.4	−4.4
Net present value (NPV, $B)	−9.5	.013	4.1	−9.9	−12.1	−7.4
Investment ($B)	17.7	.017	5.3	17.8	14.0	21.4
Revenues ($B)	7.5	.024	7.7	5.8	3.4	7.0
Profit ($B)	−10.0	.023	7.4	−11.5	−14.9	−7.5
Number of prevented epidemics (N_{ep})	31	.04	13	34	19	42

Note: NPV is computed with an annual discount rate $r = 10\%$. The standard deviation of preclinical trial cost is zero because the megafund invests in the preclinical trials of all 120 vaccine candidates at the initial time 0.

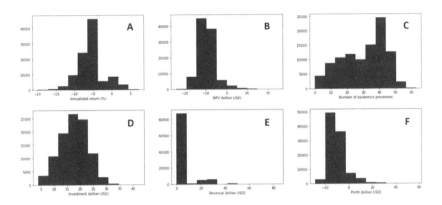

Fig. 4. Histograms of key performance metrics of vaccine megafund. (A) Annualized return, R_a. (B) Net present value (NPV). (C) Number of epidemics prevented, N_{ep}. (D) Total investment. (E) Total revenue. (F) Net profit. Color version available as an online enhancement.

unimodal distribution), and the distribution of revenues has two peaks (i.e., a bimodal distribution): although revenues are mostly likely to fall below $10 billion, there is a sizable probability that revenues exceed $20 billion. The latter corresponds to the rare scenarios when a disease X pandemic occurs, generating revenues of $20 billion from vaccine sales. This bimodality of revenues leads to significant variance in the annualized return and NPV of the megafund.

To gain additional insight into the major costs that reduce the financial performance of the megafund, we present a breakdown of megafund investment in figure 2 and find that the costs of clinical trials constitute 94% of the total cost, with phase 3 trials alone accounting for 59%. The net cost of vaccine manufacturing and its supply chain constitute only 6% of the total cost, and the higher efficiency of mRNA vaccine manufacturing is not sufficient to generate financial profits for investors. Our finding is consistent with the "valley of death" in financing translational medicine (Butler 2008), in which the main bottleneck is the risk associated with the uncertainty of revenues at the early stages of drug discovery versus the enormous cost of clinical trials. Even with more efficient vaccine manufacturing technologies and supply chain designs, the significant cost of clinical trials still prevents the vaccine megafund from generating positive financial value to its investors.

VI. Sensitivity Analysis

The simulated financial performance of the vaccine megafund hinges on the assumed values of key simulation parameters calibrated using inputs from mRNA domain experts and estimates from the literature. We perform a sensitivity analysis to test the robustness of our simulation results against the assumed parameter values. The results are summarized in table A1 and discussed in detail in Section II of the Appendix. We highlight the key findings for public policy consideration in this section.

A.   Vaccine Price

The price per vaccine dose, π, is the most important driver of financial performance. To achieve a positive expected annualized return (or a positive NPV), the list price per vaccine dose needs to be set above \$69.00 (or in the case of positive NPV, \$78.00), much higher than the assumed price of \$20.00. Although prices above \$100.00 for a vaccine dose are not uncommon in the United States (CDC 2022), high vaccine prices are a major obstacle for low-to-middle income countries to conduct massive vaccine campaigns and may increase vaccine hesitancy.

B.   Improved PoS of mRNA Vaccines

Increasing the PoS of mRNA vaccine clinical trials leads to higher investment in clinical trials and the a larger number of vaccines approved by the FDA. However, due to cannibalization between vaccines targeting the same EID and the stochastic nature of EID outbreaks, the ultimate revenues increase by a much smaller amount than the investment. The net effect is that the expected NPV decreases with the PoS and the expected annualized return becomes less negative (due to higher increase in investment than revenue).

C.   Correlations between Clinical Trial Outcomes

Increasing the correlation between vaccine trial outcomes decreases both the expected return and the expected NPV of the vaccine megafund, and significantly increases the volatility of the annualized return because the portfolio becomes less diversified.

D.   Human Challenge Trials

Increasing the probability, p_{HCT}, of conducting an HCT for vaccine clinical trials during an EID outbreak reduces the cost and duration of clinical trials, because a smaller group of subjects is enrolled. Although the expected annualized return and NPV both increase with p_{HCT}, they still remain negative. We conclude that the HCT design is insufficient to generate positive financial value.

E. Megafund Portfolio Size

Increasing the number of vaccine candidates for each EID by 50% increases both the investment in clinical trials and the likelihood that at least one vaccine candidate for the EID will be approved by the FDA. Although the expected investment increases by almost 50%, the expected revenue only increases by about 5%, due to cannibalization and the stochastic occurrence of EID outbreaks. Decreasing the number of vaccine candidates for each EID improves the expected annualized return and NPV, but both remain negative. Furthermore, the number of EID outbreaks prevented decreases from 31 to 27, resulting in a greater loss to society that is not captured by our financial analysis.

VII. Discussion

Our analysis illustrates three major challenges to the portfolio approach of financing mRNA vaccines for EIDs. First, the portfolio approach reduces the supply-side risk of vaccine R&D by increasing the probability of having at least one effective vaccine against an EID. However, it does not mitigate the demand-side risk in the revenues generated by vaccine sales, because vaccine demand is mainly determined by the natural occurrence of EID outbreaks. The stochastic nature of outbreaks limits the revenues generated by the approved vaccines, unless we increase the list price to $78.00 per dose. But with such a high list price, local governments and populations may not be able to afford the vaccines, which further reduces their demand and revenues. In addition, because mRNA vaccines share the same therapeutic mechanism, it is reasonable to expect that there will be no differentiated efficacy of different vaccines against the same disease. As a result, there will be significant market cannibalization between approved vaccines, because the total revenues of vaccine sales will not increase if there is more than one approved vaccine. Finally, the significant costs of clinical trials constitute 94% of megafund investment and severely limit its financial performance. One potential solution is to use more cost-effective clinical trial designs such as adaptive trials (Berry 2011) and platform trials (Woodcock and LaVange 2017), which simultaneously test multiple vaccine candidates using a shared control arm. These innovative trial designs have been shown to significantly reduce clinical trial costs and expedite the R&D process for glioblastoma therapeutic candidates (Siah et al. 2021). In addition, they do not elicit the ethical controversies of HCTs.

We also note that the primary goal of the vaccine megafund is to prevent future EID outbreaks and minimize the overall burden of disease. In light of this goal, our simulation assumes that we invest in clinical trials for all vaccine candidates simultaneously without optimizing for financial performance using sophisticated investment strategies (Gouglas and Marsh 2021) or financial engineering techniques such as dynamic leverage (Montazerhodjat, Frishkopf, and Lo 2016). For example, if three vaccine candidates for the same infectious disease successfully complete their phase 2 trials, we may instead first conduct phase 3 trials for two vaccine candidates, initiating the phase 3 trial for the third vaccine only if the first two have failed. This will reduce the costs of late-stage clinical trial development and improve its financial value. However, the increased financial value must be weighed against potential delays in FDA approvals of life-saving vaccines. A robust and multicriteria optimization framework is needed to ensure that their value to society is not compromised by optimizing financial returns for investors.

VIII.   Conclusion

Despite an increased PoS due to mRNA vaccine technology, diversification across a large number of vaccine candidates, and the potential benefits of conducting HCTs, the vaccine megafund model does not generate positive financial value for private-sector investors. The three bottlenecks of its financial performance are the limited revenues of vaccine sales, the cannibalization of approved vaccines for the same infectious disease, and the significant costs of late-stage clinical trials. Nonetheless, the vaccine megafund does generate tremendous social value by preventing future epidemic outbreaks; if endowed with public sector funding of $10 billion, it may also generate positive financial value for investors.

Our analysis indicates that continued collaboration between government agencies and the private sector will be necessary if the goal is to create a sustainable business model and robust vaccine ecosystem for addressing future pandemics. Strategies such as stockpiling vaccines for the most dangerous EIDs, putting in place advance market commitments or subscription fees to purchase/reserve mass quantities of vaccines in case of outbreaks, creating government-sponsored manufacturing and distribution facilities that can supplement private-sector resources, and providing limited government guarantees to investors funding vaccine programs for a prespecified list of priority diseases may all play a role in helping us reduce the impact of, or even prevent, future pandemics.

Appendix

I. Simulating Correlated Clinical Trial Outcomes

The key to simulating the financial performance of the vaccine mega-fund is to simulate the correlated binary outcomes of vaccine clinical trials. As in the previous biomedical megafund simulations (e.g., Siah et al. 2021), we use the technique proposed by Emrich and Piedmonte (1991) to simulate correlated Bernoulli variables; for example, variables that can only take the values 0 or 1, representing the failure or success of a clinical trial.

Vaccine clinical trials have five development phases (preclinical, phase 1, phase 2, phase 3, and EUA) and need to go through four phase transitions before receiving the EUA. Let the Bernoulli variable $B_{ij} \in \{0, 1\}$ denote whether vaccine candidate i has entered the development phase j, with $j \in \{0, 1, 2, 3, 4\}$. Initially, all vaccines are in the preclinical stage; that is, we set $B_{i0} = 1$. If the vaccine trial advances from phase $j - 1$ to j, where $j \in \{1, 2, 3\}$, we set $B_{ij} = 1$. If the vaccine receives EUA from the FDA, we set $B_{i4} = 1$.

To simulate the correlated phase transitions of clinical trials from phase j to $j + 1$, we first draw a vector of multivariate standard normal variables $\epsilon_j = [\epsilon_{1j}, \ldots, \epsilon_{nj}]$ with independent components ϵ_{ij}, where the length n is the number of vaccines in the portfolio. Next, we compute $z_j = \Sigma^{1/2}\epsilon_j$, where $\Sigma^{1/2}$ is the Cholesky decomposition of the correlation matrix Σ (fig. 1). The resulting vector z_j then follows a multivariate normal distribution with zero mean and covariance matrix equal to Σ, key to our simulation. Given the PoS, p_j, for phase transition from j to $j + 1$ (table 2), we can now simulate the binary clinical trial outcome as

$$B_{i,j+1} = \begin{cases} 1, z_{ij} > \alpha_j \\ 0, z_{ij} \leq \alpha_j \end{cases}, \tag{A1}$$

where z_{ij} is the i-th component of z_j, $\alpha_j = \Phi^{-1}(1 - p_j)$, and Φ^{-1} is the inverse cumulative distribution function of the standard normal variable. The clinical trial outcomes, B_{ij}, generated this way are positively correlated in each phase transition and used in our financial calculations.

In each Monte Carlo simulation, if we observe that $B_{ij} = 0$, the clinical trial for vaccine i terminates in phase j, and all subsequent B_{ik} (with $k > j$) are set to 0. If we observe $B_{ij} = 1$, the megafund incurs the clinical trial cost for phase j. If an epidemic outbreak occurs and there is at least one vaccine i with $B_{i4} = 1$ (i.e., it has received EUA), we manufacture the vaccine and collect the revenues from vaccine sales.

II. Sensitivity Analysis

We perform a sensitivity analysis to test the robustness of the simulation results against the assumed parameter values. The results are summarized in table A1.

A. Vaccine Price

The price per vaccine dose, π, is the key driver of financial performance. In the baseline model, we assume $\pi = \$20.00$, where both the annualized return and NPV are negative. Increasing π to $\$69.00$ (row 2 of table A1) achieves the break-even point for the annualized return. Increasing π further to $\$78.00$ (row 3 of table A1) achieves the break-even point for NPV. Assuming $\pi = \$100.00$ (row 4 of table A1), the megafund generates a small but positive expected annualized return of 1.9%, with a volatility of 7.2% and an expected NPV of $3.6 billion (SE $55 million). Such a high list price of $100.00 per vaccine dose is not unusual in the United States. As of April 14, 2022, 13 common adult vaccines have list prices above $100.00 in the United States (CDC 2022). However, these may be impossible to afford in low-to-middle income countries and may even increase vaccine hesitancy among the affected population.

B. Improved PoS of mRNA Vaccines

To test whether the increased PoS of mRNA vaccines leads to improved financial performance, we multiply the PoS of vaccine trials for six diseases by the technology factor, α_{tech}, to reflect the higher efficacy of mRNA vaccines for diseases with humoral immune protection. In the baseline model, we set $\alpha_{tech} = 1.2$ (i.e., a 20% increase in PoS). Surprisingly, increasing α_{tech}

from 1.0 to 1.3 (rows 5–7 of table A1) achieves a mixed effect: the expected annualized return increases from −6.7% to −5.8%, and the expected NPV decreases from −$8.1 to −$9.9 billion. As we increase α_{tech} from 1.0 to 1.3, the average number of approved vaccine candidates increases from 28 to 49, and the expected investment also increases from $15.2 to $18.4 billion. However, the reason for the mixed effect is that the expected revenues undergo a much smaller increase, from $7.1 to $7.6 billion, because, on average, only three additional EID outbreaks are prevented by the approved vaccines (due to the stochastic occurrence of EID outbreaks). The smaller ratio of revenues to investment causes the annualized return to be less negative and increase, and the larger increase in investment causes the NPV to be more negative and decrease. We conclude that the higher PoS of mRNA technology alone does not generate positive financial value for the megafund unless we also reduce the clinical trial costs or raise the price of the vaccine.

C. Correlations between Clinical Trial Outcomes

The correlation between vaccine trial outcomes measures the tendency for multiple vaccine trials to simultaneously succeed or fail due to a common target disease or mechanism of action. In the baseline model, we estimate the correlation via the novel virus distance metric, d_{ij}. However, we cannot simply rescale d_{ij} in the sensitivity analysis because the resulting correlation matrix is not guaranteed to remain PD. Instead, we gauge the impact of correlation by assuming an equicorrelated correlation matrix, in which $\rho_{ij} = \rho$ is the same for all diseases, and vary the value of ρ from 0% (independent) to 80% (highly correlated), as shown in rows 8–12 in table A1. As expected, we observe that higher values of ρ lead to worse financial performance, as the expected annualized return decreases from −3.5% to −11.7% and the expected NPV decreases from −$8.3 to −$9.5 billion. In addition, the volatility of the annualized return dramatically increases from 2.5% to 23.6%. This shows the importance of diversity in the megafund portfolio to generate positive financial value.

D. Human Challenge Trials

If deemed ethical, an HCT may be able to significantly reduce the cost and duration of the clinical development of vaccine candidates by testing a smaller group of participants than traditional vaccine trials. We

Table A1
Sensitivity Analysis of Key Simulation Parameters Computed
with 100K Monte Carlo Simulations

Portfolio	$E[R_a]$ (%)	$SD[R_a]$ (%)	E [NPV]	SD [NPV]	E [Inv]	SD [Inv]	E [Rev]	SD [Rev]	E [N_{ep}]	SD [N_{ep}]
Baseline	−6.0	6.7	−9.5	4.1	17.7	5.3	7.5	7.7	31	13
π = $69/dose	0	7.1	−1.4	11.9	17.7	5.3	25.8	26.7	31	13
π = $78/dose	.7	7.1	0	13.5	17.7	5.3	29.2	30.2	31	13
π = $100/dose	1.9	7.2	3.6	17.4	17.7	5.3	37.4	38.7	31	13
α_{tech} = 1.0	−6.7	11.9	−8.1	4.1	15.2	5.3	7.1	7.8	28	14
α_{tech} = 1.1	−6.2	9.1	−8.8	4.1	16.4	5.4	7.3	7.8	29	14
α_{tech} = 1.3	−5.8	4.8	−9.9	4.1	18.4	5.1	7.6	7.7	31	13
ρ = 0%	−3.5	2.5	−8.3	3.7	18.1	2.5	10.7	8.9	43	7
ρ = 20%	−3.8	2.7	−8.5	4.0	18.0	3.9	10.2	8.7	41	9
ρ = 40%	−4.2	4.2	−8.7	4.3	17.9	5.0	9.6	8.6	38	11
ρ = 60%	−5.9	11.1	−9.0	4.6	17.8	6.0	8.7	8.3	35	14
ρ = 80%	−11.7	23.6	−9.5	4.8	17.7	7.1	7.5	7.9	31	17
p_{HCT} = 10%	−5.7	6.7	−8.8	4.1	16.7	5.1	7.5	7.7	31	13
p_{HCT} = 30%	−5.1	6.7	−7.6	3.9	14.7	4.6	7.5	7.7	31	13
γ = .5	−4.1	8.9	−3.7	3.0	9.3	2.9	6.5	7.3	27	14
γ = 1.5	−7.3	5.7	−15.3	5.4	25.7	7.6	7.9	7.9	32	13

Note: R_a denotes annualized return (p.a.); NPV denotes net present value; Inv denotes net investment; Rev denotes net revenue, in billion US dollars; N_{ep} denotes the number of emerging infectious disease outbreaks contained by vaccines from the portfolio; π denotes the price per vaccine dose in US dollars; α_{tech} denotes the technology factor; p_{HCT} denotes the probability of human challenge trials; ρ denotes the pairwise correlation between vaccine trial outcomes; and γ denotes portfolio size factor. NPV is computed with an annual discount rate r = 10%.

investigate the effect of HCTs on the megafund performance by assigning the probability, p_{HCT}, that an HCT is allowed for each EID. The baseline portfolio does not use HCTs; that is, p_{HCT} = 0. Increasing p_{HCT} from 0% to 30% (rows 13–14 of table A1) reduces the expected investment and increases both the annualized return and the NPV, although both remain negative. We find that utilizing an HCT alone is also insufficient to generate positive financial value for investors.

E. Megafund Portfolio Size

The parallel vaccine development strategy not only increases the probability that at least one vaccine candidate will be approved but also increases the investment in clinical trials. To investigate the effect of portfolio size, we multiply the number of vaccine candidates for each infectious disease by a factor γ. The baseline portfolio corresponds to γ = 1. Increasing the portfolio size by 50% (γ = 1.5, row 16 of table A1) leads to worse financial performance, because the expected investment increases from $17.7 to $25.7 billion and the expected revenues increase by a much smaller amount, from $7.5 to $7.9 billion, as the natural occurrence of EID outbreaks remains the same. Decreasing the portfolio size by 50% (γ = 0.5, row 15 of table A1) increases both the expected return and the NPV, though both remain negative. In addition, the average number of epidemics prevented decreases from 31 to 27, which reflects a higher loss to society not captured by our financial analysis.

Endnotes

Author email address: Lo (alo-admin@mit.edu). We thank Regina Dugan, Ken Gabriel, Ben Jones, and Josh Lerner for valuable comments and suggestions, and Amanda Hu for research assistance. The views and opinions expressed in this article are those of the authors only and do not necessarily represent the views and opinions of any institution or agency, any of their affiliates or employees, or any of the individuals acknowledged above. For acknowledgments, sources of research support, and disclosure of the authors' material financial relationships, if any, please see https://www.nber.org/books-and-chapters/entrepreneurship-and-innovation-policy-and-economy-volume-2/accelerating-vaccine-innovation-emerging-infectious-diseases-parallel-discovery.

1. Phase 1 trials typically involve 10–50 patients, with the sole goal of establishing the safety and the maximum tolerable dose of a given drug candidate. If no significant side effects are encountered in phase 1, a phase 2 trial is initiated in which 50–500 patients who suffer from the targeted disease are carefully selected to test the drug candidate's efficacy. If significant benefits are detected in that trial, a much larger phase 3 trial involving thousands of patients is launched to test the drug candidate's efficacy in a broader and less carefully curated sample of patients. If significant benefits are detected in phase 3 with no serious side effects, the drug is approved for general use. Because vaccines are administered much more widely than other drugs, and given to healthy subjects rather than only those with a given disease, the regulatory hurdle for determining safety and efficacy is considerably higher. A typical phase 3 trial for a vaccine involves 30,000 subjects (as in the case of the COVID-19 vaccines), hence the outsized costs of phase 3 trials. See Lo and Chaudhuri (2022, chapter 8) for further details.

2. See Lo and Thakor (2022) for a systematic review of financing issues in the biopharma industry.

3. Positive definiteness is a mathematical property that guarantees the positivity of the variance of a weighted average of random variables. Given that the risk (as measured by variance) of a portfolio is never negative, it is important to impose this property on any correlation matrix; otherwise, nonsensical numerical results such as negative risk may occur.

References

Ahuja, A., S. Athey, A. Baker, E. Budish, J. C. Castillo, R. Glennerster, S. Duke, et al. 2021. "Preparing for a Pandemic: Accelerating Vaccine Availability." *AEA Papers and Proceedings* 111:331–35. https://doi.org/10.1257/pandp.20211103.
Arora, A., S. Belenzon, A. Patacconi, and J. Suh. 2020. "The Changing Structure of American Innovation: Some Cautionary Remarks for Economic Growth." *Innovation Policy and the Economy* 20:39–93. https://doi.org/10.1086/705638.

Berry, D. A. 2011. "Adaptive Clinical Trials in Oncology." *Nature Reviews Clinical Oncology* 9 (4): 199–207. https://doi.org/10.1038/nrclinonc.2011.165.

Berry, D. A., S. Berry, P. Hale, L. Isakov, A. W. Lo, K. W. Siah, and C. H. Wong. 2020. "A Cost/Benefit Analysis of Clinical Trial Designs for COVID-19 Vaccine Candidates." *PLoS ONE* 15 (12): e0244418. https://doi.org/10.1371/journal.pone.0244418.

Butler, D. 2008. "Translational Research: Crossing the Valley of Death." *Nature* 453:840–42. https://doi.org/10.1038/453840a.

Callaway, E. 2020. "Dozens to Be Deliberately Infected with Coronavirus in UK 'Human Challenge' Trials." *Nature* 586:651–52. https://doi.org/10.1038/d41586-020-02821-4.

CDC (Centers for Disease Control and Prevention). 2022. "CDC Vaccine Price List." https://www.cdc.gov/vaccines/programs/vfc/awardees/vaccine-management/price-list/index.html.

CEPI (Coalition for Epidemic Preparedness Innovations). 2022. "Our Portfolio." https://cepi.net/research_dev/our-portfolio.

Chaudhary, N., D. Weissman, and K. A. Whitehead. 2021. "mRNA Vaccines for Infectious Diseases: Principles, Delivery and Clinical Translation." *Nature Reviews Drug Discovery* 20:817–38. https://doi.org/10.1038/s41573-021-00283-5.

Chaudhuri, S. E., K. Cheng, A. W. Lo, S. Pepke, S. Rinaudo, L. Roman, and R. Spencer. 2019. "A Portfolio Approach to Accelerate Therapeutic Innovation in Ovarian Cancer." *Journal of Investment Management* 17 (2): 5–16.

Das, S., R. Rousseau, P. C. Adamson, and A. W. Lo. 2018. "New Business Models to Accelerate Innovation in Pediatric Oncology Therapeutics: A Review." *JAMA Oncology* 4 (9): 1274–80. https://doi.org/10.1001/jamaoncol.2018.1739.

Davis, M. M., A. T. Butchart, J. R. C. Wheeler, M. S. Coleman, D. C. Singer, and G. L. Freed. 2011. "Failure-to-Success Ratios, Transition Probabilities and Phase Lengths for Prophylactic Vaccines versus Other Pharmaceuticals in the Development Pipeline." *Vaccine* 29 (51): 9414–16. https://doi.org/10.1016/j.vaccine.2011.09.128.

Dolgin, E. 2021. "The Tangled History of mRNA Vaccines." *Nature* 597:318–24. https://doi.org/10.1038/d41586-021-02483-w.

Douglas, R. G., and V. B. Samant. 2018. "The Vaccine Industry." *Plotkin's Vaccines* 41–50.e1. https://doi.org/10.1016/B978-0-323-35761-6.00004-3.

Emrich, L. J., and M. R. Piedmonte. 1991. "A Method for Generating High-Dimensional Multivariate Binary Variates." *American Statistician* 45 (4): 302–4. https://doi.org/10.2307/2684460.

Fagnan, D. E., A. A. Gromatzky, R. M. Stein, J. M. Fernandez, and A. W. Lo. 2014. "Financing Drug Discovery for Orphan Diseases." *Drug Discovery Today* 19 (5): 533–38. https://doi.org/10.1016/j.drudis.2013.11.009.

Fernandez, J. M., R. M. Stein, and A. W. Lo. 2012. "Commercializing Biomedical Research through Securitization Techniques." *Nature Biotechnology* 30 (10): 964–75. https://doi.org/10.1038/nbt.2374.

Glennerster, R., and M. R. Kremer. 2000. "A Better Way to Spur Medical Research and Development." *Regulation* 23 (2): 34–39.

Gouglas, D., T. T. Le, K. Henderson, A. Kaloudis, T. Danielsen, N. C. Hammersland, J. M. Robinson, P. M. Heaton, and J.-A. Røttingen. 2018. "Estimating the Cost of Vaccine Development against Epidemic Infectious Diseases: A Cost Minimisation Study." *Lancet Global Health* 6 (12): E1386–96. https://doi.org/10.1016/S2214-109X(18)30346-2.

Gouglas, D., and K. Marsh. 2019. "Prioritizing Investments in New Vaccines against Epidemic Infectious Diseases: A Multi-Criteria Decision Analysis."

Journal of Multi-Criteria Decision Analysis 26 (3): 153–63. https://doi.org/10
.1002/mcda.1683.

———. 2021. "Prioritizing Investments in Rapid Response Vaccine Technologies for Emerging Infections: A Portfolio Decision Analysis." *PLoS ONE* 16
(2): e0246235. https://doi.org/10.1371/journal.pone.0246235.

Harbert, T. 2020. "How Moderna Is Racing to a Coronavirus Vaccine." April 3.
https://mitsloan.mit.edu/ideas-made-to-matter/how-moderna-racing-to
-a-coronavirus-vaccine.

Jain, S., A. Venkataraman, M. E. Wechsler, and N. A. Peppas. 2021. "Messenger RNA-based Vaccines: Past, Present, and Future Directions in the Context
of the COVID-19 Pandemic." *Advanced Drug Delivery Reviews* 179:114000.
https://doi.org/10.1016/j.addr.2021.114000.

Jarrett, S., S. Pagliusi, R. Park, T. Wilmansyah, S. Jadhav, P. C. Santana, K. R.
Krishnamurthy, and L. Yang. 2021. "The Importance of Vaccine Stockpiling
to Respond to Epidemics and Remediate Global Supply Shortages Affecting
Immunization: Strategic Challenges and Risks Identified by Manufacturers."
Vaccine: X 9:100119. https://doi.org/10.1016/j.jvacx.2021.100119.

Jarrett, S., L. Yang, and S. Pagliusi. 2020. "Roadmap for Strengthening the Vaccine Supply Chain in Emerging Countries: Manufacturers' Perspectives." *Vaccine*
X 5:100068. https://doi.org/10.1016/j.jvacx.2020.100068.

Jimenez, D. 2021. "COVID-19: Vaccine Pricing Varies Wildly by Country
and Company." Pharmaceutical Technology, October 26. https://www
.pharmaceutical-technology.com/features/covid-19-vaccine-pricing-varies
-country-company.

Kelland, K. 2019. "GSK Ends Development of Ebola Vaccine, Hands Work
to U.S. Institute." *Reuters*, August 6. https://www.reuters.com/article/us
-health-ebola-gsk/gsk-ends-development-of-ebola-vaccine-hands-work-to
-u-s-institute-idUSKCN1UW15S.

Kis, Z., C. Kontoravdi, R. Shattock, and N. Shah. 2021. "Resources, Production
Scales and Time Required for Producing RNA Vaccines for the Global Pandemic Demand." *Vaccines* 9 (1): 3. https://doi.org/10.3390/vaccines9010003.

Kis, Z., and Z. Rizvi. 2021. "How to Make Enough Vaccine for the World in
One Year?" Report, Public Citizen. https://www.citizen.org/article/how
-to-make-enough-vaccine-for-the-world-in-one-year.

Lo, A. W., and S. E. Chaudhuri. 2022. *Healthcare Finance: Modern Financial Analysis
for Accelerating Biomedical Innovation.* Princeton, NJ: Princeton University Press.

Lo, A. W., C. Ho, J. Cummings, and K. S. Kosik. 2014. "Parallel Discovery of
Alzheimer's Therapeutics." *Science Translational Medicine* 6 (241): 241cm5.
https://doi.org/10.1126/scitranslmed.3008228.

Lo, A. W., and R. Thakor. 2022. "Financing Biomedical Innovation." *Annual Review
of Financial Economics* 14:231–70.

Montazerhodjat, V., J. J. Frishkopf, and A. W. Lo. 2016. "Financing Drug Discovery via Dynamic Leverage." *Drug Discovery Today* 21 (3): 410–14. https://doi
.org/10.1016/j.drudis.2015.12.004.

Morens, D. M., and A. S. Fauci. 2020. "Emerging Pandemic Diseases: How We
Got to COVID-19." *Cell* 182 (5): 1077–92. https://doi.org/10.1016/j.cell.2020
.08.021.

Nathan, N., M. Barry, M. Van Herp, and H. Zeller. 2001. "Shortage of Vaccines
during a Yellow Fever Outbreak in Guinea." *Lancet* 358 (9299): 2129–30.
https://doi.org/10.1016/S0140-6736(01)07185-9.

NBTS (National Brain Tumor Society). 2021. "Brain Tumor Investment Fund."
https://braintumor.org/our-research/investment-fund.

Neilson, S., A. Dunn, and A. Bendix. 2020. "Moderna's Groundbreaking Coronavirus Vaccine Was Designed in Just 2 Days." *Business Insider*. https://www.businessinsider.com/moderna-designed-coronavirus-vaccine-in-2-days-2020-11.

Neumann, P. J., J. T. Cohen, and M. C. Weinstein. 2014. "Updating Cost-Effectiveness: The Curious Resilience of the $50,000-per-QALY Threshold." *New England Journal of Medicine* 371 (9): 796–97.

NIAID (National Institute of Allergy and Infectious Diseases). 2018. "NIAID Emerging Infectious Diseases/Pathogens." https://www.niaid.nih.gov/research/emerging-infectious-diseases-pathogens.

Pardi, N., M. J. Hogan, F. W. Porter, and D. Weissman. 2018. "mRNA Vaccines: A New Era in Vaccinology." *Nature Reviews Drug Discovery* 17 (4): 261–79. https://doi.org/10.1038/nrd.2017.243.

Plotkin, S. A., A. A. F. Mahmoud, and J. Farrar. 2015. "Establishing a Global Vaccine-Development Fund." *New England Journal of Medicine* 373 (4): 297–300. https://doi.org/10.1056/NEJMp1506820.

Project ALPHA. 2022. "Estimates of Clinical Trial Probabilities of Success (PoS)." https://projectalpha.mit.edu/pos.

Pronker, E. S., T. C. Weenen, H. Commandeur, E. H. J. H. M. Claassen, and A. D. M. E. Osterhaus. 2013. "Risk in Vaccine Research and Development Quantified." *PLoS ONE* 8:e57755. https://doi.org/10.1371/journal.pone.0057755.

Qi, H., and D. Sun. 2006. "A Quadratically Convergent Newton Method for Computing the Nearest Correlation Matrix." *SIAM Journal on Matrix Analysis and Application* 28 (2): 360–85. https://doi.org/10.1137/050624509.

Rapeport, G., E. Smith, A. Gilbert, A. Catchpole, H. McShane, and C. Chiu. 2021. "SARS-CoV-2 Human Challenge Studies: Establishing the Model during an Evolving Pandemic." *New England Journal of Medicine* 385 (11): 961–64. https://doi.org/10.1056/NEJMp2106970.

Siah, K. W., Q. Xu, K. Tanner, O. Futer, J. J. Frishkopf, and A. W. Lo. 2021 "Accelerating Glioblastoma Therapeutics via Venture Philanthropy." *Drug Discovery Today* 26 (7): 1744–49. https://doi.org/10.1016/j.drudis.2021.03.020.

SIFMA (Securities Industry and Financial Markets Association). 2021. "Capital Markets Fact Book, 2021." https://www.sifma.org/resources/research/fact-book.

Szabó, G. T., A. J. Mahiny, and I. Vlatkovic. 2021. "COVID-19 mRNA Vaccines: Platforms and Current Developments." *Molecular Therapy* 30 (5). https://doi.org/10.1016/j.ymthe.2022.02.016.

Vu, J., B. Kaplan, S. E. Chaudhuri, M. Mansoura, and A. W. Lo. 2022. "Financing Vaccines for Global Health Security." *Journal of Investment Management* 20 (2): 1–17.

WHO (World Health Organization). 2014. "A Brief Guide to Emerging Infectious Diseases and Zoonoses." https://apps.who.int/iris/handle/10665/204722.

———. 2020. "2019 Yellow Fever ICG Annual Meeting Report." https://www.who.int/publications/i/item/9789240008236.

Wong, C. H., K. W. Siah, and A. W. Lo. 2019. "Estimation of Clinical Trial Success Rates and Related Parameters." *Biostatistics* 20 (2): 273–86. https://doi.org/10.1093/biostatistics/kxx069.

Woodcock, J., and L. M. LaVange. 2017. "Master Protocols to Study Multiple Therapies, Multiple Diseases, or Both." *New England Journal of Medicine* 377 (1): 62–70. https://doi.org/10.1056/NEJMra1510062.

The Generic Drug Trilemma

Daniel J. Hemel, *New York University School of Law,* United States of America
Lisa Larrimore Ouellette, *Stanford Law School,* United States of America

Abstract

More than 90% of prescriptions dispensed in the United States each year are for off-patent drugs. Yet the bulk of scholarship on prescription drug policy focuses on patented drugs. Discussions of prescription drugs are typically oriented around the "innovation-access dilemma"—the trade-off between stronger patent-based incentives for innovators and higher prices for purchasers of patented products. But for drugs in the "patent afterlife"—the period after patent protection and other forms of market exclusivity have expired—the innovation-access dilemma is not the fundamental policy trade-off. Higher prices do not necessarily redound to the benefit of innovators, and price is not the only significant impediment to access: drug shortages—often triggered by safety concerns—also prevent patients from obtaining the medicines they need.

This chapter seeks to provide scholars and policy makers with a unifying framework for analyzing the variegated challenges of the pharmaceutical patent afterlife. We argue that the key trade-offs in off-patent drug policy take the form of a trilemma—the three corners of which are price, quantity, and quality (i.e., safety and efficacy). The generally accepted goal of off-patent drug policy is to facilitate (1) low prices and (2) sufficient quantities of drugs that are (3) equivalent or similar to brand-name drugs approved by the Food and Drug Administration. But policies that improve outcomes along one or two of those dimensions typically entail some sacrifice along the third.

The trilemma framing yields several analytical payoffs. First, it sheds light on the root causes of puzzling problems plaguing some off-patent drug markets, such as sudden price spikes and persistent mismatches between supply and demand. Second, it draws attention to the noninnovation costs of recent drug pricing reform proposals—costs that are often overlooked amid the emphasis on innovation versus access. Finally, it motivates a search for solutions that can transcend the trilemma and optimize along all three dimensions of off-patent drug policy. That search brings us, full circle, back to innovation and access—the concerns that dominate

Entrepreneurship and Innovation Policy and the Economy, volume 2, 2023.
Published by The University of Chicago Press for the National Bureau of Economic Research. https://doi.org/10.1086/723235

discussions of pharmaceutical policy at the beginning of the patent life. But this time, the focus is on innovation—and, specifically, manufacturing innovation—in service of rather than in tension with access.

JEL Codes: H51, I18, K32, O38

Keywords: pharmaceutical policy, generics, drug pricing, drug shortages, drug quality, pharmaceutical manufacturing

I. Introduction

The innovation-access dilemma is the dominant theme in discussions of patent law and policy (e.g., Landes and Posner 2003; Barnes 2010; Sampat and Williams 2019). Patent protection incentivizes innovation by offering a time-limited monopoly for novel and nonobvious inventions, but the high prices facilitated by patent monopolies limit access to knowledge goods. The stakes on both sides of the innovation-access trade-off are particularly high in the prescription drug context: pharmaceutical innovation has fueled significant health and longevity gains in recent decades (Lichtenberg 2019), but high prices prevent millions of patients in and beyond the United States from accessing medicines they need (WHO 2016; Kearney et al. 2021).

   In prior work, we have argued that the innovation-access dilemma is, in fact, less of a dilemma than the conventional framing lets on. First, policy makers can avoid the trade-off by replacing patents with nonpatent rewards, including grants, tax credits, and prizes (Hemel and Ouellette 2013). Second, even without eschewing intellectual property, policy makers can sidestep the innovation-access trade-off by "matching" patent-based rewards with nonpatent allocation mechanisms such as government procurement (Hemel and Ouellette 2019). The COVID-19 experience offers an illustration of "matching" in action: while preserving patent protection on the incentive side, the federal government provided all Americans with free access to vaccines through procurement contracts with Pfizer, Moderna, and Johnson & Johnson. That is, the price paid to innovators can be set separately from the price paid by patients.

   But whether one accepts or rejects the claim that the innovation-access dilemma is the fundamental policy problem in patent law generally or pharmaceutical patents specifically, it is clearly not the fundamental policy problem in the market for generic drugs, which constitute 90% of prescription drugs dispensed in the United States (Association for Accessible Medicines 2021).[1] Once drugs lose the protection of patents and other forms of market exclusivity—in the period we call the "patent afterlife"—many of the profits flow to firms that had no role in the development of the drug in question. Although patients still often pay high prices for off-patent drugs, high prices paid to firms that did not develop the relevant drug are not part of society's bargain for more innovation.

To be sure, drug policy in the patent afterlife is *not* free from trade-offs. The trade-offs, though, are different from—and potentially more difficult than—the innovation-access trade-off in patent law. And although these trade-offs have garnered much less attention than the innovation-access dilemma, they have significant implications for access to medicines in the United States.

This chapter argues that the key trade-offs in generic drug policy take the form of a trilemma—the three corners of which are price, quantity, and quality (encompassing efficacy as well as safety). As with other trilemmas in economics—for example, the classic macroeconomic trilemma (Fleming and Mundell 1964) and the political trilemma of the world economy (Rodrik 2000)—the trilemma framing captures the impossibility (or at least extreme difficulty) of achieving all three goals at the same time (here, low prices, sufficient quantities, and a safety and efficacy profile that mirrors the profile of originator drugs). Policy solutions that satisfy one—or even two—of the objectives identified by the trilemma are feasible, but solutions that adequately address all three remain elusive for many drugs. We can have a cheap and plentiful supply of generic drugs, a plentiful supply of high-quality generic drugs, or a cheap supply of high-quality generics, but the abiding challenge of generic drug policy is to solve for all three variables simultaneously.

To see how the goals of generic drug policy come into conflict, start with the corner of the trilemma that has recently attracted the most policy attention: price. Policies that reduce prices paid to manufacturers, such as price caps, also reduce incentives for generic entry, increase incentives for exit, and discourage manufacturers that remain in the market from building up excess supply. As a result, the probability of shortages will rise, negatively affecting the second corner: adequate quantities. (As discussed below, the US and Canadian experiences largely bear out this prediction.) Reciprocally, policy makers could minimize the risk of shortages by offering to reimburse off-patent drug manufacturers at high rates, but those generous reimbursements would (of course) come at the expense of the first corner of the trilemma: low prices.

The third corner of the trilemma—quality—implicates a similar quandary. With respect to small-molecule drugs, the US Food and Drug Administration (FDA) requires generic manufacturers to demonstrate "bioequivalence" with the brand-name product. Firms seeking to market the equivalent of generics for off-patent biologics must satisfy even more demanding requirements. The FDA also requires firms to adhere to rigorous manufacturing protocols. These prerequisites for approval raise entry barriers that reduce competition. That lack of competition, in turn, leaves the market for off-patent drugs more vulnerable to sudden price hikes and to persistent mismatches between supply and demand.

At least in theory, policy makers still can achieve any two of the three objectives straightforwardly. For example, policy makers can achieve both low prices and sufficient quantities by reducing entry barriers for off-patent drugmakers. But those entry barriers exist to protect safety and efficacy, so reduced regulatory scrutiny will entail a trade-off with drug quality. Similarly, policy makers can satisfy the price and quality corners of the trilemma by combining price caps with rigorous safety and efficacy evaluations. But the combination of low prices and high entry barriers will exacerbate the risk of shortages. To satisfy both quantity and quality objectives, policy makers can combine thorough regulatory scrutiny with price guarantees for manufacturers who meet those high standards—but at the cost of increased prices.

Our trilemma framing is not, to be sure, an axiom of futility: some reforms will improve outcomes in two corners much more than they cause harm in the third, and in some generic drug markets the trade-offs will be much less stark than in others. What the trilemma framing accomplishes is to highlight the compromises that characterize off-patent drug policy. It thus helps to explain how some of the puzzling outcomes in off-patent drug markets—sudden price spikes, persistent shortages, and safety lapses— trace back to choices by policy makers to prioritize (rightly or wrongly) other corners. And it inspires reflection on approaches that might alleviate some of the tension among the price, quantity, and quality objectives— for example, government efforts to accelerate manufacturing innovation.

In Section II, we describe the regulatory and competitive landscape for off-patent drugs in the United States. Section III introduces the trilemma. Section IV considers policies that seek to transcend the trilemma through antitrust enforcement, government manufacturing, and public investments in supply chain resilience. Section V concludes.

II. The US Pharmaceutical Patent Afterlife

The United States, like most other countries, provides 20 years of patent protection for inventions that satisfy certain statutory requirements. Congress has provided several additional protections for drugs and vaccines that sometimes extend the period of market exclusivity beyond the 20-year patent term. For example, the Orphan Drug Act of 1983 provides 7 years of exclusivity for drugs that treat rare diseases or conditions—generally, diseases or conditions affecting fewer than 200,000 people within the United States. The 7-year term starts from the date of FDA approval, so if a qualifying drug is approved late in the 20-year patent term, Orphan Drug Act exclusivity may last beyond the expiry of patent protection. Likewise, the Hatch-Waxman Act of 1984 allows a patent term restoration of up to 5 years to compensate for some of the time lost to clinical testing and FDA review of a new drug application (though the patent term cannot be stretched beyond 14 years after FDA approval).

Once patent protection and any additional periods of market exclusivity have ended, a pharmaceutical product enters what we call the "patent afterlife." Even then, though, competitors must obtain FDA approval before they can begin to sell a pharmaceutical product. This section provides an overview of the regulatory regime that governs the US pharmaceutical patent afterlife.

A.   Small-Molecule Drugs versus Biologics

Regulation in the US pharmaceutical patent life differs depending on whether the relevant product is a small-molecule drug or a biologic. Small-molecule drugs have simple chemical structures that can be described relatively easily by scientists. As a result, it is generally straightforward to determine whether two small-molecule drugs are chemically equivalent. Most small-molecule drugs are administered orally (e.g., as tablets, capsules, or liquids), but some are administered via injection (including many small-molecule chemotherapy drugs and anesthetics). Sometimes, the term "generic" is used to describe exclusively small-molecule generics.

Biologics have more complex structures and are typically derived from living material. Examples include vaccines, monoclonal antibodies, and insulin. Because of their complexity, the chemical structures of biologics are much harder (and sometimes impossible) for scientists to describe, making comparisons between biologics much more difficult. Biologics are usually—though not always—administered by injection or infusion.

The twentieth century has been termed "the era of the small molecule" (Economist 2014). Most pharmaceutical products in the United States still are small-molecule drugs, including over-the-counter products such as aspirin and ibuprofen as well as familiar prescription drugs such as fluoxetine (brand name Prozac) and atorvastatin (Lipitor). But many of the blockbuster drugs of recent decades have been biologics, including the arthritis drug adalimumab (Humira) and the autoimmune disease treatment infliximab (Remicade). By 2018, 8 of the 10 best-selling prescription drugs around the world by revenue were biologics (Yip 2020).

B.   Small-Molecule Drugs in the Patent Afterlife

Any new drug—whether it is a small-molecule drug or a biologic—must be approved by the FDA before it can be sold in the United States. Small-molecule drugs in the patent afterlife can be grouped into three categories based on their pathway to FDA approval: (1) brand-name drugs approved via a new drug application (NDA), (2) generics approved via an abbreviated new drug application (ANDA), and (3) drugs approved under section 505(b)(2) of the Federal Food, Drug, and Cosmetic Act, which offers a hybrid between an NDA and an ANDA.

Brand-Name Small-Molecule Drugs

An NDA for a small-molecule drug must show the product is safe and effective for its intended use, that its benefits outweigh its risks, and that it will be manufactured in a controlled way that will preserve its quality. To generate evidence in support of these applications, the sponsor must conduct costly clinical trials. According to one recent estimate, the average cost of clinical trials across phases I, II, and III is $114 million in 2013 dollars (DiMasi, Grabowski, and Hansen 2016).[2] The average cost per approved compound is much higher because most clinical trials are not successful.

A brand-name drug enters the patent afterlife when patent protection (and any other period of market exclusivity) expires. Patent expiration may occur less than 20 years after the drug is first marketed because some of the patent term is generally consumed by the time spent on clinical trials and regulatory approval (Budish, Roin, and Williams 2015). Firms often prolong patent life through "evergreening," or filing later patents on secondary innovations related to their drugs, though these patents tend to be lower quality (Frakes and Wasserman 2020) and are more likely to be held invalid or not infringed during litigation (Hemphill and Sampat 2013). Looking specifically at drugs for which the patent term was extended under the Hatch-Waxman Act, Lietzan and Lybecker (2020) estimate that the average effective patent life for these drugs is 11.58 years.

Once a brand-name drug enters the patent afterlife, it does not necessarily face immediate competition from generics. For a brand-name drug based on a "new chemical entity" (roughly speaking, a drug whose active ingredient has never before been approved by the FDA), the Hatch-Waxman Act grants 5 years of "data exclusivity." Data exclusivity prevents a generic firm from relying on the brand-name drugmaker's original clinical trial data. Technically, data exclusivity does not prevent market entry if the generic firm conducts its own clinical trials, whereas "market exclusivity" (as under, e.g., the Orphan Drug Act) completely blocks market entry. But as a practical matter, data exclusivity has a similar effect to market exclusivity because of the cost of conducting new clinical trials (Thomas 2017). If a brand-name drug based on a new chemical entity is approved with less than 5 years of patent protection remaining, data exclusivity is likely to extend the brand-name drugmaker's monopoly beyond the patent term.

Small-Molecule Generics

Once the patent term and any nonpatent market and data exclusivity periods are over, a would-be generic manufacturer still needs FDA approval before it can sell a small-molecule drug. The Hatch-Waxman Act created the standard pathway to FDA approval for small-molecule generics: an ANDA. Because small-molecule drugs generally comprise only 20–100 atoms, laboratory measurements can be used to show that a generic is chemically equivalent to the innovator (i.e., brand-name) drug. The regulatory standard is that an ANDA must contain evidence of "bioequivalence," meaning that there is no "significant difference in the rate and extent to which the active ingredient . . . becomes available at the site of drug action." A manufacturer of a small-molecule generic that satisfies this bioequivalence standard does not need to conduct its own clinical trials to establish safety and efficacy. Instead, it can rely on the studies that supported the brand-name drug's application (provided that the brand-name drugmaker no longer enjoys data exclusivity).

FDA approval of an ANDA for a small-molecule generic has potential state-law consequences. As of September 2019, 19 states had enacted laws that require pharmacists to substitute a lower-cost generic for a brand-name small-molecule drug when the physician's prescription references the brand-name product. The other 31 states and the District of Columbia had laws that allow—but do not require—pharmacists to substitute lower-cost generics for brand-name small-molecule drugs. State laws also vary in whether they require pharmacists to notify patients or obtain patient consent when they substitute a generic for a brand-name drug. In all states, physicians can prevent generic substitution by prescribing the brand-name drug and indicating "dispense as written" on the prescription (Sacks, Van de Wiele, and Fulchino 2021).

Historically, most ANDAs targeted drugs that were no longer covered by patents (FTC 2002). However, Hatch-Waxman allows—and encourages—generic developers to seek approval before a brand-name manufacturer's patents have expired. An ANDA seeking market entry before patent expiration must include a "paragraph IV" certification stating that the relevant patents are invalid or that the brand-name manufacturer's patents are not infringed by the generic product. Hatch-Waxman awards the first paragraph IV filer with 180 days of generic market exclusivity once its ANDA is approved, meaning that the FDA will not allow a second generic on the market during this time. The 180-day exclusivity period is intended to incentivize generic developers to challenge patents that were improperly granted or that are asserted to cover drugs beyond their proper scope.

Hybrid Drugs Approved under Section 505(b)(2)

Hatch-Waxman also created another pathway—known as a "505(b)(2) application"—for hybrid small-molecule drug products that depend on both an existing drug's clinical trial data plus new clinical trial data.[3] These hybrids typically have the same active ingredient as an already approved drug but a different formulation or delivery mechanism. Drugs approved under section 505(b)(2) are eligible for 3 years of data exclusivity before other firms can rely on the new clinical trials. One well-known example of a drug approved under section 505(b)(2) is the Narcan nasal spray, used to stop or reverse the effects of opioid and heroin overdoses. The FDA had previously approved a drug using the same active ingredient (naloxone hydrochloride) in injectable form.

Approvals under section 505(b)(2) have increased significantly since the 1990s. In 2011, the FDA for the first time approved more section 505(b)(2) applications than NDAs (Gaffney 2015). However, the ANDA route for small-molecule generics remains much more common than the

505(b)(2) pathway, with the FDA granting more than 10 times as many ANDA approvals each year as 505(b)(2) approvals (Darrow, He, and Stefanini 2019).

C. Biologics in the Patent Afterlife

Because of the relative recency of the biologics boom (Mullard 2022), comparatively few biologics have reached the patent afterlife. When they ultimately do, biologics fall into one of two categories: (1) brand-name biologics that have lost patent protection and market exclusivity and (2) "biosimilars."

Brand-Name Biologics

The analog to an NDA in the biologics context is a biologics license application (BLA). As with NDAs for small-molecule drugs, BLAs require costly clinical trials to demonstrate safety and efficacy. One salient difference between small-molecule pharmaceuticals and biologics is the length of data exclusivity for innovative drugs. Recall that under Hatch-Waxman, brand-name small-molecule drugs based on new chemical entities enjoy 5 years of data exclusivity. By contrast, the Biologics Price Competition and Innovation Act of 2010 (BPCIA)—enacted as part of the Affordable Care Act—provides 12 years of data exclusivity starting from the date that a new biologic is licensed by the FDA.

Biosimilars

In addition to its data exclusivity provisions for brand-name biologics, the BPCIA created an analog to an ANDA for biologic drugs: an abbreviated biologics license application (aBLA). The greater complexity of biologics makes it more difficult to demonstrate that a second product will have the same clinical effect, which is why generic biologics are termed "biosimilars" (rather than "bioequivalents"). To show biosimilarity, an aBLA must provide evidence that the product's characteristics are "highly similar" to the original biologic and that it has "no clinically meaningful differences" in clinical response studies.

If the aBLA also demonstrates that there is little risk in switching between the original biologic and the new biosimilar, the FDA may deem the biosimilar to be "interchangeable" with the brand-name biologic. When a biosimilar is designated as interchangeable with a brand-name biologic, no other manufacturer can receive an interchangeability designation for 12–42 months (with the length of the exclusivity period depending on the state of patent litigation). Thirteen states require pharmacists to substitute interchangeable biosimilars when a prescription references the brand-name biologic; the remaining states allow but do not require substitution (Sacks et al. 2021). As of June 2022, the FDA had approved approximately three dozen biosimilars, but it had designated only two of those biosimilars as interchangeable with a brand-name biologic.

The scientific differences between small-molecule and biologic drugs are reflected in different development costs. For small-molecule generics, the ANDA process typically takes 1–3 years and $1 million to $5 million, with no new clinical trials. By contrast, biosimilar development typically takes 8–10 years and around $100 million—including tens of millions of dollars in clinical response trials to confirm biosimilarity (Atteberry et al. 2019).

Table 1 summarizes the main categories of drugs that we will consider in this chapter.

D. Competition in the Pharmaceutical Patent Afterlife

The Hatch-Waxman Act is generally viewed as a success in increasing generic entry for small-molecule pharmaceutical drugs. By September 1994, 10 years after Hatch-Waxman's enactment, the FDA had approved

Table 1
Types of Drugs in the Patent Afterlife

Small-Molecule Drugs	Biologics
Brand-name small-molecule drug: Small-molecule drug approved under a new drug application (NDA) for which patent protection and market exclusivity have expired	Brand-name biologic: Biological product approved under a biologics license application (BLA) for which patent protection and market exclusivity have expired
Small-molecule generic: Small-molecule drug approved under an abbreviated new drug application (ANDA)	Biosimilar: Biological product approved under an abbreviated biologics license application (aBLA)
505(b)(2) hybrid: Small-molecule drug approved under hybrid review process based on existing drug's clinical trial data plus new data	Interchangeable biosimilar: Biosimilar deemed interchangeable with brand-name biologic by FDA. Noninterchangeable biosimilar: Biosimilar without interchangeability determination

1.91 ANDAs for every approved brand-name small-molecule drug (Heled 2021). Out of 206 new small-molecule drugs approved in tablet or capsule form between 1995 and 2010, the vast majority (167, or 81.1%) had at least one generic version approved by the FDA as of the end of 2021 (Gupta et al. 2022). Yet, despite these successes, there are still more than 360 small-molecule drugs that are no longer protected by patents or other forms of market exclusivity but that have no generic competitors (FDA 2022b), and many more with limited competition.

In contrast to Hatch-Waxman's qualified success, the BPCIA is generally viewed as failing at its goal of increasing access to biologics in the United States. Ten years after enactment of the BPCIA, the FDA still had approved only 0.1 follow-on products for every approved brand-name biologic (Heled 2021). And for some biologics, like vaccines, the FDA has not even issued regulations for how a firm would show that its vaccine is biosimilar to an existing vaccine. In other words, there is no such thing as a generic (or biosimilar) vaccine as a regulatory matter. Competition in vaccine markets thus requires an independent BLA based on new clinical trials.

Overall, competition in the pharmaceutical patent afterlife is far from robust. Conti and Berndt (2020) examine unique markets for off-patent small-molecule and biologic drugs from 2004 to 2016 and conclude that after a drug loses patent protection or other exclusivity, the median number of manufacturers in each market is typically only two or three. More than half of generics only have one supplier (NASEM 2018). As a number of scholars have noted, the generic markets attracting the least competition—including small-molecule drugs with limited markets (Scott Morton and Boller 2017) and most biologics (Atteberry et al. 2019)—often have a particularly high ratio of entry costs to available profits, giving them characteristics of natural monopolies.

From a social welfare perspective, competition is not an end in itself but a means to other welfare-relevant ends: lower prices, sufficient quantities, and higher quality. Yet as explained in the next section, lack of competition in the pharmaceutical patent afterlife has important—and negative—implications for patient welfare.

III.   Three Goals of Generic Drug Policy

Here, we introduce three key goals of policy in the patent afterlife—low prices, adequate quantities, and high quality—and explain why they form a trilemma: policy reforms that pursue one or two of these goals generally sacrifice on the third. The price-quantity-quality trilemma is conceptually distinct from the innovation-access dilemma that dominates discussions of the optimal patent term. In the standard economic model of patents (Nordhaus 1969), the optimal term is finite—at some point, the extra innovation incentive from a longer patent term no longer justifies the deadweight loss of monopoly. For present purposes, we will remain agnostic as to when that point is reached. Our focus here is on what happens afterward.[4]

A. Price

The most common complaint regarding drugs in the patent afterlife in the United States is their high price (e.g., Rosenthal 2014). Two dimensions of drug pricing are welfare-relevant: (1) the price paid to manufacturers by purchasers (including individual and group health plans, Medicare, and Medicaid) and (2) the out-of-pocket price paid by patients. The two dimensions are closely related, but they are also importantly distinct. Indeed, some policies that reduce out-of-pocket prices for patients may raise prices paid to manufacturers (and vice versa).

In recent years, large and abrupt increases in the list prices for generic drugs have become front-page news (e.g., Pollack and Tavernise 2015). From the first quarter of 2010 to the first quarter of 2015, more than a fifth of established generic small-molecule drugs (315 out of 1,441) experienced a sudden price increase of 100% or more (GAO 2016). In one of the most notorious examples, Turing Pharmaceuticals—then run by the since-convicted "pharma bro" Martin Shkreli—hiked the price of the 6-decade-old antiparasite drug Daraprim over 5,000% (Lupkin 2019).

Yet cross-country comparisons complicate the narrative of high US generic drug prices. A RAND Corporation study commissioned by the US Department of Health and Human Services (HHS) found that, as of 2018, US unbranded generic drug prices were 16% lower than prices in other countries within the Organization for Economic Cooperation and Development (OECD;Mulcahy et al. 2021). The same study found that unbranded generic drugs accounted for a much larger share of drug volume in the United States than elsewhere in the OECD (84% vs. 35%). In other words, relative to other high-income countries, US purchasers are paying less for unbranded generics and buying more of them.

The RAND study's findings do not imply that high prices are a spurious concern for off-patent drug policy. First, the cross-country comparison excludes biologics, which now constitute more than two-fifths of total US pharmaceutical spending (IQVIA 2020). (As noted above, biologicdrugs do not technically have "generics"—a drug designed to have the same clinical effect as a branded biologic is a "biosimilar.") Second, the comparison also excludes nonoriginator drugs sold under brand names, such as drugs approved by the FDA through the hybrid section 505(b)(2) pathway. Once all small-molecule nonoriginator drugs are included in the cross-country comparison, US purchasers pay—on average—21% more than OECD peers. Third, the category of unbranded generics does not include off-patent drugs that do not (yet) face a generic competitor, for which prices may remain high while effective market exclusivity persists. Fourth, for some small-molecule drugs (like the estrogen derivative estradiol), prices remain high even after generics enter the market (Thomas 2018). And even insofar as US generic drug prices are in line with other OECD countries, one still might conclude that OECD countries are overpaying for generic drugs across the board.

Most importantly, the RAND comparison focuses on prices paid to manufacturers, not out-of-pocket prices paid by patients. In countries with universal health coverage, patient copays for prescription drugs are generally subject to low caps. For example, under the United Kingdom's National Health Service program, copays for outpatient drugs are capped at £9.35 (NHS 2022), or approximately $11.40 in US dollars as of June 2022. Outpatient drugs are free for many patients—including all children under 16, all adults over 60, and anyone who is pregnant or has had a child within the last 12 months—and inpatient drugs are free for everyone.

For patients with health insurance in the United States, by contrast, copays for prescription drugs can be substantial even after those drugs enter the patent afterlife. For example, average out-of-pocket spending on insulin for patients covered by Medicare Part D was $49 per prescription, or $520 per year, in 2019 (Cubanski and Damico 2022). And out-of-pocket costs can be significantly higher for the roughly 10% of Americans who have no health insurance (Cohen et al. 2021). Out-of-pocket patient costs are important because they can impede access to medicines. In one recent survey, 3 in 10 US adults reported not taking medicines as prescribed at some point in the past year "due to cost" (Kearney et al. 2021).

For purposes of the analysis below, our primary focus is on prices paid to manufacturers, not out-of-pocket prices paid by patients. We focus on prices paid to manufacturers for three reasons. First, most people in the United States (more than 60%) are covered by private health insurance plans. Higher costs incurred by those plans are likely to be passed through partly or fully to patients—for example, through higher premiums or, in the case of employer-sponsored plans, potentially through lower wages (Kolstad and Kowalski 2016). Thus, prices paid to manufacturers by insurers or by self-funded employer plans remain relevant to patients even when those prices are not reflected directly in copays. And high premiums potentially push more individuals into the ranks of the uninsured. Second, in many cases, higher prices paid to manufacturers are reflected directly in higher out-of-pocket prices for patients. For example, Medicare Part B mandates a 20% copay for prescription drugs administered in an outpatient setting. Third, more than 45% of prescription drug costs in the United States are paid by federal, state, and local governments (CMS 2021). Prices paid to manufacturers by government purchasers affect fiscal capacity, including the capacity of federal, state, and local governments to provide greater relief to patients.

But although the twin goals of reducing prices paid to manufacturers and reducing out-of-pocket prices paid by patients will often align, they will sometimes come into conflict. Higher copays potentially encourage patients to economize on health-care spending (Zeckhauser 1970). For example, a patient facing a high copay for a brand-name drug may be more likely to choose a lower-priced generic (insofar as the patient faces a choice under the relevant state's substitution law) or more likely to ask their physician to prescribe a biosimilar in place of a brand-name biologic. Capping or eliminating copays may therefore result in higher health system costs, some of which may be passed back to the broader patient pool (e.g., through higher premiums).

B. Quantity

A second area of concern regarding generic drugs in the United States is quantity. As of June 2022, the FDA classified 120 drugs as "currently in shortage" (FDA 2022a). Drug shortages are not a COVID-19-specific phenomenon: in 2011, the FDA recorded 251 new shortages (FDA 2021). Although shortages can arise with respect to on-patent and off-patent drugs, the FDA reports that two-thirds of drugs that went into shortage during a 5-year period from 2013 to 2017 were drugs with a generic version on the market (FDA 2020). Shortages are especially common with respect to sterile injectables, such as anesthetics and chemotherapy treatments (Yurukoglu, Liebman, and Ridley 2017).

From an economic perspective, the very idea of a "shortage" is somewhat puzzling: unless the supply and demand curves are both vertical lines, there must be some price at which they intersect. Within a

Marshallian supply-demand framework, there are at least three ways to make sense of widespread reports of drug "shortages." First, demand for the relevant drug may be inelastic. For example, insulin is often cited in microeconomics textbooks as an example of a product with inelastic demand (e.g., Brown 1995; Cowen and Tabarrok 2009). If demand is entirely unresponsive to price, then a temporary supply shock may result in disequilibrium.[5] Second, purchasing practices may introduce rigidities that prevent prices from rising to market-clearing levels. For example, most medical centers acquire drugs through group purchasing organizations (GPOs), which act as intermediaries between purchasers and manufacturers (Bruhn, Fracica, and Makary 2018). Long-term contracts between GPOs and manufacturers—including contracts that lock a GPO into using a particular manufacturer as its sole source for a drug—may prevent prices from responding rapidly to changes in demand and supply. Third and finally, the term "shortage" might be understood to refer broadly to supply shocks that cause quantity to fall and price to rise, even if there is no extended period of disequilibrium between supply and demand. Although "shortage" is arguably a misnomer (i.e., the market clears at the new, higher price), the result is still that patients cannot obtain drugs at prices that prevailed prior to the shock.

Whether or not drug shortages are "real shortages" (Stomberg 2018) in the economic sense, the health costs of generic drug supply shocks are potentially significant. In 2018, the American Medical Association adopted a policy declaring drug shortages to be an "urgent public health crisis" (American Medical Association 2018). In several surveys, physicians and pharmacists report higher rates of adverse drug outcomes and even patient deaths due to drug shortages (for a literature review, see Phuong et al. 2019). Retrospective cohort studies document negative clinical outcomes associated with specific shortages. For example, Vail, Gershengorn, and Hua (2017) find that patients with septic shock in hospitals affected by a 2011 norepinephrine shortage experienced higher rates of in-hospital mortality. Gross et al. (2017) find higher rates of C. difficile infection among patients at hospitals that switched to other antibiotics during a nationwide shortage of piperacillin/tazobactam in 2014.

Not all shortages are associated with negative clinical outcomes. For example, Trifilio et al. (2013) find no reduction in remission rates among patients with acute myeloid leukemia who switched from the chemotherapy drug daunorubicin to an alternative (idarubicin) during a daunorubicin shortage. Indeed, there is some evidence that older patients benefited from the shortage-induced switch. Moreover, the number of new shortages appears to be on the decline. According to the FDA, new drug shortages fell from a high of 251 in 2011 to 43 in 2020, notwithstanding COVID-19-related supply chain disruptions (FDA 2021).[6]

C. Quality

A final area of concern regarding generic drugs in the United States is quality, including both safety and efficacy. From a theoretical perspective, there are several reasons to be concerned about the quality of generic drugs. Although these concerns may loom larger in theory than in practice, the theoretical perspective reminds us why the quality of generics should not be taken for granted.

First, one source of concern is extreme quality uncertainty in the prescription drug market. Patients have no real way to detect manufacturing defects even after taking a drug. In the absence of any manufacturing defect, prescription drugs typically are less than 100% effective and produce adverse reactions in a subset of patients. A patient's own experience is thus minimally informative about potential manufacturing flaws. Quality uncertainty potentially leads to a "market for lemons," in which manufacturers of high-quality products cannot monetize their quality investments (Akerlof 1970). Those manufacturers may respond by diluting their quality standards or by exiting the market.

Second, reputational mechanisms—which address quality uncertainty in other markets—are particularly weak in the market for generic drugs. As noted above, all states require or permit pharmacists to substitute a cheaper available generic when a doctor's prescription specifies a brand-name small-molecule drug (Sacks et al. 2021). Patients do not necessarily choose—and may not even know—the identity of the generic manufacturer. The low salience of reputation reduces incentives for generic manufacturers to invest in quality.

Third, no single generic firm internalizes the full costs of manufacturing defects. For example, the infamous Cutter incident—in which live polio virus contaminated 120,000 doses of the Salk polio vaccine in 1955—shook confidence in (and reduced uptake of) other vaccine manufacturers' products as well (Oshinsky 2006). Acting on its own, a generic manufacturer may choose a level of investment in quality assurance that is lower than the optimal level from the entire industry's (or society's) perspective.

Fourth and finally, ex post liability for manufacturing defects cannot resolve all the problems of quality uncertainty in the market for generic drugs. Some defects will likely go undetected, because patients and physicians will not be able to distinguish the consequences of manufacturing defects from the normal operation of a nondefective drug. Moreover, some of the social costs of manufacturing defects—for example, reduced uptake of other manufacturers' products—likely will not be recoverable in tort. And all this is on top of familiar shortcomings of tort law—most relevantly, the fact that limited liability for corporate shareholders shields actors from the full costs of their torts (Leebron 1991).

Anecdotal evidence partly bears out these theoretical concerns about generic drug quality. In 2013, generic manufacturer Ranbaxy accepted a $500 million fine for safety violations at two of its Indian factories, including delays in reporting "unknown impurities" detected in an epilepsy drug that eventually led to a 73-million-pill recall (Thomas 2013). Discoveries of the likely carcinogen NDMA have led to major FDA-initiated recalls of off-patent drugs to treat heartburn (Johnson 2019), high blood pressure (Edney, Berfield, and Yu 2019), and diabetes (Blankenship 2020a). Investigative journalists have also uncovered anecdotes of safety violations at generic manufacturing plants, such as fabrication of data for regulators (e.g., Eban 2019; Stockman 2021).

Evaluating the actual health costs of these quality failures is more challenging. The possible presence of contaminants of unknown risk at various points along the generic drug supply chain will not always translate to patient harm, and these problems may be episodic rather than systemic. It is also unclear whether quality problems are substantially higher for generics than for brand-name drugs—quality concerns also can strike before pharmaceuticals enter the patent afterlife. Although critics of the generics industry point to the outsourcing of most generic manufacturing to India and China and problems with the FDA's foreign inspection program, many brand-name drugs are also sourced from overseas, sometimes from the same factories as generics. Moreover, the FDA does not publicly disclose where a drug is made because this information is considered a trade secret, which makes it hard to determine whether manufacturing origin affects patient outcomes.

Randomized controlled trials generally have not found significant differences in the clinical efficacy of generic and brand-name products (Kesselheim et al. 2008, 2010). But these studies do not resolve the quality debate, for two reasons. First, randomized trials compare generic drugs with brand-name drugs, but if brand-name drugs also have quality problems, researchers may observe no statistically significant differences between generic and brand-name treatment groups even though quality problems plague both. Understanding the health consequences of quality issues in the drug supply would require a comparison of real-world marketed drugs with the idealized, defect-free versions. Second, blinded randomized controlled trials cannot capture the consequences that arise when patients know they are switching from brand-name drugs to generics. Some studies have found that switching from brand-name to generic drugs was associated with worse clinical outcomes and more adverse events (for a systematic review, see Straka, Keohane, and Liu 2017), possibly because of negative perceptions of generics (Colgan et al. 2015) and related psychosomatic effects (Goldszmidt et al. 2019). FDA efforts to bolster confidence in generic drug quality may have positive health consequences even if those consequences flow through psychosomatic channels.

D.   The Generic Drug Trilemma

Each of these three goals—low prices, sufficient quantity, and high quality—theoretically lies within reach. But efforts to advance one or two of these goals predictably conflict with the third. We first consider policies that would satisfy one corner of the trilemma (i.e., would achieve one of the three goals), and then consider policy combinations that would satisfy two corners.

Price

The most straightforward way to reduce prices of prescription drugs is to impose price caps. For example, in 1998, the government of Ontario—Canada's most populous province—introduced the so-called 70/90 regulations under which the first generic entrant was prohibited from charging more than 70% of the brand-name product price and subsequent generic entrants were initially capped at 90% of the first generic price (Zhang et al. 2016). Since 2018, several US states have created prescription drug affordability boards authorized to establish price ceilings for prescription drugs (Williamson 2021). The Inflation Reduction Act, which Congress passed in 2022, effectively caps the price of insulin and a limited number of single-source drugs, including some off-patent drugs without generic competitors.

Price caps, to be sure, are not certain to achieve their immediate goal of reducing prices. For example, Anis, Guh, and Woolcott (2003) find that price caps set by the Ontario 70/90 regulations served as focal points for generic manufacturers: firms offered the maximum price allowable under the regulation even when they might have set lower prices in an unregulated market. But even well-designed price caps cannot escape from the law of unintended consequences. Price caps reduce incentives for generic entry and increase incentives for exit, as evidenced by increased generic exit in Ontario (Zhang et al. 2016). Policies laser-targeted at reducing prices are therefore likely to have negative effects on quantity (Scott Morton 2001; Rye 2012).

Policy makers also can push down prices by reducing regulatory barriers to market entry. Conrad and Lutter (2019) find a strong negative correlation between the median generic price of a particular drug (relative to the brand price before generic entry) and the number of generic producers of the drug: the median price with one generic producer is 61% of the brand-name price, falling to 21% of the brand-name price with four producers. The number of generic producers per drug would likely increase—and prices would fall—if the FDA's ANDA review process were less demanding. But that review process exists to ensure quality, and although it may be possible for the FDA to make some cost-cutting changes to the ANDA process without any serious impacts on safety or efficacy, agency efforts to reduce regulatory barriers to entry will ultimately come into conflict with the quality objective.

Quantity

For the same reason that price caps negatively affect quantity, the most straightforward way to address drug shortages is to guarantee higher prices. When Congress asked the FDA to analyze the "drug shortage crisis" in 2018, the agency concluded that the root cause of shortages was economic forces that lead to a "race to the bottom" in generic drug pricing (FDA 2020). But by construction, price guarantees would run counter to the goal of lowering drug prices. Quality issues, meanwhile, are the immediate reason for most drug shortages in the United States: according to the FDA, 62% of new drug shortages from 2013 to 2017 were triggered by quality issues (FDA 2020). Relaxing quality standards would thus reduce the number of shortages—but of course, safety and efficacy would suffer as a result.

Quality

To address concerns about generic drug quality, regulators could impose more rigorous quality requirements on new entrants, coupled with strict liability regimes targeting firms whose generics have manufacturing defects. Heightened ex ante scrutiny or ex post liability, however, raise the costs of supplying the market and thus are likely to undermine the other two corners of the trilemma by decreasing quantity and raising prices. For example, Atal, Cuesta, and Sæthre (2022) examine Chile's introduction of bioequivalence requirements for generic drugs and find that this "stronger quality regulation decreased the number of drugs in the market by 25% [and] increased average paid prices by 10%."

Price Plus Quantity

Just as a rigorous quality standard will increase both prices and the risk of shortages, policy makers could achieve both lower prices and higher quantities by reducing ex ante regulatory barriers and ex post liability risks. For example, Sachs (2019) proposes that after a price spike exceeding a certain threshold for a particular drug, the FDA could "preclear" generic manufacturers to make and sell that drug before completing the full ANDA or aBLA approval process. (One could imagine a similar "pre-clearance" mechanism triggered by drug shortages.) Yet as Sachs acknowledges, shortcutting the generic drug approval process "creates serious problems" for safety and efficacy.

Similarly, Cohen et al. (2019) note that the FDA already has statutory authority to authorize importation from Canada, and they suggest that the agency use this authority to allow generic drug imports when prices rise suddenly in the United States. (They also argue for expanding the FDA's importation authority to include a select group of other countries beyond Canada.) Yet as Bruser and McLean (2014) note, the FDA's safety standards are often more stringent than those of Canada's pharmaceutical regulator. In other words, importation can lower prices and reduce the risks of shortages because it effectively reduces the quality threshold. Although US patients may be better off on balance if the FDA were to allow generic imports in response to price spikes, the choice would not be trade-off-free.

Price Plus Quality

Like price and quantity, price and quality are mutually realizable goals. For example, policy makers could combine binding price caps with rigorous safety and efficacy regulations. But the combination of price caps and stringent quality standards would heighten the risk of shortages.

Exacting quality standards would raise manufacturer costs, spurring exit and deterring entry without high prices as an inducement.

Arguably, the US childhood vaccine experience in recent years reflects the consequences of policies that prioritize price and quality over quantity. The 1993 Vaccines for Children program provides eligible children with covered vaccines at no out-of-pocket cost to their families. Eligible children are those who are uninsured or eligible for Medicaid, as well as children who receive vaccines at Federally Qualified Health Centers and all children who are members of an Indian tribe. More than half of young children in the United States are eligible for vaccines through the program (HHS 2020). Covered vaccines are all pediatric vaccines included on a list maintained by the Centers for Disease Control and Prevention's Advisory Committee on Immunization Practices. One provision in the 1993 law imposes price caps on preexisting pediatric vaccines: HHS is prohibited from paying more through the program for any vaccine than the May 1993 price adjusted for subsequent increases in the Consumer Price Index.[7]

Congress's choice to cap prices for a significant portion of the childhood vaccine market without making any downward adjustments to quality standards puts the trilemma framework to the test. Sure enough, the United States subsequently saw a rash of childhood vaccine shortages. By 2004, 8 of 11 routine childhood vaccines had gone into shortage, with the probability of shortages correlated to low prices for the relevant vaccine (Ridley, Bei, and Liebman 2016). Thirty-five states temporarily suspended or reduced immunization requirements for day care and/or school programs—evidently in response to supply constraints (GAO 2002).

The childhood vaccine experience illustrates the perils of transplanting the framework of an innovation-access trade-off into the generic drug space, where a different policy trade-off dominates. As Ridley et al. (2016) summarize, one of the reasons why Congress imposed price caps through the Vaccines for Children program was a belief that it is "no longer necessary to worry about incentives for innovation for these vaccines because the costs of innovation were paid long ago by manufacturers." But in the patent afterlife, prices affect dimensions other than innovation as well. Specifically, when prices are constrained to be low but quality standards raise production costs, manufacturers are less likely to invest in maintaining and expanding supply. Whether or not Congress made the "right" trade-off among price, quality, and quantity as part of the 1993 act, the choice to cap prices without conceding on quality clearly entailed a trade-off—though one not immediately acknowledged at the time.

Fig. 1. The generic drug trilemma

Quantity Plus Quality

Finally, policy makers could ensure sufficient quantities and maintain rigorous quality standards if they were willing to guarantee high prices for generic drugs. In this respect, "money answereth all things" (Ecclesiastes 10:19). Manufacturers would have strong incentives to invest in spare capacity—and in measures to protect safety and efficacy—if profit margins on drugs in the patent afterlife were wide enough. But, of course, the one objective that cannot be satisfied by throwing money at a problem is economizing on price.

Figure 1 illustrates the three corners of the trilemma and some of the policy reforms that satisfy one or two corners.

IV. Partial Solutions to the Trilemma

Although policy makers cannot escape the price-quantity-quality trilemma, certain solutions will manage the trilemma better than others. In some cases, policy reforms can achieve gains for one or two goals that far outweigh the losses for the remaining corner. The trilemma also helps illustrate that no single goal is worth pursuing at any cost. Rather, ideally, society should seek gains in any one corner of the trilemma only up to the point that marginal benefit of those gains for social welfare equals the marginal cost of welfare losses at the other corners. Reaching this optimum, however, is easier said than done.

In some circumstances, competitive markets may be the best mechanism for balancing these trade-offs, and greater antitrust scrutiny may help facilitate such competition. But the government also can generate competition itself by entering the market as a producer (or by contracting with other entities to manufacture off-patent drugs). In addition, the trilemma highlights the potential contributions of policies to reduce price-quality-quantity trade-offs, such as public investments in supply chain resilience. Here, we describe generic drug policies grounded in each of these three approaches—antitrust enforcement, government production, and promotion of manufacturing innovation. Although none of these approaches offers a complete solution, each set of policies offers promise for improving outcomes in the patent afterlife.

A.   Antitrust Enforcement

One consequence of the United States' choice to allow unregulated pricing with restricted entry into the off-patent drug market is to leave the market vulnerable to anticompetitive conduct. Robust enforcement of antitrust laws can address some anticompetitive practices, but it does not offer a total escape from the price-quantity-quality trilemma.

Much of the literature on generic drug entry focuses on the period before patent protection expires—the patent life rather than the patent afterlife. A significant policy concern during a drug's patent life is that the relevant patents may have been erroneously granted by the US Patent and Trademark Office (Frakes and Wasserman 2019), or that they may not actually cover the drug in question. One of the innovations of the Hatch-Waxman Act—the paragraph IV process described in Section 2.2.2—was to create a route for generic drug manufacturers to challenge a patent as invalid or not infringed. In effect, Congress has sought to enlist generic drugmakers as "patent police."[8]

Patent policing by generic manufacturers does implicate the innovation-access trade-off. The paragraph IV process is designed to reveal instances in which brand-name drugs do not merit the innovation incentive that comes with patent protection. However, paragraph IV has not fully lived up to its designers' high hopes. One threat to the integrity of the process is the practice of "pay for delay," in which a brand-name manufacturer pays or otherwise compensates a generic firm in exchange for the generic firm dropping a patent challenge (Hemphill 2006). A further threat is common ownership: when generic drug manufacturers and brand-name counterparties have the same institutional shareholders, they are more likely to settle paragraph IV disputes (Xie and Gerakos 2020). Finally, when generic drug manufacturers also have patented products in their portfolios, they are less likely to pursue paragraph IV challenges to judgment—possibly for fear of establishing precedents that will undermine their own patents (Carrier, Lemley, and Miller 2020).

Antitrust enforcement could potentially help invigorate patent policing by generic manufacturers. Stricter scrutiny of pay-for-delay deals might deter generic and brand-name manufacturers from entering anticompetitive agreements. Policy interventions to reduce common ownership (Elhauge 2016; Posner, Scott Morgan, and Weyl 2017) might encourage more aggressive patent challenges under Hatch-Waxman and the BPCIA. Merger review might play a role in preventing brand-name and generic manufacturers from combining.

Our focus here, though, is not on the ways in which generic manufacturers fulfill their patent policing function, but on outcomes after the relevant patents have expired or been invalidated. Anticompetitive practices continue into the patent afterlife, but they differ from the practices associated with on-patent drugs. Often, anticompetitive practices in the patent afterlife exploit elements of the regulatory infrastructure designed to ensure the safety and efficacy of generic drugs. And the market for off-patent drugs is more vulnerable to anticompetitive conduct as a result of entry barriers erected with safety and efficacy in mind.

Historically, one mainspring of anticompetitive conduct in the patent afterlife has been the requirement—borne out of concerns regarding generic drug quality—that generic drug manufacturers demonstrate bioequivalence. To satisfy the requirement, a potential generic drug manufacturer must test its own product against samples of the corresponding brand-name drug. Some brand-name manufacturers have sought to prevent potential generic competitors from performing those tests by refusing to provide samples of the brand-name drug (Pear 2018)—what one former Federal Trade Commission official has described as a "sample blockade" (Kades 2021). Turing Pharmaceuticals—the company once led by Martin Shkreli, who was later convicted of securities fraud—used this strategy to maintain its monopoly over the antiparasite drug Daraprim long after all the relevant patents expired.[9]

"Safety protocol filibusters" (Kades 2021) are another anticompetitive practice that brand-name manufacturers have used to block generic entry during the patent afterlife. These "filibusters" involve drugs that are part of the FDA's risk evaluation and mitigation strategies (REMS) program. For drugs that carry a risk of serious adverse effects, the FDA requires manufacturers to develop safety protocols to reduce the risk of adverse outcomes. For example, a REMS protocol might require health-care professionals to complete a training module and obtain certification before prescribing or dispensing a particular drug. Historically, the FDA has required brand-name and generic manufacturers of the same drug to develop a single, shared REMS system. The generic manufacturer could not begin to sell the drug until the shared REMS was in place. That requirement encouraged brand-name manufacturers to engage in foot-dragging—or "filibustering"—during negotiations to establish the shared REMS, thus delaying generic entry. The FDA had the authority to waive the single, shared REMS requirement, but the agency rarely used that power (Dabrowska 2018).

The CREATES Act of 2019 seeks to address both the sample blockade and safety protocol filibuster issues. The statute—signed into law as part of a larger budget bill in December 2019—allows a potential generic entrant to sue to obtain samples of the brand-name drug. The statute also gives the FDA greater flexibility to allow generic manufacturers to establish their own REMS. Anecdotal evidence suggests that these reforms have, at least in part, achieved their goals (Kades 2021). However, sample blockades and safety protocol filibusters are not the only anticompetitive practices in the patent afterlife. For example, brand-name manufacturers still may—and do—use "citizen petitions" to challenge generic drugmakers' assertions that the brand-name and generic products are bioequivalent (Carrier 2018). These citizen petitions can delay generic approval for months or more even when they are ultimately denied.

Sample blockades, safety protocol filibusters, and sham citizen petitions all are distinct anticompetitive practices, but they are connected by a common thread: in each case, brand-name manufacturers exploit the fact that prices of off-patent drugs are unregulated while entry remains restricted. Those entry restrictions, in turn, are designed with safety and efficacy in mind. In other words, efforts to protect quality enable brand-name manufacturers to take actions that inflate price.

Even when anticompetitive conduct does not involve direct exploitation of quality protections, the entry barriers erected for quality-related reasons leave the market for off-patent drugs more vulnerable to collusion. For example, two executives at the generic manufacturer Heritage Pharmaceuticals pled guilty in 2017 to charges that they conspired with competitors to fix prices (DOJ 2017). A third executive at Sandoz, the generic unit of Novartis, pled guilty to related charges in 2020 (Blankenship

2020b). An ongoing set of lawsuits filed by 48 states alleges "rampant" collusion among generic manufacturers of prescription topical products (Stuart 2020). Quality controls—such as rigorous requirements to establish bioequivalence—facilitate this type of collusion by limiting the number of players in the market for any given drug and making it harder for new entrants to undermine existing cartels. In largely denying a motion to dismiss the states' antitrust claims, a federal district court emphasized that the states "plausibly outline a regulatory regime" that would provide a motive for price-fixing because "high barriers to entry . . . make an industry more conducive to collusion."[10]

Robust enforcement of antitrust laws—as well as legislative changes such as the CREATES Act—may help to alleviate some of the costs of a market with unregulated prices plus significant barriers to entry. Ultimately, though, antitrust enforcement is treating a symptom of the underlying choice to prioritize quantity and quality over price. As long as prices are unregulated and barriers to entry are high, antitrust enforcement will continue to play an important role in the off-patent drug market—but even the most rigorous antitrust scrutiny will not escape the trilemma. For example, in an empirical study of high off-patent drug prices in the United States compared with other countries, Ganapati and McKibbin (2021) note the greater market power of US drug suppliers as a factor limiting price decreases in US generic markets. But they also conclude that given the high fixed costs of entry, price controls are likely needed to substantially lower generic prices. Of course, capping prices without adjusting quality requirements will implicate concerns about quantity.

B.   Government Manufacturing

The primary strategy for managing the price-quantity-quality trilemma in the United States has been to promote competition through antitrust enforcement and to ensure quality through FDA oversight. One open question is whether these targeted interventions are superior to a more direct government role in supplying generic and biosimilar drugs. In other words, can the federal government manage the price-quantity-quality trade-off more effectively by acting as a police officer and seeking to root out anticompetitive behavior and unsafe manufacturing practices or—alternatively—by manufacturing safe and effective generics and biosimilars itself?

The proposed Affordable Drug Manufacturing Act—first introduced in 2018 by Representative Jan Schakowsky and Senator Elizabeth

Warren—would pursue the latter pathway. The bill would create an Office of Drug Manufacturing, located within HHS, which would be authorized to manufacture—or enter into contracts with other entities to manufacture—certain drugs. The authorization would apply only to drugs for which patent protection and any period of market or regulatory exclusivity under Hatch-Waxman and the BPCIA has expired. Moreover, the authorization would be limited to drugs marketed in the United States by fewer than three manufacturers—and, even then, only if the price has increased faster than the rate of inflation within the past 5 years, the drug is included on the FDA's drug shortage list, or the drug is listed by the World Health Organization as an essential medicine and the HHS secretary determines that the current price is a barrier to patient access (Warren 2018, 2020). The federal government then would sell the manufactured drugs at a "fair price" determined by the new HHS office.

The government manufacturing approach merits consideration. As Warren (2018) notes, the idea has some precedent in the Strategic National Stockpile, an HHS-managed cache of vaccines and antidotes accumulated in preparation for a possible bioterrorist attack or other public health emergency. And the federal government is already a large direct purchaser of pharmaceuticals through the Department of Defense (DoD), the Department of Veterans Affairs (VA), the Indian Health Service, the Federal Bureau of Prisons, and the Department of State. The two largest purchasers, the DoD and the VA, spent nearly $15 billion on pharmaceutical procurement in 2018, which accounted for nearly 5% of total US drug expenditures (CBO 2021). Federal pharmaceutical contracting has had a direct impact on an even larger number of Americans during the COVID-19 pandemic, when all Americans could freely access vaccines that the government procured from Pfizer, Moderna, and Johnson & Johnson.

One key difference between the Schakowsky-Warren proposal and the COVID-19 vaccine experience is that under the Schakowsky-Warren proposal, the federal government would not necessarily control the entire US supply of the drugs that it manufactures or procures. The federal government would simply be an additional source from which pharmacies, hospitals, GPOs, and other prescription drug buyers could procure the drugs they need. Thus, the federal government would not have primary responsibility for allocating and distributing drugs across the country. Moreover, by overshooting on quantity and contracting with a diverse set of suppliers, the government could minimize the risk that a quality-control issue at one plant will trigger a national shortage.

To be sure, government manufacturing is not a panacea to the trilemma. Manufacturing (or arranging for the manufacture of) millions of prescription drug doses lies far outside HHS's core competency—it remains to be seen whether the agency could amass the requisite expertise and logistical capacity to implement a large-scale manufacturing effort. And the risks of waste and mismanagement—familiar from other government procurement programs (e.g., Liebman and Mahoney 2017; Decarolis et al. 2020)—would remain. At the same time, it bears emphasis that the status quo approach already imposes significant burdens on federal authorities, who bear responsibility for enforcing antitrust laws amid legal and economic uncertainty. Rooting out anticompetitive conduct in the patent afterlife is not necessarily easier for the federal government than introducing competition itself.

C.   Promoting Innovation in Manufacturing

At the heart of the price-quantity-quality trilemma lies the challenge of scaling up production of high-quality drugs in response to a price spike or shortage. The substantial cost and time required to bring a generic drug or biosimilar to market means that an incumbent manufacturer can raise prices and reap large profits for an extended period before new entrants can undercut it, and drug shortages can persist for months or years before anyone else fills the void. A final set of solutions strikes at the heart of the trilemma by enabling faster, more flexible manufacturing processes that do not compromise on safety or efficacy. And unlike for patented drugs, where efforts to encourage innovation often come at the expense of access, innovation and access are aligned in the patent afterlife. That is, manufacturing innovations have the potential to increase access to a cheap and plentiful supply of high-quality off-patent drugs.

One of the most promising manufacturing innovations is a switch from batch processing to continuous production. Batch processing of pharmaceuticals can be analogized to baking cookies in a home kitchen. The various steps (assembling ingredients, mixing the cookie dough, dropping the dough onto a cookie sheet, baking in the oven, and cooling on a rack) occur sequentially. The entire batch moves on to the next step only after all the members of the batch have passed through the preceding step. By contrast, continuous manufacturing looks something like an assembly line. New ingredients may be fed into the assembly line even as fully finished products are rolling off the end. The switch from batch processing to continuous manufacturing has the potential to cut production times dramatically. As an FDA publication notes, "Manufacturing that takes a month with batch technology might take only a day with continuous manufacturing" (FDA 2019a). The fast ramp-up means that continuous manufacturing methods could—in theory—respond rapidly to price spikes or shortages.

Notwithstanding the benefits of switching from batch to continuous processing, the FDA—as of early 2022—had approved only six drugs that utilize continuous manufacturing (FDA 2022c). A recent report by the National Academies of Sciences, Engineering, and Medicine attributes the slow adoption of continuous manufacturing partly to regulatory barriers (NASEM 2021). As the National Academies report notes, the FDA evaluates manufacturing practices in the context of individual drug approvals. A manufacturer that sought to switch from batch to continuous production would need to obtain FDA approval for each drug affected by the switch. Although the FDA has expressed support for continuous manufacturing (FDA 2019b, 2022c), the costs—including regulatory costs—of changing to continuous manufacturing have dissuaded firms from making the switch for existing drugs.

Policy makers seeking to accelerate the switch to continuous manufacturing could pursue several strategies (Price 2014). For example, an expedited FDA review pathway for NDAs based on continuous manufacturing could incentivize more firms to make the switch for more drugs. Federal funding for the development and implementation of continuous manufacturing could add further impetus. To that end, a statute passed by Congress in 2022 authorizes $100 million in funding over a 5-year period for new "National Centers of Excellence in Advanced and Continuous Pharmaceutical Manufacturing" at institutions of higher education. If the federal government assumed a more active role in drug manufacturing—as under the Schakowsky-Warren proposal—it also could encourage or require the firms with which it contracts to implement continuous manufacturing themselves.

V. Conclusion

This chapter introduces the generic drug trilemma as a conceptual framework for evaluating policy reforms in the pharmaceutical patent afterlife. By highlighting the trade-offs among three key goals of generic drug policy—low prices, adequate quantities, and high quality—the trilemma can help policy makers and analysts assess whether interventions that improve outcomes in one corner justify sacrifices elsewhere. The trilemma framework also inspires a search for policies that can loosen the tension among price, quantity, and quality—such as government manufacturing of generic drugs and government promotion of manufacturing innovations that enable rapid responses to price spikes and shortages. Finally, our analysis has focused on the US context, but the price-quantity-quality trilemma is global in scope. One reason to begin with the domestic context is that the problems of price, quantity, and quality are more tractable in the United States, where resource constraints are less binding and a strong quality regulation regime already exists. Successful navigation of the policy trilemma in the US context is likely to yield lessons for abroad. In the global context, access-to-medicines advocates have primarily emphasized one element of the trilemma—price—and have focused on removing barriers to generic entry. Yet serious quantity and quality concerns apply in less developed countries as well (Chokshi, Mongia, and Wattal 2015; WHO 2016). Our analysis of the US context serves as a reminder that price is only one element of the global access-to-medicines challenge and that a holistic approach to access-to-medicines problems will need to be three-dimensional.

Endnotes

Author email addresses: Daniel J. Hemel (daniel.hemel@nyu.edu), Lisa Larrimore Ouellette (ouellette@law.stanford.edu). For acknowledgments, sources of research support, and disclosure of the authors' material financial relationships, if any, please see https://www.nber.org/books-and-chapters/entrepreneurship-and-innovation-policy-and-economy-volume-2/generic-drug-trilemma.

1. "Off-patent" drugs constitute even more than 90% of prescription drugs dispensed. The category of off-patent drugs includes not only generics but also biosimilar versions of biologic products as well as branded drugs that are no longer patent-protected.

2. The $114 million estimate is an average for small-molecule drugs and biologics. For phase I and phase III clinical trials, the authors find no statistically significant cost differences between small-molecule drugs and biologics. Phase II clinical trials appear to be more expensive for biologics than for small-molecule drugs (DiMasi et al. 2016, online app. B).

3. The 505(b)(2) pathway has also been used for some biologic drugs, but as of March 23, 2020, new drugs that rely on an existing biologic drug's clinical trial data must be approved under the "biosimilar" pathway described below.

4. We thus bracket the question of whether patent terms or market exclusivity should be extended for some types of drugs and/or shortened for others (Buccafusco and Masur 2021).

5. Notwithstanding insulin's utility as a textbook example of inelastic demand, many patients actually appear to be price-sensitive: a study of patients at the Yale Diabetes Center found that more than a quarter had cut back on insulin use due to cost (Herkert, Vijayakumar, and Luo 2019).

6. For a critique of the FDA's methodology for identifying shortages, see Lutter (2022). The University of Utah Drug Information System reports a higher number of shortages but a similar trend: from a high of 267 new shortages in 2011 to 129 in 2020 and 114 in 2021 (ASHP 2022).

7. Omnibus Budget Reconciliation Act of 1993, Pub. L. No. 103–66, 107 Stat. 312, 636–645 (codified at 42 U.S.C. § 1396s).

8. The BPCIA sets forth an elaborate process—colloquially known as the "patent dance"—through which makers of brand-name biologics and biosimilars may resolve patent disputes.

9. *FTC v. Shkreli*, No. 20-CV-706, 2022 WL 135026 (S.D.N.Y. Jan. 14, 2022).
10. *In re Generic Pharms. Pricing Antitrust Litig.*, 338 F. Supp. 3d 404, 448 (E.D. Pa. 2018).

References

Akerlof, George A. 1970. "The Market for 'Lemons': Quality Uncertainty and the Market Mechanism." *Quarterly Journal of Economics* 84 (3): 488–500.

American Medical Association. 2018. "New AMA Policy Reflects Frustration over Ongoing Drug Shortages." https://www.ama-assn.org/press-center/press-releases/new-ama-policy-reflects-frustration-over-ongoing-drug-shortages.

Anis, Aslam H., Daphne P. Guh, and John Woolcott. 2003. "Lowering Generic Drug Prices: Less Regulation Equals More Competition." *Medical Care* 41 (1): 135–41.

ASHP. 2022. "Drug Shortages Statistics." https://www.ashp.org/drug-shortages/shortage-resources/drug-shortages-statistics.

Association for Accessible Medicines. 2021. "The U.S. Generic and Biosimilar Medicines Savings Report." https://accessiblemeds.org/sites/default/files/2021-10/AAM-2021-US-Generic-Biosimilar-Medicines-Savings-Report-web.pdf.

Atal, Juan Pablo, Jose Ignacio Cuesta, and Morten Sæthre. 2022. "Quality Regulation and Competition: Evidence from Pharmaceutical Markets." Working Paper no. 22-17, Stanford Institute for Economic Policy Research. https://siepr.stanford.edu/publications/working-paper/quality-regulation-and-competition-evidence-pharmaceutical-markets.

Atteberry, Preston, Peter B. Bach, Jennifer A. Ohn, and Mark R. Trusheim. 2019. "Biologics Are Natural Monopolies (Part 1): Why Biosimilars Do Not Create Effective Competition." *Health Affairs Forefront.* https://www.healthaffairs.org/do/10.1377/forefront.20190405.396631.

Barnes, David W. 2010. "The Incentives/Access Tradeoff." *Northwestern Journal of Technology and Intellectual Property* 9 (3): 96–127.

Blankenship, Kyle. 2020a. "FDA Pushes Metformin Recalls for 5 Drugmakers after Carcinogen Contamination." *Fierce Pharma*, May 29, 2020. https://www.fiercepharma.com/manufacturing/fda-recommends-metformin-recalls-for-5-drugmakers-after-carcinogen-contamination.

———. 2020b. "Former Novartis Exec Pleads Guilty in Generics Price-Fixing Conspiracy." *Fierce Pharma*, February 18, 2020. https://www.fiercepharma.com/pharma/former-novartis-sandoz-exec-pleads-guilty-generics-price-fixing-investigation.

Brown, William S. 1995. *Principles of Economics.* St. Paul, MN: West.

Bruhn, William E., Elizabeth A. Fracica, and Martin A. Makary. 2018. "Group Purchasing Organizations, Health Care Costs, and Drug Shortages." *JAMA* 320 (18): 1859–60.

Bruser, David, and Jesse McLean. 2014. "Canadians Kept in Dark about Defective Drugs." *Toronto Star*, September 11, 2014. https://www.thestar.com/news/canada/2014/09/11/canadians_kept_in_dark_about_defective_drugs.html.

Buccafusco, Christopher, and Jonathan S. Masur. 2021. "Drugs, Patents, and Well-Being." *Washington University Law Review* 98 (5): 1403–60.

Budish, Eric, Benjamin N. Roin, and Heidi Williams. 2015. "Do Firms Underinvest in Long-Term Research? Evidence from Cancer Clinical Trials." *American Economic Review* 105 (7): 2044–85.

Carrier, Michael A. 2018. "Five Actions to Stop Citizen Petition Abuse." *Columbia Law Review Online* 118:82–93.

Carrier, Michael A., Mark A. Lemley, and Shawn Miller. 2020. "Playing Both Sides? Branded Sales, Generic Drugs, and Antitrust Policy." *Hastings Law Journal* 71 (2): 307–58.

CBO (Congressional Budget Office). 2021. "A Comparison of Brand-Name Drug Prices among Selected Federal Programs." https://www.cbo.gov/system/files/2021-02/56978-Drug-Prices.pdf.

Chokshi, Maulik, Rahul Mongia, and Vasudha Wattal. 2015. "Drug Quality and Safety Issues in India." Policy Brief no. 2, Indian Council for Research on International Economic Relations, New Delhi. https://think-asia.org/bitstream/handle/11540/6703/Drug-Quality.pdf.

CMS (Centers for Medicare and Medicaid Services). 2021. "NHE Fact Sheet." Last updated December 15, 2021. https://www.cms.gov/Research-Statistics-Data-and-Systems/Statistics-Trends-and-Reports/NationalHealthExpendData/NHE-Fact-Sheet.

Cohen, Matthew, Ravi Gupta, Thomas J. Bollyky, Joseph S. Ross, and Aaron S. Kesselheim. 2019. "Policy Options for Increasing Generic Drug Competition through Importation." *Health Affairs Forefront*, January 7, 2019. https://www.healthaffairs.org/do/10.1377/forefront.20190103.333047.

Cohen, Robin A., Michael E. Martinez, Amy E. Cha, and Emily P. Terlizzi. 2021. "Health Insurance Coverage: Early Release of Estimates from the National Health Interview Survey, January–June 2021." *National Center for Health Statistics*, November 2021. https://www.cdc.gov/nchs/data/nhis/earlyrelease/insur202111.pdf.

Colgan, Sarah, Kate Faasse, Leslie R. Martin, Melika H. Stephens, Andrew Grey, and Keith J. Petrie. 2015. "Perceptions of Generic Medication in the General Population, Doctors and Pharmacists: A Systematic Review." *BMJ Open* 5: e008915.

Conrad, Ryan, and Randall Lutter. 2019. "Generic Competition and Drug Prices: New Evidence Linking Greater Generic Competition and Lower Generic Drug Prices." https://www.fda.gov/media/133509/download.

Conti, Rena M., and Ernst R. Berndt. 2020. "Four Facts Concerning Competition in US Generic Prescription Drug Markets." *International Journal of the Economics of Business* 27 (1): 27–48.

Cowen, Tyler, and Alex Tabarrok. 2009. *Modern Principles of Economics.* New York: Worth.

Cubanski, Juliette, and Anthony Damico. 2022. "Insulin Out-of-Pocket Costs in Medicare Part D." *Kaiser Family Foundation*, May 17, 2022. https://www.kff.org/medicare/issue-brief/insulin-out-of-pocket-costs-in-medicare-part-d/.

Dabrowska, Agata. 2018. "FDA Risk Evaluation and Mitigation Strategies (REMS): Description and Effect on Generic Drug Development." CRS Report No. R44810. Congressional Research Service, Washington, DC. https://sgp.fas.org/crs/misc/R44810.pdf.

Darrow, Jonathan J., Mengdong He, and Kristina Stefanini. 2019. "The 505(b)(2) Drug Approval Pathway." *Food and Drug Law Journal* 74 (3): 403–39.

Decarolis, Francesco, Leonardo M. Giuffrida, Elisabetta Iossa, Vincenzo Mollisi, and Giancarlo Spagnolo. 2020. "Bureaucratic Competence and Procurement Outcomes." *Journal of Law, Economics, and Organization* 36 (3): 537–97.

DiMasi, Joseph A., Henry G. Grabowski, and Ronald W. Hansen. 2016. "Innovation in the Pharmaceutical Industry: New Estimates of R&D Costs." *Journal of Health Economics* 47:20–33.

DOJ (Department of Justice). 2017. "Division Update Spring 2017." https://www.justice.gov/atr/division-operations/division-update-spring-2017/division-secures-individual-and-corporate-guilty-pleas-collusion-industries-where-products.

Eban, Katherine. 2019. *Bottle of Lies: The Inside Story of the Generic Drug Boom.* New York: HarperCollins.

Economist. 2014. "Going Large." *Economist*, December 30, 2014. https://www.economist.com/business/2014/12/30/going-large.

Edney, Anna, Susan Berfield, and Evelyn Yu. 2019. "Carcinogens Have Infiltrated the Generic Drug Supply in the U.S." *Bloomberg Businessweek*, September 12, 2019. https://www.bloomberg.com/news/features/2019-09-12/how-carcinogen-tainted-generic-drug-valsartan-got-past-the-fda.

Elhauge, Einer. 2016. "Horizontal Shareholding." *Harvard Law Review* 129 (5): 1267–317.

FDA (Food and Drug Administration). 2019a. "Impact Story: Regulatory Science Is Strengthening U.S. Drug Product Manufacturing." February 5, 2019. https://www.fda.gov/drugs/regulatory-science-action/impact-story-regulatory-science-strengthening-us-drug-product-manufacturing.

———. 2019b. "Quality Considerations for Continuous Manufacturing: Guidance for Industry." https://www.fda.gov/regulatory-information/search-fda-guidance-documents/quality-considerations-continuous-manufacturing.

———. 2020. "Drug Shortages: Root Causes and Potential Solutions." https://www.fda.gov/media/131130/download.

———. 2021. "Drug Shortages for Calendar Year 2020." https://www.fda.gov/media/150409/download.

———. 2022a. "FDA Drug Shortages." Last updated March 22, 2022. https://www.accessdata.fda.gov/scripts/drugshortages/default.cfm.

———. 2022b. "List of Off-Patent, Off-Exclusivity Drugs without an Approved Generic." Last updated June 16, 2022. https://www.fda.gov/drugs/abbreviated-new-drug-application-anda/list-patent-exclusivity-drugs-without-approved-generic.

———. 2022c. "An FDA Self-Audit of Continuous Manufacturing for Drug Products." June 27, 2022. https://www.fda.gov/drugs/cder-small-business-industry-assistance-sbia/fda-self-audit-continuous-manufacturing-drug-products-audio-transcript.

Fleming, J. Marcus, and Robert A. Mundell. 1964. "Official Intervention on the Forward Exchange Market: A Simplified Analysis." *IMF Staff Papers* 11 (1): 1–19.

Frakes, Michael D., and Melissa F. Wasserman. 2019. "Irrational Ignorance at the Patent Office." *Vanderbilt Law Review* 72 (3): 975–1030.

———. 2020. "Investing in Ex Ante Regulation: Evidence from Pharmaceutical Patent Examination." Working Paper no. 27579, NBER, Cambridge, MA. https://www.nber.org/papers/w27579.

FTC (Federal Trade Commission). 2002. "Generic Drug Entry Prior to Patent Expiration." https://www.ftc.gov/sites/default/files/documents/reports/generic-drug-entry-prior-patent-expiration-ftc-study/genericdrugstudy_0.pdf.

Gaffney, Alexander. 2015. "An Increasing Number of Companies Are Using a Once-Obscure FDA Drug Approval Pathway." *Regulatory Focus*, April 8, 2015. https://www.raps.org/regulatory-focus%E2%84%A2/news-articles/2015/4/an-increasing-number-of-companies-are-using-a-once-obscure-fda-drug-approval-pathway.

Ganapati, Sharat, and Rebecca McKibbin. 2021. "Markups and Fixed Costs in Generic and Off-Patent Pharmaceutical Markets." Working Paper no. 29206, NBER, Cambridge, MA. https://www.nber.org/papers/w29206.

GAO (Government Accountability Office). 2002. "Childhood Vaccines: Ensuring an Adequate Supply Poses Continuing Challenges." GAO Report no. GAO-02-987. https://www.gao.gov/assets/gao-02-987.pdf.

———. 2016. "Generic Drugs under Medicare: Part D Generic Drug Prices Declined Overall, but Some Had Extraordinary Price Increases." GAO Report no. GAO-16-706. https://www.gao.gov/assets/gao-16-706.pdf.

Goldszmidt, Rafael B., André R. Buttendorf, Guenther Schuldt Filho, Jose M. Souza Jr., and Marco A. Bianchini. 2019. "The Impact of Generic Labels on the Consumption of and Adherence to Medication: A Randomized Controlled Trial." *European Journal of Public Health* 29 (1): 12–17.

Gross, Alan E., Richard S. Johannes, Vikas Gupta, Ying P. Tabak, Arjun Srinivasan, and Susan C. Bleasdale. 2017. "The Effect of a Piperacillin/Tazobactam Shortage on Antimicrobial Prescribing and *Clostridium difficile* Risk in 88 US Medical Centers." *Clinical Infectious Diseases* 65 (4): 613–18.

Gupta, Ravi, Christopher J. Morten, Angela Y. Zhu, Reshma Ramachandran, Nilay D. Shah, and Joseph S. Ross. 2022. "Approvals and Timing of New Formulations of Novel Drugs Approved by the US Food and Drug Administration between 1995 and 2010 and Followed Through 2021." *JAMA Health Forum* 3 (5): e221096.

Heled, Yaniv. 2021. "The Biologics Price Competition and Innovation Act at 10—A Stocktaking." *Texas A&M Journal of Property Law* 7 (1): 81–109.

Hemel, Daniel J., and Lisa Larrimore Ouellette. 2013. "Beyond the Patents–Prizes Debate." *Texas Law Review* 92 (2): 303–82.

———. 2019. "Innovation Policy Pluralism." *Yale Law Journal* 128 (3): 544–614.

Hemphill, C. Scott. 2006. "Paying for Delay: Pharmaceutical Patent Settlement as a Regulatory Design Problem." *New York University Law Review* 81 (5): 1553–623.

Hemphill, C. Scott, and Bhaven Sampat. 2013. "Drug Patents at the Supreme Court." *Science* 339 (6126): 1386–87.

Herkert, Darby, Pavithra Vijayakumar, and Jing Luo. 2019. "Cost-Related Insulin Underuse among Patients with Diabetes." *JAMA Internal Medicine* 179 (1): 112–14.

HHS (US Department of Health and Human Services). 2020. "Putting America's Health First: FY 2021 President's Budget for HHS." https://www.hhs.gov/sites/default/files/fy-2021-budget-in-brief.pdf.

IQVIA. 2020. "Biosimilars in the United States 2020–2024." https://www.iqvia.com/insights/the-iqvia-institute/reports/biosimilars-in-the-united-states-2020-2024.

Johnson, Carolyn Y. 2019. "A Tiny Pharmacy Is Identifying Big Problems with Common Drugs, Including Zantac." *Washington Post*, November 8, 2019.

Kades, Michael. 2021. "The CREATES Act Shows Legislation Can Stop Anticompetitive Pharmaceutical Industry Practices." *Washington Center for Equitable Growth*, May 27, 2021. https://equitablegrowth.org/the-creates-act-shows-legislation-can-stop-anticompetitive-pharmaceutical-industry-practices/.

Kearney, Audrey, Liz Hamel, Mellisha Stokes, and Mollyann Brodie. 2021. "Americans' Challenges with Health Care Costs." Kaiser Family Foundation. https://www.kff.org/health-costs/issue-brief/americans-challenges-with-health-care-costs.

Kesselheim, Aaron S., Alexander S. Misono, Joy L. Lee, Margaret R. Stedman, M. Alan Brookhart, Niteesh K. Choudhry, and William H. Shrank. 2008. "Clinical

Equivalence of Generic and Brand-Name Drugs Used in Cardiovascular Disease: A Systematic Review and Meta-analysis." *JAMA* 300 (21): 2514–26.

Kesselheim, Aaron S., Margaret R. Stedman, Ellen J. Bubrick, Joshua J. Gagne, Alexander S. Misono, Joy L. Lee, M. Alan Brookhart, Jerry Avorn, and William H. Shrank. 2010. "Seizure Outcomes Following the Use of Generic versus Brand-Name Antiepileptic Drugs." *Drugs* 70:605–21.

Kolstad, Jonathan T., and Amanda E. Kowalski. 2016. "Mandate-based Health Reform and the Labor Market: Evidence from the Massachusetts Reform." *Journal of Health Economics* 47:81–106.

Landes, William M., and Richard A. Posner. 2003. *The Economic Structure of Intellectual Property Law*. Cambridge, MA: Harvard University Press.

Leebron, David W. 1991. "Limited Liability, Tort Victims, and Creditors." *Columbia Law Review* 91 (7): 1565–650.

Lichtenberg, Frank R. 2019. "How Many Life-Years Have New Drugs Saved? A Three-Way Fixed-Effects Analysis of 66 Diseases in 27 Countries, 2000–2013." *International Health* 11 (5): 403–16.

Liebman, Jeffrey B., and Neale Mahoney. 2017. "Do Expiring Budgets Lead to Wasteful Year-End Spending? Evidence from Federal Procurement." *American Economic Review* 107 (11): 3510–49.

Lietzan, Erica, and Kristina M. L. Acri née Lybecker. 2020. "Distorted Drug Patents." *Washington Law Review* 95 (3): 1317–82.

Lupkin, Sydney. 2019. "A Decade Marked by Outrage over Drug Prices." *NPR*, December 31, 2019. https://www.npr.org/sections/health-shots/2019/12/31/792617538/a-decade-marked-by-outrage-over-drug-prices.

Lutter, Randall. 2022. "How Not to Fix Medical Supply Chains." *City Journal*, February 23, 2022. https://www.city-journal.org/how-not-to-fix-medical-supply-chains.

Mulcahy, Andrew W., Christopher M. Whaley, Mahlet Gizaw, Daniel Schwam, Nathaniel Edenfield, and Alejandro U. Becerra-Ornelas. 2021. "International Prescription Drug Price Comparisons: Current Empirical Estimates and Comparisons with Previous Studies." RAND Report no. RR2956. http://www.rand.org/t/RR2956.

Mullard, Asher. 2022. "2021 FDA Approvals." *Nature Reviews Drug Discovery* 21 (1): 83–88.

NASEM (National Academies of Sciences, Engineering, and Medicine). 2018. *Making Medicines Affordable: A National Imperative*. Washington, DC: National Academies Press.

———. 2021. *Innovations in Pharmaceutical Manufacturing on the Horizon: Technical Challenges, Regulatory Issues, and Recommendations*. Washington, DC: National Academies Press.

NHS (National Health Service). 2022. "NHS Prescription Charges." Last updated March 31, 2021. https://www.nhs.uk/nhs-services/prescriptions-and-pharmacies/nhs-prescription-charges/.

Nordhaus, William D. 1969. *Invention, Growth, and Welfare: A Theoretical Treatment of Technological Change*. Cambridge, MA: MIT Press.

Oshinsky, David M. 2006. *Polio: An American Story*. New York: Oxford University Press.

Pear, Robert. 2018. "Drug Company 'Shenanigans' to Dodge Generics Come under Scrutiny." *New York Times*, April 15, 2018, A20.

Phuong, Jonathan Minh, Jonathan Penm, Betty Chaar, Lachlan Daniel Oldfield, and Rebekah Moles. 2019. "The Impacts of Medication Shortages on Patient Outcomes: A Scoping Review." *PLoS One* 14 (5): e0215837.

Pollack, Andrew, and Sabrina Tavernise. 2015. "A Drug Company's Price Tactics Pinch Insurers and Consumers." *New York Times*, October 5, 2015, A1.

Posner, Eric A., Fiona M. Scott Morton, and E. Glen Weyl. 2017. "A Proposal to Limit the Anticompetitive Power of Institutional Investors." *Antitrust Law Journal* 81 (3): 669–728.

Price, W. Nicholson, II. 2014. "Making Do in Making Drugs: Innovation Policy and Pharmaceutical Manufacturing." *Boston College Law Review* 55 (2): 491–562.

Ridley, David B., Xiaoshu Bei, and Eli B. Liebman. 2016. "No Shot: US Vaccine Prices and Shortages." *Health Affairs* 35 (2): 235–41.

Rodrik, Dani. 2000. "How Far Will International Economic Integration Go?" *Journal of Economic Perspectives* 14 (1): 177–86.

Rosenthal, Elisabeth. 2014. "Lawmakers Question Drug Makers on Rising Costs of Generics." *New York Times*, October 8, 2014, B9.

Rye, Brian. 2012. "Medicare Price Controls Worsen Drug Shortages, Boost Gray Market." *Bloomberg Government*. http://glacialblog.com/userfiles/76/BGov_Drug_Shortage_Report(2).pdf.

Sachs, Rachel E. 2019. "Addressing Pharmaceutical Price Spikes through Generic Preclearance." *Journal of Legal Medicine* 39:169–76.

Sacks, Chana A., Victor L. Van de Wiele, and Lisa A. Fulchino. 2021. "Assessment of Variation in State Regulation of Generic Drug and Interchangeable Biologic Substitutions." *JAMA Internal Medicine* 181 (1): 16–22.

Sampat, Bhaven, and Heidi L. Williams. 2019. "How Do Patents Affect Follow-on Innovation? Evidence from the Human Genome." *American Economic Review* 109 (1): 203–36.

Scott Morton, Fiona M. 2001. "The Problem of Price Controls." *Regulation* 24 (1): 50–55.

Scott Morton, Fiona M., and Lysle T. Boller. 2017. "Enabling Competition in Pharmaceutical Markets." Hutchins Center Working Paper #30, Hutchins Center on Fiscal & Monetary Policy at Brookings, Washington, DC. https://www.brookings.edu/wp-content/uploads/2017/05/wp30_scottmorton_competitioninpharma1.pdf.

Stockman, Farah. 2021. "Our Drug Supply Is Sick. How Can We Fix It?" *New York Times*, September 19, 2021, SR4.

Stomberg, Christopher. 2018. "Drug Shortages, Pricing, and Regulatory Activity." In *Measuring and Modeling Health Care Costs*, ed. Ana Aizcorbe, Colin Baker, Ernst R. Berndt, and David M. Cutler, 323–48. Chicago: University of Chicago Press.

Straka, Robert J., Denis J. Keohane, and Larry Z. Liu. 2017. "Potential Clinical and Economic Impact of Switching Branded Medications to Generics." *American Journal of Therapeutics* 24 (3): e278–e289.

Stuart, Christine. 2020. "Sandoz, Pfizer and 2 Dozen Others Accused of Fixing Generic Drug Prices." Courthouse News Service, June 10, 2020. https://www.courthousenews.com/sandoz-pfizer-and-2-dozen-accused-of-fixing-generic-drug-prices/.

Thomas, John R. 2017. *Regulatory Exclusivity Reform in the 115th Congress*. CRS Report no. R44951. Congressional Research Service, Washington, DC. https://sgp.fas.org/crs/misc/R44951.pdf.

Thomas, Katie. 2013. "Generic Drug Maker Pleads Guilty in Federal Case." *New York Times*, May 14, 2013, B1.

———. 2018. "A Polite Silence on Sex Raises Women's Costs." *New York Times*, June 4, 2018, B1.

Trifilio, Steven, Zheng Zhou, Jayesh Mehta, Colleen Czerniak, Judy Pi, Deborah Greenberg, Molly Koslosky, Mihaela Pantiru, and Jessica Altman. 2013. "Idarubicin Appears Equivalent to Dose-Intense Daunorubicin for Remission Induction in Patients with Acute Myeloid Leukemia." *Leukemia Research* 37 (8): 868–71.

Vail, Emily, Hayley B. Gershengorn, and May Hua. 2017. "Association between US Norepinephrine Shortage and Mortality among Patients with Septic Shock." *JAMA* 317 (14): 1433–42.

Warren, Elizabeth. 2018. "It's Time to Let the Government Manufacture Generic Drugs." *Washington Post*, December 17, 2018.

———. 2020. S.3162, 116th Congress. Affordable Drug Manufacturing Act of 2020.

WHO (World Health Organization). 2016. "Medicines Shortages." *WHO Drug Information* 30 (2): 180–85.

Williamson, Kirk. 2021. "Part 2: In Quest to Lower Rx Prices, States Deploy New Tools." *Arnold Ventures*, September 29, 2021. https://www.arnoldventures .org/stories/part-2-in-quest-to-lower-rx-prices-states-deploy-new-tools.

Xie, Jin, and Joseph Gerakos. 2020. "The Anticompetitive Effects of Common Ownership: The Case of Paragraph IV Generic Entry." *AEA Papers and Proceedings* 110:569–72.

Yip, Stephanie. 2020. "Top 10 Best-Selling Drugs of 2019." *PharmaIntelligence*. https://pharmaintelligence.informa.com/~/media/informa-shop-window /pharma/2020/files/reports/top-10-best-selling-drugs-of-2019.pdf.

Yurukoglu, Ali, Eli Liebman, and David B. Ridley. 2017. "The Role of Government Reimbursement in Drug Shortages." *American Economic Journal: Economic Policy* 9 (2): 348–82.

Zeckhauser, Richard. 1970. "Medical Insurance: A Case Study of the Tradeoff between Risk Spreading and Appropriate Incentives." *Journal of Economic Theory* 2 (1): 10–26.

Zhang, Wei, Daphne Guh, Huiying Sun, Carlo A. Marra, Larry D. Lynd, and Aslam H. Anis. 2016. "The Impact of Price-cap Regulations on Exit by Generic Pharmaceutical Firms." *Medical Care* 54 (9): 884–90.

Innovating to Net Zero: Can Venture Capital and Start-Ups Play a Meaningful Role?

Silvia Dalla Fontana, *University of Lugano and Swiss Finance Institute,* Switzerland

Ramana Nanda, *Imperial College London and CEPR,* United Kingdom

Abstract

We show that patents related to clean energy generation and storage, changes to industrial production, and carbon capture and sequestration—where breakthroughs are seen as being particularly critical to addressing climate change—are more than twice as likely to cite fundamental science than other net-zero emissions patents, highlighting their "deep tech" focus compared with innovation in areas such as energy efficiency, information and communication technologies, and transportation. Interestingly, firms backed by venture capital (VC) have patents that are significantly more likely to cite fundamental science compared with other firms, including in these deep tech sectors. Net-zero related patents granted to VC-backed firms are also three to five times more likely to be among the group of highest-cited patents, indicating the distinctive nature of innovations commercialized by VC-backed firms. However, VC still accounts for a tiny share of all patents related to net zero, and the patenting focus of VC-backed firms has shifted away from deep tech in recent years. We discuss the growing literature on the potential frictions facing the commercialization of science-based deep tech innovations and touch on potential solutions that might enable VC to play a more meaningful role in supporting the transition to net zero in the coming decades.

JEL Codes: Q55, Q56, G24, G30, G32

Keywords: venture capital, net zero, financing deep tech, innovation

Entrepreneurship and Innovation Policy and the Economy, volume 2, 2023.

I. Introduction

As the consequences of rising global temperatures and related climate change are becoming more apparent, a growing number of countries—covering more than 70% of global CO_2 emissions—have committed in recent years to work toward achieving net-zero emissions by 2050, in an effort to limit long-term increase in global temperatures to 1.5°C. Despite this progress, a seminal report released by the International Energy Agency (IEA 2022) notes that about half the projected CO_2 reductions that will be required to achieve net-zero by 2050 will depend on technologies that are currently not commercially viable—highlighting the critical need for breakthrough innovations to mitigate the impacts of climate change.

In this chapter, we discuss the prevalence and focus of US innovation related to achieving net-zero targets, with a particular focus on the potential role played by start-ups backed by venture capital (VC). We identify patents related to the mitigation of climate change using tags developed by the Cooperative Patent Classification (CPC).[1] The classification scheme was put together with the help of experts in the field, including the Intergovernmental Panel on Climate Change, and was developed to tag technologies with certain attributes rather than to replace the classification of technologies themselves. As described in table 1, the Y02 subclasses include not only areas related to specific clean energy technologies but also technologies related to energy efficiency, transportation, industrial production, and carbon capture and sequestration that have the potential to mitigate climate change through lowering greenhouse gases (GHG) in the atmosphere. Together, these technologies account for about 6.5% of all utility patents in the US Patent and Trademark Office (USPTO) between 2000 and 2020 but have grown at more than twice the rate of other patents in the USPTO since 2010.

The IEA (2022) report notes that breakthrough innovations are likely to be particularly important in areas such as energy generation and storage, industrial production, and carbon capture and sequestration, given their current contribution to CO_2 emissions relative to what is required by 2050. Using a measure of a patent's reliance on fundamental science developed by Marx and Fuegi (2020), we show that patents in these sectors tend to cite fundamental science much more intensively than other sectors such as energy efficiency, information and communication technologies (ICT), and transportation. We refer to these three more science-intensive sectors as the subset of net-zero patents that are "deep tech."

Table 1
Cooperative Patent Classification of "Green Innovations"

Y02E	Reduction of Greenhouse Gas (GHG) Emissions, Related to Energy Generation, Transmission, or Distribution
10/00	Energy generation through renewable energy sources
30/00	Energy generation of nuclear origin
20/00	Combustion technologies with mitigation potential
40/00	Technologies for an efficient electrical power generation, transmission, or distribution
50/00	Technologies for the production of fuel of nonfossil origin
60/00	Enabling technologies; technologies with a potential or indirect contribution to GHG emissions mitigation
70/00	Other energy conversion or management systems reducing GHG emissions

Y02C	Capture, Storage, Sequestration, or Disposal of GHG
20/00	Capture or disposal of GHG
20/10	of nitrous oxide (N_2O)
20/20	of methane
20/30	of perfluorocarbons (PFC), hydrofluorocarbons (HFC), or sulfur hexafluoride (SF_6)
20/40	of CO_2

Y02P	Climate Change Mitigation Technologies in the Production or Processing of Goods
10/00	Technologies related to metal processing
20/00	Technologies relating to chemical industry
30/00	Technologies relating to oil refining and petrochemical industry
40/00	Technologies relating to the processing of minerals
60/00	Technologies relating to agriculture, livestock, or agroalimentary industries
70/00	Climate change mitigation technologies in the production process for final industrial or consumer products
80/00	Climate change mitigation technologies for sector-wide applications
90/00	Enabling technologies with a potential contribution to GHG emissions mitigation

Y02T	Climate Change Mitigation Technologies Related to Transportation
10/00	Road transport of goods or passengers
30/00	Transportation of goods or passengers via railways, e.g., energy recovery or reducing air resistance
50/00	Aeronautics or air transport
70/00	Maritime or waterways transport
90/00	Enabling technologies or technologies with a potential or indirect contribution to GHG emissions mitigation

Table 1
Continued

	Climate Change Mitigation Technologies Related to Buildings, e.g., Housing,
Y02B	House Appliances, or Related End-User Applications

10/00	Integration of renewable energy sources in buildings
20/00	Energy efficient lighting technologies, e.g., halogen lamps or gas discharge lamps
30/00	Energy efficient heating, ventilation, or air conditioning (HVAC)
40/00	Technologies aiming at improving the efficiency of home appliances; e.g., induction cooking or efficient technologies for refrigerators, freezers, or dishwashers
50/00	Energy efficient technologies in elevators, escalators, and moving walkways, e.g., energy saving or recuperation technologies
70/00	Technologies for an efficient end-user side electric power management and consumption
80/00	Architectural or constructional elements improving the thermal performance of buildings
90/00	Enabling technologies or technologies with a potential or indirect contribution to GHG emissions mitigation

	Climate Change Mitigation Technologies in Information and Communication Technologies [ICT], i.e., Information and Communication Technologies
Y02D	Aiming at the Reduction of Their Own Energy Use

10/00	Energy efficient computing, e.g., low power processors, power management, or thermal management
30/00	Reducing energy consumption in communication networks

Y02A	Technologies for Adaptation to Climate Change

10/00	at coastal zones; at river basins
20/00	Water conservation; Efficient water supply; Efficient water use
30/00	Adapting or protecting infrastructure or their operation
40/00	Adaptation technologies in agriculture, forestry, livestock, or agroalimentary production
50/00	in human health protection, e.g., against extreme weather
90/00	Technologies having an indirect contribution to adaptation to climate change

	Climate Change Mitigation Technologies Related to Wastewater Treatment
Y02W	or Waste Management

10/00	Technologies for wastewater treatment
30/00	Technologies for solid waste management
90/00	Enabling technologies or technologies with a potential or indirect contribution to GHG emissions mitigation

Note: This table reports the description of different Cooperative Patent Classification groups used to tag green innovation. Green patents include the categories Y02A and Y02W, but these have been excluded from our analysis as the focus of this paper is on technologies that can directly contribute to meeting net-zero targets.

The fact that these deep tech sectors coincide with the areas that require the biggest breakthrough innovations is important in light of growing evidence that large corporations have pulled back considerably from fundamental innovation in recent years (Arora, Belenzon, and Patacconi 2018; Arora et al. 2020). Moreover, a large body of academic research has highlighted how the organizational form associated with the commercialization of innovations can have first-order effects on the degree to which radical versus incremental innovations are brought to market (Akcigit and Kerr 2018). The bureaucratic organizational structure and related incentives in large firms are often not conducive to radical innovations (Kortum and Lerner 2000). Moreover, large corporations often have weaker incentives to commercialize technologies that compete with core lines of business (Reinganum 1983; Cunningham, Ederer, and Ma 2021). This suggests an important role for deep tech inventions emerging from universities and the related importance of sources of finance such as VC to help support their commercialization.

Consistent with this view, we find that patents associated with mature firms have the lowest citations to science, whereas VC-backed start-ups, which tend to be the most science-intensive on average, have more than three times the number of scientific citations that mature firms do. In addition, when examining the influence of patents, we find that net-zero patents granted to VC-backed start-ups are three to six times more likely to be in the top percentile of patents in terms of citations received, when compared with USPTO patents granted to mature firms in a same technology class and granted in the same year. This higher influence of VC-backed patents compared with mature firms within net-zero patents is even larger than the differential identified by Howell et al. (2020) in their analysis of VC-backed patenting in general.

Despite the greater influence and scientific reliance of VC-backed patents that are likely to be of particular relevance in deep tech sectors, we nevertheless also note that VC-backed patents comprise less than 3% of all net-zero patents, and moreover have disproportionately grown in non–deep tech areas such as energy efficiency and transportation in recent years. In Sections III and IV, we discuss potential frictions and possible solutions related to the commercialization of climate-related deep tech that might enable VC-backed start-ups to play a more meaningful role in supporting the transition to net-zero in the coming decades.

II.   Innovations Related to Net-Zero

A.   *Identifying Net-Zero Patents*

We focus on patents granted by the USPTO from 2000 and 2020, restricting the analysis to utility patents.[2] To identify innovations related to net zero, we use a novel classification scheme that is part of the CPC system. The CPC system is the result of a partnership between the European Patent Office and the USPTO that was implemented in 2013. The aim of this project was to harmonize the different classification systems in place and to bring the best practices from both offices together.[3] The Y02 category that identifies environmental technologies was first introduced in January 2013.[4] More subclasses of that same category were added in 2015 and 2018, and the scheme is now considered to be complete, with eight main categories, reported in table 1.[5]

The aim of this categorization is to extend the reach of patents related to "green" technologies to a wider range of stakeholders, including nonexperts. As such, the Y02 categorization works as a separate class applied by the patent office that is considered additional to standard classifications of technology. An important feature of this categorization is that it spans many different fields and is able to capture innovations in both mitigation and adaptation technologies (Haščič and Migotto 2015). This allows for a compelling way to classify ICT and related energy efficiency technologies that are typically harder to classify in terms of their contribution to climate change mitigation.[6]

As shown in table 1, the classification system of climate change technologies includes innovations related both to climate change mitigation and to adaptation. A deeper examination of the adaptation technologies tagged in Y02A shows that they are largely related to technologies helping to address growing threats of vector-borne, fly-borne, or waterborne diseases whose impact is exacerbated by climate change. Y02W is focused on waste management and wastewater. Although technologies in these two groups can play a role in climate change, they are less related to addressing the specific goals related to reaching net-zero targets, so we exclude them from our analysis.

For our analysis, we therefore focus on the six main categories related to net-zero. Panel *A* of figure 1 reports the number of net-zero patents granted by the USPTO from 2000 to 2020 in relation to all other USPTO patents, where net-zero patents refer to the six categories of Y02 patents noted above that are related to achieving net-zero targets. As can be seen

A

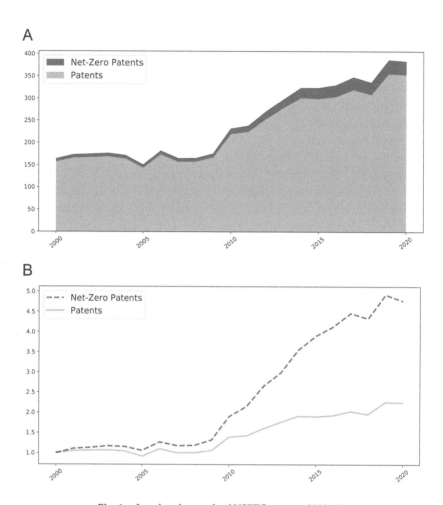

Fig. 1. Level and growth of USPTO patents 2000–20.
Notes: This figure shows the number of net-zero and all other patents granted by the US Patent and Trademark Office from 2000 to 2020 (panel *A*). Net-zero patents include the six groups identified using the Cooperative Patent Classification system and reported in table 1. Panel *B* reports the growth of these two groups relative to the number of patents in each group in 2000.

from panel *A*, net-zero patents constitute a small share of total patents in the USPTO but have grown from 4% in 2000 to 8% in 2020.

Panel *B* reports the growth of net-zero patents and all other patents relative to the baseline year 2000. As can be seen from panel *B*, net-zero patents have grown more than twice as fast as other patents in the USPTO, with a large inflection emerging in 2010. The inflection seen in 2010 could represent changing fundamentals that drive an increase in net-zero innovation or could be driven at least in part by the new classification implemented in those years, leading to a greater focus on these technologies.[7]

We turn next to validating the CPC system using text taken from the titles of all net-zero patents and identifying distinctive words associated with patents in each category. The distinct words associated with each category are derived using a Term Frequency–Inverse Document Frequency (TF-IDF) procedure, where the frequency of each word in a document (TF) is weighted by the inverse of the frequency across all documents in the corpus (IDF).[8] Panels A to F of figure 2 report word clouds of the content of patent titles in the six net-zero categories. The types of keywords emerging from the patent titles in each of these categories appear intuitive, which is reassuring in terms of the quality of the classification. Figure 3 shows the total trend of patents in each of these categories from 2000 to 2020. In relative terms, the highest growth was reported in the category of mitigation technologies related to household appliances and ICT. Column 1 of table 2 reports the precise number of net-zero patents issued in each category over the 2000–20 period, ranging from more than 4,000 patents for GHG capture to nearly 110,000 patents related to generation and storage.

B.   Deep Tech Sectors That Rely More on Fundamental Science

As noted in the introduction, one of our goals is to understand differences in the net-zero sectors in terms of their reliance on fundamental science because this is likely to affect the commercialization frictions they face. The word clouds reported in figure 2 provide an intuitive sense that the first three categories—renewable energy generation and storage, carbon capture and sequestration, and industrial production—are likely to be much more reliant on fundamental science relative to the categories related to energy efficiency and transportation. However, we also validate this intuition using data provided by Marx and Fuegi (2021), which identifies citations that a patent makes to scientific papers.[9]

Column 2 of table 2 reports the share of patents in each category that cites at least one scientific paper. The first three rows correspond to sectors with a much greater reliance on science. Between a third and half of all patents cite science in these sectors, compared with 27% for all utility patents over the 2000–20 period. Columns 3–8 report the means and

Fig. 2. Distinctive words in each category of net-zero patents granted 2000–20.

Notes: This figure uses text taken from the titles of all net-zero patents to identify distinctive words associated with each net-zero subcategory. The distinct words associated with each category are derived using a TF-IDF procedure, in which the frequency of each word in a document (TF) is weighted by the inverse of the frequency of all documents in the corpus (IDF).

quantiles of scientific paper citations of these patents, conditional on citing at least one science paper. They reinforce the stark difference in reliance on science across these categories. Not only do the first three sectors have a much greater propensity to cite science at the extensive margin, but they also have a significantly greater intensity of reliance on science, as can be seen by the larger number of scientific papers cited

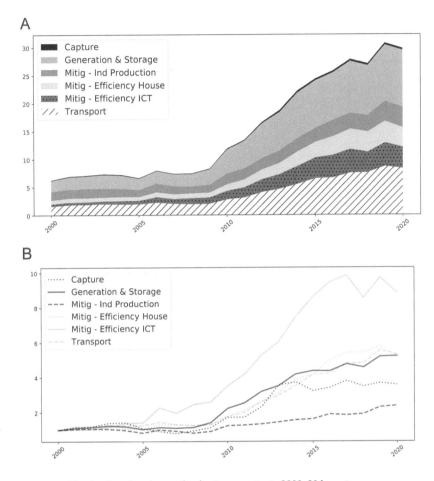

Fig. 3.   Level and growth of net-zero patents 2000–20 by category.

Notes: This figure reports details on net-zero patents granted by the US Patent and Trademark Office from 2000 to 2020 by the six net-zero categories used in this paper. The six net-zero groups are identified using the Cooperative Patent Classification tagging system and are: Energy Generation and Storage (class Y02E in table 1), Technologies for GHG Capture (class Y02C in table 1), Technologies for Mitigation in Industrial Production (class Y02P in table 1), Technologies Related to Transportation (class Y02T in table 1), Technologies Related to Energy Efficiency in Buildings (class Y02B in table 1), and Information and Communication Technologies (class Y02D in table 1). Panel A is a stacked chart that reports the overall number of patents in each class. Panel B reports the growth of these groups relative to the number of patents in each group in 2000.

at all points above the 25th percentile. As noted before, these deep tech categories coincide with the sectors where we need some of the most important breakthrough innovations to reach net-zero targets. We return to this fact and the implications for policy in the subsequent sections.

Table 2
Citation to Fundamental Science by Net-Zero Patents, by Category

		# Patents	% with 1 or More Scientific Citation	Mean	p10	p25	p50	p75	p90
Deep tech	GHG capture	4,248	48	13	1	2	4	10	37
	Mitigation in industrial prod.	43,641	39	12	1	1	4	10	28
	Generation and storage	108,691	33	11	1	1	3	9	24
Non–deep tech	Energy efficiency in ICT	42,053	29	7	1	1	2	5	14
	Energy efficiency in buildings	37,358	18	6	1	1	2	5	13
	Mitigation in transport	84,843	12	7	1	1	2	5	13

Note: This table reports the propensity to cite science for net-zero patents and heterogeneity across subcategories. Column 2 reports the share of net-zero patents that cite at least one scientific article for each category. Columns 3–8 report the intensity of scientific citations by category, conditional on citing at least one scientific paper. Data on scientific citations are obtained through the open-source data set provided by Marx and Fuegi (2020). Citations include front-page citations to scientific papers as described in Section II. Energy Generation and Storage, GHG (greenhouse gas) Capture, and Technologies for Mitigation in Industrial Production cite science more intensively and hence are labeled as "deep tech." ICT = information and communication technologies.

C. The Role of VC

We turn next to understand differences in net-zero patenting by the type of assignee. To do so, we first distinguish firms from other assignees such as universities, government laboratories, and individuals by supplementing the USPTO classification of assignees (as reported in the disambiguated assignee data) with text analysis to better distinguish institutions, hospitals, and universities from the company or corporation group.[10]

Within firms, we further distinguish between mature firms, young firms, and those backed by VC. We define "young" firms as those whose first patent was granted less than 10 years before the focal patent. In other words, the same firm could have some of its patents categorized as being associated with a young-firm indicator and others being associated with mature-firm indicator. Finally, we merge the patent data with the Refinitiv VentureXpert database, following a similar procedure to Bernstein, Giroud, and Townsend (2016) to identify VC-backed start-ups.[11]

In light of the fact that corporations have been documented to be pulling back from fundamental research in recent years (Arora et al. 2018,
2020), we look specifically at firm-type differences in net-zero patents,
given the particular importance of deep tech innovations to achieving
net-zero targets. As seen in table 3, mature companies account for about
two-thirds of the net-zero patents granted between 2000 and 2020. A
further fifth is accounted for by young firms. VC-backed firms account
for just under 3% of net-zero patents. Universities, government labs, and
individuals account for the balance. Columns 3–8 examine variation in
the share of these patents by the different net-zero sectors. Generation
and storage accounts for the largest relative share of patents for all assignees. However, it can be seen that, although all the other assignees
have 40%–50% of their net-zero patents in this category, mature companies have a relatively smaller 30% share in generation and storage. In
comparison, mature companies have a much larger relative share of patents related to mitigation in transport. Energy efficiency in buildings
and ICT account for between 30% and 35% of patents for all the firms.
GHG capture has a very small share of patents across all assignees, with
the greatest relative share coming from universities, government labs,
and individuals.

Looking at the sum of shares for deep tech patents (cols. 3–5) versus
non–deep tech (cols. 6–8) for different assignees in table 3, it can be seen
that deep tech constitutes a larger share of VC-backed firms' overall patenting (60%), compared with young firms (55%) and mature firms
(44%). In table 4, we document the degree to which patents granted
to different assignees rely on fundamental science, broken down by
whether or not the patent is in one of the three deep tech categories.
The difference between the average number of scientific citations between deep tech and non–deep tech for all assignee groups is consistent
with the pattern documented in table 2. However, it is also striking that
VC-backed firms are much more likely to cite fundamental science
relative to firms in general. This is driven by both the extensive and intensive margin, as well as the fact that, as seen in table 3, VC-backed
firms have a larger share of deep tech patents among the set of patents
they have been granted.

Another way of examining differences in the nature of patenting by
assignees is to look at the impact of these patents through their citations.
In table 5, we report the share of patents granted to each type of assignee
that are in the top (10th and 1st) percentiles in terms of citations received, relative to all other patents granted in the same year across the

Table 3
Net-Zero Patenting by Sector and Assignee Type

	# of Tot Patents	% of Tot Patents	Share of Total Patents of Each Assignee in Each Class					
			Generation and Storage (%)	GHG Capture (%)	Mitigation in Industrial Prod. (%)	Mitigation in Transport (%)	Energy Eff. in Buildings (%)	Energy Eff. in ICT (%)
VC-backed start-ups	8,806	2.6	45.5	.6	13.9	11.6	13.9	14.5
Young firms	70,001	20.8	38.7	1.2	15.6	21.6	14.3	8.4
Mature firms	218,417	64.8	30.4	1.3	12.6	29.9	10.2	15.5
Others	39,935	11.8	45.9	2.0	15.6	19.9	12.0	4.5

Note: The first two columns of this table document the number and share of net-zero patents that are associated with different assignee types. Columns 3–8 report the share of each assignee type's patents that correspond to each sector. For example, 45.5% of venture capital (VC)-backed start-up patents are related to Generation and Storage, and 1.3% of mature firm patents are related to GHG (greenhouse gas) Capture.

Table 4
Citation to Science Associated with Different Assignee Types

	All Patents	Net-Zero Patents	Net-Zero DT	Net-Zero Non-DT
	Panel A: Unconditional Mean of Citations to Science			
VC-backed start-ups	11.6	12.4	17.3	5
Young firms	3.6	2.9	4.2	1.3
Mature firms	3.1	2.2	3.7	1
Others	3.9	2.5	3.4	1.1
	Panel B: Conditional on Having at Least One Citation to Science			
VC-backed start-ups	23.3	24.4	29.7	12.7
Young firms	13.6	10.6	12.1	7
Mature firms	11.3	9	10.9	6
Others	13.8	4	8.3	6

Note: This table reports differences in propensity to cite science by patents granted to different assignee types. Columns report results for all patents in the US Patent and Trademark Office database 2000–20 and separately for net-zero, deep tech (DT), and non-DT patents and defined in table 2. Data on scientific citations are obtained through the open-source data set provided by Marx and Fuegi (2020). VC = venture capital.

Table 5
Patent Impact by Assignee Type

	All Patents (%)	Net-Zero Patents (%)	Net-Zero DT (%)	Net-Zero Non-DT (%)
	Panel A: Share of Patents Being in the Top 10% of Citations Received			
VC-backed start-ups	21.4	27.3	23.6	33.4
Young firms	10.6	13.3	11	16.3
Mature firms	9	10.2	8.8	11.5
Others	6.9	9.7	8.1	12.5
	Panel B: Share of Patents Being in the Top 1% of Citations Received			
VC-backed start-ups	2.9	4.6	3.7	6
Young firms	1.1	1.6	1.2	2
Mature firms	.9	1.0	1.1	1
Others	.6	.9	.6	1.2

Note: This table reports the share of each assignee's patents that are in the top 10% (panel A) and top 1% (panel B) of influential patents, normalized within a given grant year and US Patent and Trademark Office technology class. The sample includes patents granted 2000–17 because patents granted extremely recently have not accumulated a sufficient number of citations to accurately identify outliers. DT = deep tech; VC = venture capital.

entire USPTO patent database. The reason for looking at the right tail of citations is that some patenting is "defensive." Looking at the most highly cited patents gives a better indication of the degree to which there is a pattern in terms of the firms where the most influential patents are being developed. Given the large share of patents comprised by these assignees, we see that net-zero patents filed by other—particularly mature—firms are about proportional to what might be expected at random, albeit a bit less influential. These results are consistent with mature firms focusing more on incremental, sustaining innovations. On the other hand, and consistent with the findings of Howell et al. (2020), we find that VC-backed start-ups are disproportionately likely to have top-cited patents. They are almost three times more likely than random to have net-zero patents that are in the top 10% of citations and almost five times more likely to have patents in the top 1% of citations. Given the role that VC can play in stimulating breakthrough innovation (Kortum and Lerner 2000; Bernstein et al. 2016; Lerner and Nanda 2020), these results suggest that VC has the potential to play an increasingly important role in helping to drive the breakthrough innovations needed to achieve net-zero targets.

Despite the outsized impact the VC-backed patents appear to have among net-zero patenting, one potential limitation of VC impact is the small number of firms and net-zero patents it is associated with. Although this is equally true of VC-backed innovations in general, VC-backed firms are associated with some of the most innovative, transformational, and valuable firms in the world (Lerner and Nanda 2020). Of potentially greater concern is that, following a brief increase during a boom in venture financing for renewable energy start-ups (Nanda, Younge, and Fleming 2014; Popp et al. 2020), VC funding within net zero is increasingly associated with non–deep tech patents. Figure 4 shows that, although VC-backed start-ups continue to dominate mature firms in terms of the share of deep tech patenting in net zero, the share has declined from more than 70% in 2012 to about 55% in 2020.

III. Potential Frictions in Financing Deep Tech

VC investment in the United States—encompassing all investments, not just those related to net zero—has grown substantially since the early 2000s. The number of start-ups doubled over this period and the amount of capital being invested has risen more than five-fold since the early 2000s. However, as Lerner and Nanda (2020) note, this growth has

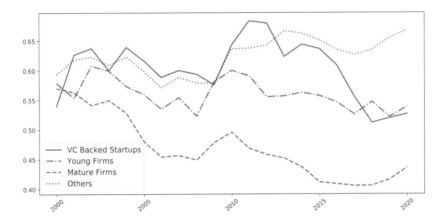

Fig. 4. Share of net-zero patents that are deep tech, by assignee type.

Notes: This figure reports the share of net-zero patents that are classified as deep technologies, by assignee type over the 2000–20 time period. Deep technologies are identified using patents to science citations as described in table 2, and this group includes Energy Generation and Storage, GHG (greenhouse gas) Mitigation in Industrial Production, and Carbon Capture Technologies.

not been uniform. It has come disproportionately from sectors such as software and related services including consumer internet, enterprise software, and media and communication. Hardware, energy, materials, and resources combined accounted for about 10% of capital invested by VCs in 2020, falling from a high of 40% in earlier part of the sample. To some extent, these ebbs and flows of funding across sectors reflect technology life cycles, the huge wave of application-related innovations made possible by the internet revolution in the late 1990s, and the subsequent rise of cloud computing in the mid-2000s (Nanda 2020). Nevertheless, growing academic research has begun to articulate certain aspects of start-ups that tend to make them have lower risk-adjusted returns and hence are less attractive to VC investors. We turn next to reviewing this work.[12]

A. Capital Intensity and Time Scale of Experimentation Cycles

VC investors do not shy away from investing large sums of money, particularly when financing the scale-up of successful ventures. Many business-to-consumer social networks and business-to-business enterprise software firms have raised hundreds of millions, or even billions, of dollars of equity financing from VC investors in the prior decade.

However, VCs are particularly sensitive to how much time and money it takes to achieve initial derisking milestones. To see why, it is useful to recognize the skewed nature of risk and return in VC: more than half of the investments that even the most successful VCs make fail entirely, and the majority of return for VC firms is generated by one or two extremely successful investments that are very hard to predict (Kerr, Nanda, and Rhodes-Kropf 2014). VCs therefore invest in stages; each stage or round of financing by the VC can be thought of as an experiment that generates information about whether or not a start-up can achieve its potential. Staged financing is tied to milestones and effectively gives VCs real options—they can choose to invest further in the next round of financing when start-ups achieve milestones, or they can choose to abandon follow-on financing if they do not believe the start-up is showing sufficient promise. VCs are therefore naturally drawn to start-ups where early experiments are quicker and cheaper, because it means their real option to reinvest or abandon at the next round is more valuable and the returns from their investments can be higher.

Ewens, Nanda, and Rhodes-Kropf (2018) highlight how the introduction of cloud computing services dramatically lowered the cost of learning about the ultimate potential of risky web-based start-ups. Specifically, it allowed those start-ups to rent hardware in small increments from providers like Amazon Web Services, use this to quickly gauge customer demand, and postpone expensive investments to scale up until after learning about the size and nature of demand from consumers. This, in turn, led to a disproportionate rise in the number of start-ups that could benefit from such lowered cost of experimentation and faster experimentation cycles. Related to this, VC investors are often drawn to start-ups with limited technical risk and where the key uncertainty relates to market demand for the product or service. Rapid iteration around early customer validation can either show a lack of demand or help reduce market risk substantially, thereby making the initial derisking cheap and efficient.

It is true that there is increasing scope for software and related information technologies to play a role in addressing climate and related challenges because products emerging from energy technologies are now more likely to be smaller, modular, and able to rely on innovation in high-tech sectors (Popp et al. 2020). However, our analysis of VC-backed net-zero patents has also shown that the deep tech patents that rely more on fundamental science are disproportionately related to start-ups in sectors such as semiconductors, computer hardware, and industrial production. These are areas in which early prototypes still embody substantial technical risk, and initial experiments involved in technical derisking are expensive and do not always benefit from the faster experimentation cycles that VC investors are drawn to. This friction is consistent with the relative decline in such innovations coming from VC firms in recent years.

B.   Learning Efficiency of Lab Experiments

When considering the role of experiments in early derisking, it is also helpful to recognize that real options are more valuable in sectors where initial experiments generate more information; in other words, where achieving or missing initial milestones helps VCs learn more about the ultimate potential of a venture (Nanda and Rhodes-Kropf 2016). This is because more informative experiments help VCs learn faster about firms that might ultimately fail, enabling them to "throw less good money after bad." More informative experiments also show firms achieving their promise earlier in their life, enabling start-ups to raise their next round of financing at much higher valuation step-ups. VCs that fund the initial rounds of financing in these ventures are therefore less diluted—that is, they maintain greater equity ownership—and hence generate a larger return for any given exit value.

Some of the challenges associated with deep tech commercialization stem from the fact that it is difficult to project how successful lab experiments might work at scale. For example, forecasting the unit costs at scale associated with energy storage using a new battery material or carbon capture and sequestration technology can be extremely difficult, even if the technology has been shown to work in a controlled laboratory environment. Moreover, because demand is tied to the ability of firms to produce at certain price points, this also implies that technology and market risk can often be intricately tied to each other in the energy sector (Arora, Fosfuri, and Roende 2022). In such instances, the costs and timelines associated with the lower learning efficiency and derisking process can be prohibitively large for commercial investors, as they may need to finance a full-scale demonstration pilots before learning whether the technology is sufficiently good to disrupt a market. The equity needed by a profit-seeking investor in such instances can be prohibitively large, leading projects with potential to not make it past the early derisking phase.

Advances in digital chemistry and synthetic biology, as well as huge increases in computational power that enable more accurate simulation of material properties at scale, are helping to improve the ability to forecast from successful lab experiments to success at scale. However, Siegmund et al. (2021) also point to the fact that lab experiments are often not conducted with a view to increasing learning efficiency. In the context of new catalysts, they point to specific examples of how success defined on a different temperature, pressure, and time scale can lead to a large number of false positives, potential solutions deemed promising in lab experiments but that could have been identified as having "failed" in the lab if the thresholds used were more consistent with the requirements of at-scale commercial applications. Some of this is due to the fact that the early derisking is increasingly done in university environments, where there can often be a lack of understanding of the particular specifications or bottlenecks that need to be optimized in an industrial setting. Even within large organizations, however, the research and development (R&D) and product teams may not work to jointly set early-stage technical milestones in a manner that increases the information value of the early experiments.

C. *Human Capital Involved in Deep Tech Translation*

There are numerous challenges to building a new venture that faces large amounts of technical risk in addition to having to sell into highly regulated industries with large entrenched incumbents that are averse to adopting new technologies unless they have a huge economic benefit. This makes the challenge of having the right entrepreneurial talent to build such ventures and sell these products to commercial customers nontrivial (Nanda et al. 2014). Those with technical talent may not have the skill or inclination to get involved in commercialization, and those with entrepreneurial talent can find it hard to evaluate the quality of technical ideas at the nascent stages, making it unappealing to select into entrepreneurship for those with very high opportunity costs (Hall and Woodward 2010). This is likely to be particularly true when the experimentation cycles and hence time to product is longer, as is the case with many science-based deep tech ventures (Ewens, Nanda, and Stanton 2020).

D. *Appropriating Value Being Created*

The discussion above has focused on supply-side frictions that make it harder to reduce the technical, market, and execution risk associated with building deep tech ventures relative to sectors such as information technology, software, and services.

It is also the case that software ventures often have the potential to more easily generate return. One of the attractive features of information technology is the highly scalable and asset-light businesses it is associated with. This leads to high levels of profitability and more cash flow to investors per unit of revenue, which in turn creates enormous opportunities for outsized returns.

In many deep tech sectors such as energy generation, storage, capture, and industrial production, new firms are typically selling to large incumbents with substantial market power and low willingness to adopt new technologies, thereby making it hard to command high profit margins when selling to them. Many of these customers could also be competitors, making it harder to appropriate value. Finally, to the extent that these require substantial investment in physical assets to generate cash, the path to becoming a valuable company can be slower. Indeed, as van den Heuvel and Popp (2022) note, a combination of "lackluster demand and a lower potential for outsized returns" makes clean energy firms less attractive to VC investors.

IV. Policy Implications

Having discussed some of the key frictions making deep tech investment less attractive to VC investors, we turn to a discussion of some policy implications. We note that innovation is clearly an important part of environmental policy, and encouraging innovation is often an explicit goal of policy makers. A large literature on the links between environmental policy and innovation is beyond the scope of this paper (see, e.g., Fu et al. 2018; Popp 2019). Similarly, the speed required to develop COVID-19 vaccines underlines how much society depends on the pace of scientific research and how effective science funding can be. A bias against funding risky research has also been discussed in the literature (Stephan 2014; Franzoni, Stephan, and Veugelers 2021), but we do not focus on this. We focus more narrowly on policies that might help address the specific sets of frictions outlined above that have been argued to reduce the risk-adjusted return of deep tech opportunities for VC investors.[13]

A. Government's Role in Stimulating Demand

Many successful examples of government involvement in the commercialization of tough tech have been related to the government's role as a customer (Mowery 2010; Mazzucato 2013). A key reason for this may have to do with such advance market commitments substantially reducing market risk through a willingness to pay for early versions of an emerging technology. A large military contract can also help to establish standards and coordinate the direction of technology trajectories.

Mazzucato (2013) notes the spillovers to ICT from the decade-long mission of the National Aeronautics and Space Administration (NASA) to put a man on the moon. In a compelling case study of the iPhone, she also shows how several of its key components—global positioning system, touchscreen glass, accessibility of the internet, and voice recognition technology—benefited either directly or indirectly from state funding. Evidence has also been found that federal investment during World War II subsequently led to increased private-sector investment. It is also suggested that a very substantial increase in federal investment in the life sciences and the growth of the biotechnology revolution was triggered by President Nixon's declaration of a "War on Cancer" in 1971 and the substantial commitments to federal funding of biomedical science in subsequent years through the National Institutes of Health.

Mowery (2010) discusses the role of the US military R&D and procurement budgets in driving substantial innovation and technological change in the United States in the post–World War II era. The government's role as a customer was very important in the 1960s and 1970s to the semiconductor industry—the one sector downstream from materials science where VC have profited at scale. The US Department of Defense and NASA played the role of collaborative customer, pulling the new industry down the learning curve to low-cost, reliable production, as military customers had done for the preceding microelectronics industry up to and during World War II. Similarly, the US government's role in reimbursement of new drugs and devices through Medicare and Medicaid substantially reduces market risk for drug development, implying that biotechnology ventures have enjoyed very high rates of access to the initial public offering (IPO) market, despite the high degree of technology risk, the long and expensive path to regulatory approval, and hence substantial cash flow deficits (Pisano 2006). In the context of clean energy, Germany's role in committing to purchase electricity generated from renewable energy sources is likely to have played a role in driving the growth of the industry and bringing the cost of photovoltaics down. Paying part of the contract value in advance can substantially reduce start-ups' dependence on external finance. This important role of the government as customer is often underappreciated when considering the role that policy makers can play in jump-starting innovation.

Government's role as a customer can also be used in outlining property rights, particularly those that help level the playing field for and enable innovation by start-ups. Program managers of the Defense Advanced Research Projects Agency, especially in its early years when it was funding general-purpose information technology (IT)-related research, conceived of their mission as including protection of the new entrants from the established incumbents (Azoulay et al. 2019). Related to this, strong intellectual property rights and well-functioning markets for technology (Arora, Belenzon, and Suh 2021) help start-ups monetize the value of their innovations.

B.   Supporting Financing and Certification of Technical Derisking

The record of government involvement in trying to directly subsidize the financing of start-ups has been mixed at best. Nevertheless, one setting where start-ups engaged in innovation have been shown to benefit substantially is the US Department of Energy's Small Business Innovation Research grant program, which has helped start-ups finance the prototyping of new technologies and thereby substantially increase the odds of receiving VC (Lerner 1999; Howell 2017). This ties in directly to the friction outlined above—where start-ups in some sectors cannot attract VC due to the difficulty they face in learning about the effectiveness of a new technology in the field as opposed to the lab and hence have trouble convincing investors they can achieve product-market fit and generate sufficient customer demand.

In the context of net-zero innovations, organizations such as Advanced Research Projects Agency–Energy also play an important certification role in helping to vet promising technologies. This can help provide independent validation that a technology is meeting technical milestones, because VC and other commercial investors often do not have the technical capability to assess and evaluate the efficacy and promise of a new technology.

C.   Supporting New Organizational and Financing Models

As noted above, deep tech solutions to global challenges such as achieving net-zero targets are increasingly being developed within universities.

Many of the frictions noted above relate to the challenge of effective handoff from a university lab environment to a commercial setting.

Given that they already have a lot of the specialized equipment, talent, and technical expertise needed to support and validate technical derisking, academic institutions have the potential to play a central role in helping to support the initial technical derisking and development prior to start-ups raising risk capital from investors. Beyond cost, another potential key benefit of derisking in a university environment is the potential to recycle knowledge arising from failure. Because most early-stage experiments fail and the insights from the failure of such technical experiments are instructive for future generations of entrepreneurs, the different incentive system of a university related to scaling knowledge can be extremely valuable in this context, particularly in settings where there are strong externalities, as is the case with knowledge around early-stage derisking and translation.

Another role that universities can play is in helping founders of deep tech ventures, who often have technical background but less business training, to understand the appropriate customer segments, business models, and financing sources for their new ventures (Sauermann and Stephan 2010; Cohen, Sauermann, and Stephan 2020). In addition to helping to stimulate the supply of technical talent that is also trained for building ventures, universities can play a role in helping to match strong technical projects with similarly strong entrepreneurial talent.

In terms of the transition from universities to VC, VC firms typically raise closed-end funds, implying that they are required to invest the money they raise and return the proceeds within a fixed period, usually 10 years. Given that investments are made over the first few years, this implies that VCs are naturally drawn to investments where they can realize a return through an exit—either an acquisition or an IPO—within a short time. Not all ventures are amenable to this timeline. For example, start-ups that have a physical component to generating cash flows often take longer to build, particularly if the venture needs to build factories to produce new products—as is the case with energy production, storage, and many industrial production methods. Although VCs have some leeway to extend the fund life a few years, the fixed limit to a fund's life can become a binding constraint for investors, although the use of evergreen funds can overcome such constraints (Lerner and Nanda 2020).

As noted by Nanda (2020), universities, government labs, corporate R&D, VC firms, corporate VC firms, and longer-term "patient capital" associated with family offices each brings different incentives, funding models, ability to experiment, and tolerance for failure. Each has different benefits and constraints. Understanding the degree to which these can be adapted to most effectively help commercialize deep tech addressing net-zero challenges—perhaps while also harnessing nondilutive capital from philanthropy for initial experiments—is a promising area of further inquiry.

Endnotes

Author email addresses: Dalla Fontana (silvia.dalla.fontana@usi.ch), Nanda (ramana .nanda@imperial.ac.uk). Parts of this chapter draw extensively on work by Nanda et al. (2014), Nanda and Rhodes-Kropf (2016), Nanda (2020), and Janeway, Nanda, and Rhodes-Kropf (2021). We thank Ben Jones, Josh Lerner, and participants at the May 2022 NBER EIPE conference for helpful suggestions. For acknowledgments, sources of research support, and disclosure of the authors' material financial relationships, if any, please see https://www .nber.org/books-and-chapters/entrepreneurship-and-innovation-policy-and-economy-vol ume-2/innovating-net-zero-can-venture-capital-and-startups-play-meaningful-role.

1. The CPC is a patent classification system jointly developed by the European Patent Office and the USPTO.

2. We obtain patent data from PatentsView.org, a platform that provides data from the USPTO. We only keep patents for which we observe the date it was applied for, the date it was granted, the patent title, the organization it was assigned to, the type of organization, and its CPC technology classification. With these restrictions, our sample comprises 90.3% of the 5,367,164 patents granted over this period.

3. https://www.cooperativepatentclassification.org/about.

4. https://www.epo.org/news-events/news/2013/20130102.html.

5. Cohen et al. (2020) use the same classification system to examine patenting differences between mature publicly traded firms to the link between the environmental, social, and governance ratings of these firms and their innovation. Our analysis focuses on the universe of firms regardless of whether they are publicly traded.

6. In the CPC tagging, a patent can belong to multiple Y02 classes. However, this happens for a minority of patents: 293,278 out of 356,996 (82.2%) belong to one group only. In the case of patents assigned to more than one Y02 class, we proceed to allocate each patent to a unique group as follows: first, we sum the number of subcategories for each group. We allocate the patent to the group that has the highest number of subclasses with the rationale that a patent with more tags in one group suggests that this group is the most relevant for the patent. This procedure is applied to 20,191 patents (6% of total). Second, for patents that do not have a prevalent subclass, we allocate them to one group after considering the different combinations of subclasses. When carbon capture technologies are combined with energy efficiency classes, this is usually because GHG obtained with carbon capture can be also used for other purposes. In this case, we consider carbon capture as the main technology group. When technologies related to transportation, efficiency in buildings, and ICT are combined with classes such as energy generation, this is because they are related to technologies that improve energy efficiency and make use of energy from renewable sources; in this case, we keep the main intended use of the technology (home appliances, car engines and batteries, etc.) as the main technology group. Last, when the subclass of energy generation is combined with waste, it is because these are technologies related to fuels obtained from waste, so we consider them as generation technologies. Overall this second step is applied to 41,694 of patents, which represents 11.7% of the total.

7. Although the classification was applied retrospectively, it is possible that it was more effective for identifying patents applied for from that moment on.

8. In our data set, each list of patent titles belonging to a certain category is a separate document, and the corpus is composed of all documents. We start by cleaning the text of

titles and removing all punctuation and special characters and use lemmatization to group together the inflected forms of a word to be analyzed as a single term. We then apply a list of stop-words to be excluded from the frequency count. The list includes standard English stop-words, as well as USPTO stop-word lists that are specific for technical language processing. With TF-IDF, we then add a list of stop-words created from terms that are recurrent in all documents of the corpus. The frequency of the remaining words is then adjusted for how rarely a word is used in the corpus.

9. The authors link data from the USPTO to a broad set of scientific articles not limited by industry or field. Their algorithm can capture up to 93% of patent citations to science with an accuracy rate of 99% or higher.

10. This is performed taking into account that inventors are international; a word that indicates, for example, a university must be considered in different languages.

11. We start by matching each standardized name of a company in VentureXpert with standardized names from the USPTO data set: if an exact match is found, this is taken to be the same company and removed from the list. For the remaining companies, we use a fuzzy matching technique that gives a similarity score to matches of stem names weighted by the inverse frequency of use of each word in the names list. If a similarity score higher than 85% is found, we combine this information with other identifying information, such as founding dates and patent grant dates, and standardized city/nation combination. In the overall sample of international start-ups, we identify 18,987 that have at least one patent granted by the USPTO. This is approximately 20% of the overall VentureXpert data set of VC-backed start-ups, and this ratio is in line with other papers matching these two data sets. Because we want to identify innovations that are in the portfolios of VC and not all innovations belonging to companies that were funded by VCs many years before, we apply two more restrictions: first, we define a patent to be VC-backed if it was applied for between the first and last round of financing by VC funds. Second, we restrict patent level that indicates if a patent is applied for within 10 years since the first patent was issued by that same firm.

12. This section draws extensively on Nanda et al. (2014), Nanda and Rhodes-Kropf (2016), and Nanda (2020).

13. This section draws extensively on Janeway et al. (2021).

References

Akcigit, Ufuk, and William R. Kerr. 2018. "Growth through Heterogeneous Innovations." *Journal of Political Economy* 126 (4): 1374–443. https://doi.org/10.1086/697901.

Arora, Ashish, Sharon Belenzon, and Andrea Patacconi. 2018. "The Decline of Science in Corporate R&D." *Strategic Management Journal* 39 (1): 3–32.

Arora, Ashish, Sharon Belenzon, Andrea Patacconi, and Jungkyu Suh. 2020. "The Changing Structure of American Innovation: Some Cautionary Remarks for Economic Growth." *Innovation Policy and the Economy* 20 (1): 39–93.

Arora, Ashish, Sharon Belenzon, and Jungkyu Suh. 2021. "Science and the Market for Technology." Working Paper no. 28534 (March), NBER, Cambridge, MA.

Arora, Ashish, Andrea Fosfuri, and Thomas Roende. 2022. "Caught in the Middle: The Bias against Startup Innovation with Technical and Commercial Challenges." Working Paper no. 29654 (January), NBER, Cambridge, MA.

Azoulay, Pierre, Erica Fuchs, Anna P. Goldstein, and Michael Kearney. 2019. "Funding Breakthrough Research: Promises and Challenges of the ARPA Model." *Innovation Policy and the Economy* 19:69–96.

Bernstein, Shai, Xavier Giroud, and Richard R. Townsend. 2016. "The Impact of Venture Capital Monitoring." *Journal of Finance* 71 (4): 1591–622.

Cohen, Wesley M., Henry Sauermann, and Paula Stephan. 2020. "Not in the Job Description: The Commercial Activities of Academic Scientists and Engineers." *Management Science* 66 (9): 4108–17.

Cunningham, Colleen, Florian Ederer, and Song Ma. 2021. "Killer Acquisitions." *Journal of Political Economy* 129 (3): 649–702. https://doi.org/10.1086/712506.

Ewens, Michael, Ramana Nanda, and Matthew Rhodes-Kropf. 2018. "Cost of Experimentation and the Evolution of Venture Capital." *Journal of Financial Economics* 128 (3): 422–42. https://doi.org/10.1016/j.jfineco.2018.03.001.

Ewens, Michael, Ramana Nanda, and Christopher T. Stanton. 2020. "Founder-CEO Compensation and Selection into Venture Capital-Backed Entrepreneurship." Working Paper no. 27296 (June), NBER, Cambridge, MA. https://ideas.repec.org/p/nbr/nberwo/27296.html.

Franzoni, Chiara, Paula Stephan, and Reinhilde Veugelers. 2021. "Funding Risky Research." Working Paper no. 28905 (June), NBER, Cambridge, MA.

Fu, Wancong, Chong Li, Jan Ondrich, and David Popp. 2018. "Technological Spillover Effects of State Renewable Energy Policy: Evidence from Patent Counts." Working Paper no. 25390 (December), NBER, Cambridge, MA.

Hall, Robert E., and Susan E. Woodward. 2010. "The Burden of the Non-diversifiable Risk of Entrepreneurship." *American Economic Review* 100 (3): 1163–94.

Haščič, Ivan, and Mauro Migotto. 2015. "Measuring Environmental Innovation Using Patent Data." Environment Working Paper no. 89, OECD, Paris.

Howell, Sabrina T. 2017. "Financing Innovation: Evidence from R&D Grants." *American Economic Review* 107 (4): 1136–64.

Howell, Sabrina T., Josh Lerner, Ramana Nanda, and Richard R. Townsend. 2020. "How Resilient Is Venture-Backed Innovation? Evidence from Four Decades of U.S. Patenting." Working Paper no. 27150 (May), NBER, Cambridge, MA.

IEA (International Energy Agency). 2022. "Net Zero by 2050: A Roadmap for the Global Energy Sector." https://www.iea.org/reports/net-zero-by-2050.

Janeway, William H., Ramana Nanda, and Matthew Rhodes-Kropf. 2021. "Venture Capital Booms and Start-Up Financing." *Annual Review of Financial Economics* 13 (1): 111–27.

Kerr, William R., Ramana Nanda, and Matthew Rhodes-Kropf. 2014. "Entrepreneurship as Experimentation." *Journal of Economic Perspectives* 28 (3): 25–48. https://ideas.repec.org/a/aea/jecper/v28y2014i3p25-48.html.

Kortum, Samuel, and Josh Lerner. 2000. "Assessing the Contribution of Venture Capital to Innovation." *RAND Journal of Economics* 31 (4): 674–92.

Lerner, Josh. 1999. "The Government as Venture Capitalist: The Long-Run Impact of the SBIR Program." *Journal of Business* 72 (3): 285–318.

Lerner, Josh, and Ramana Nanda. 2020. "Venture Capital's Role in Financing Innovation: What We Know and How Much We Still Need to Learn." *Journal of Economic Perspectives* 34 (3): 237–61.

Marx, Matt, and Aaton Fuegi. 2020. "Reliance on Science: Worldwide Front-Page Patent Citations to Scientific Articles." *Strategic Management Journal* 41:1572–94.

———. 2021. "Reliance on Science: Worldwide Front-Page Patent Citations to Scientific Articles." *Journal of Economic and Management Strategy* 31:369–92.

Mazzucato, Mariana. 2013. *The Entrepreneurial State: Debunking Public vs. Private Sector Myths*. London: Anthem.

Mowery, David C. 2010. "Military R&D and Innovation." In *Handbook of the Economics of Innovation*, Vol. 2, ed. Bronwyn H. Hall and Nathan Rosenberg, 1219–56. Amsterdam: North-Holland.

Nanda, Ramana. 2020. "Financing Tough Tech Innovation." In *Global Innovation Index 2020: Who Will Finance Innovation?*, ed. Soumitra Dutta, Bruno Lanvin, and Sacha Wunsch-Vincent, 113–19. Ithaca, NY: Cornell University Press.

Nanda, Ramana, and Matthew Rhodes-Kropf. 2016. "Financing Entrepreneurial Experimentation." *Innovation Policy and the Economy* 16 (1): 1–23. https://doi.org/10.1086/684983.

Nanda, Ramana, Ken Younge, and Lee Fleming. 2014. "Innovation and Entrepreneurship in Renewable Energy." In *The Changing Frontier: Rethinking Science and Innovation Policy*, ed. Adam B. Jaffe and Benjamin F. Jones, 199–232. Chicago: University of Chicago Press.

Pisano, Gary P. 2006. *Science Business: The Promise, the Reality, and the Future of Biotech*. Boston: Harvard Business School Press.

Popp, David. 2019. "Environmental Policy and Innovation: A Decade of Research." Working Paper no. 25631 (March), NBER, Cambridge, MA.

Popp, David, Jacquelyn Pless, Ivan Haščič, and Nick Johnstone. 2020. "Innovation and Entrepreneurship in the Energy Sector." Working Paper no. 27145 (May), NBER, Cambridge, MA.

Reinganum, Jennifer F. 1983. "Uncertain Innovation and the Persistence of Monopoly." *American Economic Review* 73 (4): 741–48. https://ideas.repec.org/a/aea/aecrev/v73y1983i4p741-48.html.

Sauermann, Henry, and Paula E Stephan. 2010. "Twins or Strangers? Differences and Similarities between Industrial and Academic Science." Working Paper no. 16113 (June), NBER, Cambridge, MA.

Siegmund, Daniel, Sebastian Metz, Volker Peinecke, Terence E. Warner, Carsten Cremers, Anna Grevé, Tom Smolinka, Doris Segets, and Ulf-Peter Apfel. 2021. "Crossing the Valley of Death: From Fundamental to Applied Research in Electrolysis." *JACS Au* 1 (5): 527–35. https://doi.org/10.1021/jacsau.1c00092.

Stephan, Paula. 2014. "The Endless Frontier: Reaping What Bush Sowed?" In *The Changing Frontier: Rethinking Science and Innovation Policy*, ed. Adam B. Jaffe and Benjamin F. Jones, 321–66. Chicago: University of Chicago Press.

van den Heuvel, Matthias, and David Popp. 2022. "The Role of Venture Capital and Governments in Clean Energy: Lessons from the First Cleantech Bubble." Working Paper no. 29919 (April), NBER, Cambridge, MA.

To Starve or to Stoke? Understanding Whether Divestment versus Investment Can Steer (Green) Innovation

Jacquelyn Pless, *Massachusetts Institute of Technology*, United States of America

Abstract

More than 1,500 organizations and investors representing more than $40 trillion in assets have committed to fossil fuel divestment to combat climate change. Will it work? This chapter explores whether divestment might induce green innovation, a critical component of the transition to a cleaner economy. Divestment could theoretically steer innovation by increasing the cost of capital for "dirty firms," but it is unclear whether the effects will be large enough to significantly reduce investment opportunities. I argue that continuing to invest in dirty industries could drive green innovation conditional on investors being socially conscious and governing through "voice." This hinges upon understanding which firm strategies actually foster green innovation, though, and the commonly used environmental, social, and governance indicators come with several limitations. I demonstrate how decomposing them and using alternative approaches to measuring environmental performance can improve investment, strategy, and management decision-making and policy design. I examine the relationship between 14 specific practices and whether large firms in 16 pollution-intensive sectors are on track for meeting the Paris Agreement emissions targets ("carbon performance"). I find no correlation between carbon performance and the most basic practices, such as disclosing emissions, but a positive correlation for five more explicit strategies: setting long-term quantitative emissions targets, having a third party verify emissions data, incorporating environmental performance into executive remuneration policies, supporting governmental climate change efforts, and setting an internal price of carbon. I construct a new "best practices" score based on these results and find that it has a much higher correlation with carbon performance than some other composite measures.

JEL Codes: O32, O35, G3, Q4, Q5

Keywords: divestment, direction of innovation, management practices, corporate governance

Entrepreneurship and Innovation Policy and the Economy, volume 2, 2023.

I. Introduction

Climate change is arguably one of today's greatest threats to the economy, the environment, and humanity. As sea levels rise to dangerous levels and extreme weather events such as droughts and hurricanes intensify, the effects are damaging ecosystems, harming human health, and hampering economic activity. Scientific evidence suggests that warming must not exceed 1.5°C above preindustrial levels to avoid the most catastrophic consequences, and reaching this goal will require deep and immediate cuts to global greenhouse gas emissions (IPCC 2018).[1]

But the policies and regulations that could help achieve such reductions tend to be controversial and uncertain. Although climate change policy in the United States recently made remarkable progress when President Biden signed the Inflation Reduction Act into law—a sweeping climate bill that allocates more than $300 billion for energy and climate reform, the largest single investment in climate in US history, such policy action, is unprecedented.[2] Brewing frustrations around inaction have thus motivated a search for additional approaches to mitigate climate change, and a global movement toward divesting from fossil fuels and industries that rely upon them has emerged. The idea is that, if investors reduce the supply of capital to firms in pollution-intensive industries, and if consumers reduce demand for their goods and services, "dirty firms" might become less competitive and eventually shut down. As of August 2022, more than 1,500 organizations and investors representing more than $40 trillion in assets have committed to some form of fossil fuel divestment as a means of combating climate change.

Will it work? In this chapter, I explore whether divestment could be an effective tool for inducing innovation in cleaner technologies, practices, and processes (henceforth "green innovation"), which will be critical for the transition to a cleaner economy. Doing so quickly enough to reach the Paris Agreement targets will undoubtedly still require new and affordable solutions for reducing pollution. I discuss how the main mechanism through which starving dirty firms of finance could play such a role is by increasing their cost of capital, which then might, at least in theory, reduce their investment opportunity sets. This could change the composition of innovation activities throughout the economy and increase demand for clean companies.

However, whether divestment can increase the cost of capital enough to substantially induce green innovation, and do so quickly enough to help meet the Paris Agreement emissions reduction targets, remains unclear.

Divestment also could even dampen investments in green solutions if firms would have otherwise allocated such capital to improving their environmental performance or developing clean technologies. In addition, socially conscious shareholders might be able to reshape firms' strategies and innovation pursuits by engaging with management. Could investing in polluting industries therefore more effectively steer the direction of innovation than divesting? How can investors help guide firms such that they improve their environmental performance? Are there specific management practices and strategies that are more likely to foster green innovation than others? How are green innovation and environmental performance measured in the first place?

The aim of this chapter is to provide insight into these questions. To limit the scope, I focus on firms in polluting industries (e.g., transportation, manufacturing, oil and gas) as opposed to innovation by firms in clean industries (e.g., those strictly focused on developing clean technology). So-called dirty firms could innovate in their processes and practices to reduce their environmental footprint—for example, improving operational efficiency and using cleaner fuels—or they could develop and adopt clean technologies themselves as well. The exact form of innovation will not be relevant for my analysis, but it is important to keep in mind that I am focusing on firms in dirty industries even when referring to investment.

Note that this type of investment differs from what is often referred to as "impact investing." The latter often refers to investing in firms that are already socially conscious (e.g., those making efforts to improve their environmental performance, or at least claiming to do so) and companies that are strictly focused on developing clean technologies or other pollution-reducing innovations. In this paper, I am referring to investments even in firms that score poorly on measures of environmental performance, such as the commonly used environmental, social, and governance (ESG) indicators.

The first part of this chapter provides background on the divestment movement and considers how divestment versus continued investment in polluting industries could induce green innovation. I start Section II by discussing the unique characteristics of green innovation that can theoretically dampen the incentive for firms to invest. Green innovation is characterized by a unique "double-externality" challenge. Firstly, as is the case for innovations of all types, imperfect appropriability leads to knowledge spillovers, and this can dampen the incentive for firms to invest because they cannot fully capture the value of their innovations. Secondly, though environmental externalities also lead to prices not reflecting the true social cost of production, which can further dampen the incentive to invest in green innovation specifically. These market failures are often invoked to justify government intervention, but as noted, climate policy has been historically controversial and uncertain. Furthermore, although mechanisms implemented around the world so far—such as putting a price on carbon—have been shown to increase innovation to some degree, whether they do so substantially and quickly enough remains unclear. I discuss this literature in Section II.

In Section III, I discuss recent divestment trends and the rationale behind why they might continue. Investors are not motivated solely by a sense of moral obligation. Rather, there are climate-related risks that affect firm performance and thus the value of financial assets, such as the physical effects of climate change on production, increasing stringency in environmental policy, changing consumer preferences, and labor supply risk.

Section IV explores how reducing the supply of capital for dirty firms could induce green innovation. I discuss the main mechanism through which it might do so: increasing the cost of capital for dirty firms. When investors sell, they lower share prices to attract buyers, which reduces the value of the firm and its future cost of capital. This can theoretically reduce the firm's investment opportunity set and thus its status quo pursuits that sustain pollution-intensive industries, such as the exploration and extraction of new oil and gas resources.

After reviewing the evidence in the (relatively thin) literature, I conclude that divestment will likely not have a substantial enough impact on the cost of capital to significantly reduce investment opportunities for firms in polluting industries. The most comprehensive study to date is Berk and van Binsbergen (2021), who find that the cost of capital increases by less than 20 basis points even when ESG investors hold 50% of wealth and more than 85% of investors must be socially conscious to affect the cost of capital by at least 1%. Whether this could sufficiently redirect investment activity is unclear without further research, but it seems unlikely, especially if the demand for fossil-related goods and services continues to generate enough revenue for firms to remain profitable.

Instead, I argue that, conditional on shareholders being socially conscious and effectively engaging with leadership, continuing to invest in pollution-intensive industries might be an effective avenue for promoting green innovation. Investors can steer innovation and business activities by governing through "voice," engaging with managers to inform their decision-making and shape their strategies. On the other hand, they lose their seat at the table when they sell their shares. They transfer their control rights to the buyer. The buyer is also less likely to be socially conscious if the sell is motivated by environmental objectives, so the new owners might be even less likely to encourage the firm to improve its environmental performance or invest in green innovation.

Successfully steering innovation by governing through voice, though, hinges upon understanding which management practices and strategies actually foster green innovation and improve environmental performance. There is surprisingly little evidence in the literature so far, which I explore in the latter part of the chapter (Sec. V). I first discuss the measures most commonly relied upon for assessing a firm's "greenness," such as ESG indicators, and how they come with many limitations for effectively guiding investment and management decision-making. The limitations can be broadly categorized as related to (1) inconsistencies across indicators from different ratings providers, (2) aggregation methods that mask important details and conflate inputs (i.e., management practices and strategies) with outcomes (i.e., actual environmental performance), and (3) lack of comparability between environmental performance across industries.

I then bring these critiques to the data and examine the relationship between environmental performance and specific firm strategies and management practices for large public firms in 16 pollution-intensive sectors. I use data capturing the responses to individual questions that go into the creation of many ESG indicators, focusing on those related specifically to environmental management, and complement these with a new measure of "carbon performance" developed by the Transition Pathway Initiative (TPI) that evaluates whether companies are on track for reducing their pollution levels such that they are aligned with the Paris Agreement emissions reduction targets. Using this alternative methodology allows for a scientifically based definition of "good" carbon performance and comparison of firms across industries.

Taking a descriptive approach, I examine the relationship between 14 specific management practices and strategies with the likelihood that firms are aligned with the Paris Agreement targets. I find little to no correlation between carbon performance and the most basic practices, such as simply disclosing emissions or acknowledging climate change as a risk to the business. On the other hand, there is a positive correlation between carbon performance and five arguably stronger and more explicit versions of such practices: having emissions information verified, setting long-term quantitative targets, incorporating ESG performance into executive remuneration policies, supporting domestic and international climate change efforts, and setting an internal price of carbon. Last, I construct a new "best practices" measure based on these results that is highly correlated with carbon performance—much more so than it is for some aggregate measures.

Although the results of these analyses should not be interpreted as causal, and they should not be applied to other settings without further research given the small sample size and select set of industries that I study, the exercise provides three insights that might be of interest to investors and managers. First, decomposing measures such as ESG indicators is important for developing an understanding of which practices and strategies foster green innovation, and it is particularly important to not conflate inputs (such as firm strategies) with outcomes (realized environmental performance). Second, some practices and strategies can be designed and implemented with varying degrees of strength, which reinforces the importance of decomposing these measures. For example, disclosing pollution levels or simply stating that the firm aims to reduce emissions might not be effective unless targets are long term and quantitative. Third, if constructing and using an aggregated management quality measure to inform decision-making is of interest, analyzing which specific practices and strategies are most effective first (i.e., the best practices) might be an effective approach to determine appropriate weights for each component.

The results also may be of interest to policy makers and regulators given the growing recognition that energy and environmental innovation will be critical for the transition to a cleaner economy. Stakeholder capitalism and encouraging firms in pollution-intensive industries to reduce their environmental footprint are also at the forefront of the public discourse. The Securities and Exchange Commission recently proposed a new rule that would require public companies to provide reports on their emissions, climate-related risks, and plans for reaching net zero. My findings highlight how the potential for such practices to drive change likely depends on their specificity and how well they are integrated into the firm's overall strategy.

II.   The Double-Externality Challenge

It has long been known that innovation fuels economic growth (Romer 1990; Aghion and Howitt 1992). But not all innovations are created equal. Although most generate both private and social value, some contribute more to social progress—improvements in society's capacity to meet basic human needs and create conditions that empower people to improve their quality of life—than others. For example, clean energy technologies that reduce pollution or innovation that improves health-care and education services surely contribute more to social welfare than a new payment-processing application.

Innovation for social progress faces a "double-externality" challenge, though, that introduces unique implications for the incentives that inventors and firms face to invest in such pursuits (Jaffe, Newell, and Stavins 2005). Innovation of all types can generate value that the creator cannot fully capture, including some benefits to users or knowledge spillovers that other firms can build upon, and this imperfect appropriability might lead to underinvestment in new ideas (Nelson 1959; Arrow 1962).[3] When there are also production and consumption externalities, as there are in the energy and industrial sectors, prices tend to not reflect the true costs and benefits of the good or service. Prices for, say, electricity from fossil fuel sources might be "underpriced" in the sense that they do not incorporate the harm that producing and consuming it creates, dampening the incentive to invest in alternatives.

These market failures are often invoked to justify government intervention, such as carbon taxes to address environmental externalities and direct funding or fiscal incentives that reduce the cost of research and development (R&D) to address the appropriability challenge. There is indeed growing evidence that some mechanisms increase innovative activity. For example, Popp (2002), Martin, De Preux, and Wagner (2014), Aghion et al. (2016), Calel and Dechezleprêtre (2016), and Calel (2020) find that putting a price on carbon induces green innovation. Research is also increasingly showing that direct grants and tax credits for R&D have positive effects on innovation inputs and outcomes in various settings.[4] However, there is little work so far on how they affect energy and environmental innovation specifically or on the effects of energy-specific funding. More research is also needed on the optimal policy mix and the ways in which these mechanisms interact.[5]

Why is this relevant in the context of fossil fuel divestment? Although recent climate policy is making unprecedented progress, historically it has been controversial and uncertain. Supporters of the divestment movement argue that reducing the supply of capital for firms in polluting industries and the demand for their products and services could offer a complementary tool for transitioning to a cleaner economy and driving green innovation. However, whether divestment has or will have such effects remains unclear. Continuing to invest even in the dirtiest industries also has the potential to direct innovation. I explore this tension and the underlying mechanisms in Section IV.

III.   The Divestment Movement

The fossil fuel divestment movement dates to at least a decade ago when students at Swarthmore College urged their administration to move its money out of dirty industries. Advocates argue that, by no longer financing the fossil fuel industry, investors can help address climate change by driving polluting firms out of business. Recent trends are cultivating a renewed optimism about its potential. More than 1,500 organizations and investors—including universities, foundations, governments, private equity firms, and individuals—with a total of about $40 trillion in assets under management made public commitments to divest to some degree as of August 2022, a more than 75,000% increase in total assets under management since 2014 (Invest-Divest 2021).

These figures can be misleading, though, if one is interested in tracking divestment trends. The assets under management totals are only equal to actual divestment if the investor currently has 100% of its assets in fossil fuels and if it commits to fully divesting. Many have made only partial commitments, promising to divest from some types of fossil fuels and not others, and they may not divest from nonenergy industries that are still high polluting because they rely on fossil fuels as inputs, such as manufacturing.

Promised divestment also does not represent actual or current divestment and the timelines over which will occur can be opaque. Significant amounts of funds are still flowing into heavily polluting industries. Recent analyses have shown that the energy holdings of the world's 10 largest alternative asset managers, making up $3 trillion in assets combined, include more than 300 portfolio companies in the energy sector, and 80% of their energy assets go toward fossil fuels (PESP 2021).[6]

A.   Climate-Related Risks

There are several reasons to think that shareholders might continue divesting, though. Divestment is not driven only by a sense of moral obligation. Companies and investors are increasingly recognizing that climate change creates real risks that threaten their operations and financial performance. For example, nearly all respondents to Deloitte's (2021) survey of 750 executives around the world indicated that climate change has negatively affected their business already. I discuss the risks firms and investors face in this section.

Physical Risk

For many industries, the physical manifestations of climate change can be economically costly because of how they can affect operations and asset values. Increasingly frequent and extreme weather events such as hurricanes, blizzards, high temperatures, and droughts can disrupt operations and the interdependent global supply chains that firms rely upon. They interrupt production, reducing revenues and raising costs (and prices) associated with the need to repair damage. Severe weather also can be dangerous for workers. For example, many manufacturing industries involve combustible and flammable materials, so lightning can cause injuries and death. Operations must be shut down to protect worker safety.

In Deloitte's (2021) survey of executives, the operational impact of climate-related disasters was identified as the leading environmental sustainability challenge. Because physical risks affect firms' output, productivity, and financial performance, they can reduce long-term returns on investments and thus the value of financial assets. Dietz et al. (2016) examine the impact of climate change on the present market value of global financial assets and find that the expected "climate value at risk" is 1.8% when considering business as usual, amounting to $2.5 trillion.[7] Investors may consider these risks in their investment decisions.

Policy Risk

More stringent climate policies also impose costs for fossil fuel companies and the industries that rely upon them, which ultimately affects asset values. Furthermore, costs are passed through to prices, which puts downward pressure on demand. Although the prospects and consistency of policies aiming to tackle climate change historically have been uncertain, recent activity suggests this is changing. Increasingly salient extreme weather events along with the scientific evidence on the consequences of global warming are bringing climate change to the forefront of public discourse, and the Inflation Reduction Act that President Biden recently signed into law includes unprecedented measures for addressing climate change.

Demand Risk

Relatedly, changing consumer preferences creates demand risk. Consumers are increasingly boycotting fossil fuels and the goods and services that rely upon them in their production processes, or "exiting" from the fossil fuel market more generally by seeking alternatives (e.g., electric vehicles), which can dampen long-run returns to investments and threaten the survival of the firm. Reduced demand, or the threat thereof, may contribute to continued divestment moving forward.

Labor Supply Risk

Shifting preferences and increasing stigma associated with polluting companies also creates labor supply risk such that it could be increasingly difficult for dirty firms to attract workers. Human capital is an important input into firm productivity. A reduction in the supply of workers willing to work for dirty firms, and especially high-skilled labor, poses financial risks for investors as well.

IV.   How Can Divestment versus Investment Steer Innovation?

Can divestment induce green innovation and do so quickly enough to meet the Paris Agreement goals? On the one hand, divestment reduces the supply of capital for polluting industries (and those relying upon them in their production processes), making it more difficult for them to invest in new polluting activities or projects that advance their status quo dirty activities. On the other hand, providing capital could enable them to pursue innovations that reduce their environmental impact. Investing also provides shareholders with a seat at the table so they can influence management decision-making and strategy. This section explores how these opposing strategies might (or might not) steer innovation.

A.   Cost of Capital Channel

The primary mechanism through which divestment can induce green innovation (and contribute toward the transition to a less pollution-intensive economy more generally) is by increasing the cost of capital for dirty firms. When investors sell their shares in a company, they lower the price to attract buyers, implying that the firm will then face a higher cost of capital. In theory, this should reduce their investment opportunity set, dampening dirty innovation if they would have otherwise allocated capital to expanding their status quo activities (e.g., further oil and gas exploration), and lowering their growth rates. It also could induce dirty firms to exit and increase demand for clean companies, changing the composition of firms within the economy and enhancing green innovation investments.[8]

For these dynamics to have a meaningful effect on the direction of innovation, the change in the cost of capital must be substantial enough to actually reduce dirty firms' investment opportunity set, and the effect probably must be immediate to be on track for achieving the pollution reduction targets laid out in the Paris Agreement. Polluting firms must have an incentive to promptly improve their environmental performance (or exit), especially given the uniquely long innovation cycles in capital-intensive industries.[9]

The literature on how divestment affects the cost of capital for dirty firms is relatively thin, but evidence from one of the more comprehensive studies to date suggests that its effects would likely be far too small to significantly redirect innovation. Berk and van Binsbergen (2021) show how the change in the cost of capital can be derived from a simple formula based on the fraction of the economy that socially conscious investors choose to target and their correlation with the rest of the market.[10] They then bring their theory to the data to study how socially conscious investment strategies have affected the cost of capital in the United States in recent years using the largest social index fund in the world—the Vanguard FTSE Social Index Fund—to identify the subset of clean stocks in the FTSE4Good Index.

Using data for December 2015 through December 2020, the authors first find that a little less than half of US market capitalization fell in the dirty portfolio. They then show that, when applying their formula and assuming a market risk premium of 6%, the cost of capital increases by only 0.35 basis points. This increase is very small, and it is highly unlikely that this would be enough to meaningfully influence investment decision-making. Strikingly, when calibrating their model to study what it would take to have such an impact, they find that the cost of capital increases by less than 20 basis points even when ESG investors hold 50% of wealth. More than 85% of investors must be socially conscious to affect the cost of capital by at least 1% according to their study. The authors test these theoretical predictions empirically by exploiting changes in firms' ESG classifications and find that inclusion in the 4 Good index has no effect on the cost of capital.[11] The main implication from this analysis is that, even if divestment continues to rise, the effects on the cost of capital will likely be very small.

Trends in the Cost of Capital

At the same time, although it is not likely that divestment is a central driver, recent trends in the cost of capital for various energy technologies suggest that it is increasingly expensive to finance investments in dirty energy. In figure 1, I examine the cost of capital for dirty and clean energy projects by plotting the required rate of return for top dirty and clean energy projects calculated by Goldman Sachs (2020), which measures the average internal rate of return for fossil fuel and renewable energy projects by year of project sanction.[12] There appears to be a premium emerging for borrowers investing in fossil fuel projects, as the cost of capital for dirty energy and renewables is diverging. Justifying investments in new offshore oil projects required more than a 20% projected return in 2020 over a project's lifetime, relative to somewhere around 3%–5% for renewables according to these calculations.

It is also important, though, to consider the cost of capital for firms in other high-polluting sectors that use dirty fuels in their production processes, because their continued demand can keep the fossil fuel industry alive. In figure 2, I plot the weighted average cost of capital calculated by the International Energy Agency (IEA 2021) for the cement, iron and steel, and chemicals industries in advanced economies (panel A) and China (panel B). It has been decreasing for all three industries in advanced economies. In the chemicals industry, for example, it fell sharply from about 8% in 2018 to 4% in 2020. In China, it has remained mostly flat for the chemicals and cement industries, and declined for iron and steel since 2018.

Is Divestment Driving These Trends?

Although divestment can, in theory, reduce the cost of capital, there are many other factors at play, and it is difficult to identify the underlying mechanisms without further research. At the same time, the timing of recent trends in the cost of capital suggests that divestment has not been a central driver. The cost of capital for fossil fuels and renewable energy began to diverge in 2014 (see fig. 1), several years before divestment commitments took off. Commitments of some form totaled only about $52 billion in total assets under management in 2014. This has since grown substantially, but a very high proportion of that change occurred more recently. Commitments still only totaled $15 trillion in 2021 and then increased to $39.2 trillion today.

This suggests that other forces are behind the cost of capital divergence. For example, the costs of renewable energy technologies, particularly solar, were falling dramatically during this time period. Initial deployment

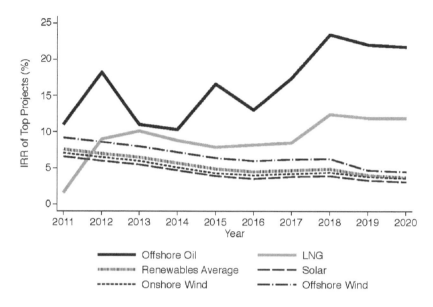

Fig. 1. Required internal rate of return (IRR) (2010–20). Color version available as an online enhancement.

Notes: Created by author using the internal rate of return (IRR) calculations in Goldman Sachs (2020). Data for 2020 are estimates. LNG = liquefied natural gas.

of solar can be largely attributed to public support mechanisms, including subsidies and tax incentives, and costs came down over time, most likely due to learning-by-doing as adoption increased. Renewable energy projects thus became more profitable and less risky and could have simply been the more rational investments.

Furthermore, although the climate-related risks discussed in Subsection III.A can drive divestment and thus affect the cost of capital indirectly through the divestment channel, they also can directly affect the cost of capital. Pollution-intensive industries are exposed to climate-related risks, so investors may increase the cost of capital for dirty firms and projects, even if they do not reduce their access to capital. For example, recent work has shown that, as economic policy uncertainty increases, firms face a higher cost of capital and the effects increase in risk exposure (Xu 2020).[13]

B. Losing (or Gaining) a Seat at the Table

Another way in which investors can influence the direction of innovation is by leveraging their voice. That is, they can actively engage with

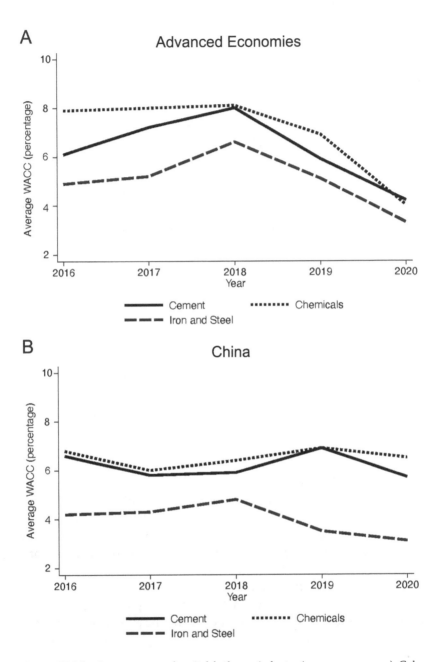

Fig. 2. Weighted average cost of capital for heavy industry (company averages). Color version available as an online enhancement.

Notes: Created by author using weighted average cost of capital (WACC) calculations in IEA (2021) . Panel *A* shows advanced economies; panel *B* shows China.

management to steer a firm's direction rather than divesting. In fact, when Deloitte (2021) surveyed executives around the world about their motivations for increasing sustainability efforts, investor or shareholder demands was the number one driver.

Voice as a form of corporate governance can come in various forms. One common approach is voting in shareholder meetings. For example, in 2021, DuPont lost a vote to more than 80% of shareholders who supported a proposal requiring the company to assess its pollution policies and disclose how much plastic it dumps each year (Crowley 2021). This might not be the most powerful approach, however. It might pressure companies to address issues that are raised, but they are not always bound to meeting the demands of such proposals. Voting also becomes complex when answers to the questions at hand entail more than two options (e.g., yes or no) due to preference aggregation (Arrow 1951).

Investors can take more involved approaches, though, such as having direct conversations with managers (Dimson, Karakas, and Li 2015). They can propose strategy changes, suggest or block projects, and even directly monitor management. Investors can also vote to elect socially conscious board members, or back managers who initiate important changes. This was recently executed successfully when the investment firm Engine No. 1 replaced two Exxon board members with its own candidates (with BlackRock's support) who have leadership experience in green energy innovation (Ambrose 2021).

Naturally, influencing management and shaping corporate strategy through active engagement requires continuing to invest rather than divesting, as shareholders lose their "seat at the table" when they sell. Divestment is a transfer of control rights—for every seller there must be a buyer—and may even dampen green innovation if the seller is more socially conscious than the buyer, which is a reasonable assumption when it is socially conscious organizations that are divesting. The transfer of control rights is only likely to enhance green innovation if the buyer does happen to be more socially conscious.

Continuing to invest as a means toward enabling the green transition is also the takeaway from Berk and van Binsbergen (2021).[14] They argue that, because divestment will likely not have a sufficiently strong impact on the cost of capital to affect firms' investments, playing an active role in engaging with managers might be more effective. Broccardo, Hart, and Zingales (2022) draw a similar conclusion in their theoretical analysis of whether stakeholders (including consumers, workers, and shareholders) should divest or boycott as opposed to leverage their voice. They find that divestment only achieves the socially optimal outcome if all stake-holders are socially responsible, whereas achieving an optimal outcome through voice requires the majority of investors to be just slightly socially responsible.

Note that continuing to invest as discussed here—that is, investing in dirty industries—is distinct from what is often referred to as "impact investing." The latter usually refers to assessing a company's environmental performance and its efforts to improve it, or at least their claims of doing so, and investing in those that perform better on metrics such as ESG indicators. It also tends to include investments in companies that are directly developing clean technologies and other innovations that can reduce pollution. In this paper, I am referring to continued investments in dirty industries even if they score poorly on ESG indicators, and then influencing the firm's innovation investment decisions by governing through voice and actively engaging with management.

C. Corporate Governance and Managerial Incentives

For voice to play a meaningful role in steering innovation, it is important that investors actually exert pressure and engage with management, and the degree to which they can do so will likely depend on the type of investor and whether they are majority shareholders. Managers have a stronger incentive to meet investor demands when the lender owns large positions. Lenders owning only a small share of a company also have less of an incentive to dedicate time for monitoring managers (Shleifer and Vishny 1986; Kerr and Nanda 2015). Their stakes are lower.

Furthermore, although companies might benefit from spreading risk, concentrated ownership can provide the stability and assurance needed to take risks if they are backed by long-term commitments (Bushee 1998; Aghion, Van Reenen, and Zingales 2013; Dimson et al. 2015). Institutional investors might therefore play a particularly important role given their long-term holdings and substantial degrees of ownership. Their engagement also can help mitigate a moral hazard challenge that otherwise dampens the incentives for firms to invest in innovation. Although innovation can take many years to pay off, managers often face short-term performance expectations (e.g., quarterly reporting) and lack incentives to make long-term investments, and they might be particularly reluctant to pursue innovation activities if they are risk averse. The separation between ownership and management can lead to conflicting goals and investment strategies that do not maximize firm value in the long run, thwarting R&D projects. Institutional investor engagement can help reduce these managerial agency costs (Hall and Lerner 2010).

There is indeed some evidence that greater institutional ownership increases firm innovation outcomes (Aghion et al. 2013). Recent work has also shown that institutional investor engagement with managers might be an important channel for improving environmental performance specifically. In an analysis of the "Big Three" (i.e., BlackRock, Vanguard, and State Street Global Advisors), Azar et al. (2021) find a strong association specifically between engagement by the Big Three with large pollution-intensive firms and carbon emissions reductions. Dyck et al. (2019) also find that institutional investors improve environmental and social performance.

V. Improving Investment and Management Decision-Making

Successfully allocating capital and governing through voice such that investments help foster and steer innovation hinge upon knowing which organization strategies, processes, and practices actually lead to successful innovation outcomes and improve the firm's environmental performance. Not all companies are equally likely to engage with investors, and conditional on engagement, not all companies have the human (and physical) capital to innovate.[15] Whether a company has the potential to then achieve environmental innovation objectives is a function of characteristics that are often difficult to observe, such as management quality and innovation activities that could improve environmental performance. Assessing this potential requires not only having accurate and reliable measures of such factors but also understanding which management practices help achieve the intended outcomes.

Impact investors and divesting organizations often use ESG indicators to assess whether a company is socially conscious and to guide their decision-making. However, these measures come with a number of limitations and are increasingly controversial. Furthermore, empirical evidence pointing to the management practices and firm strategies that actually foster environmental performance improvements or innovation is sparse. In this section, I discuss these issues and recent efforts to address them, and I conduct an empirical analysis using new data and methods for measuring environmental performance and management quality to illustrate the challenges with current approaches and to shed new light on which practices and strategies are correlated with higher environmental performance.

A. *Management Practices and Performance*

Understanding the importance of managers and management practices for organizational performance has been of interest to economics, management, sociology, and policy scholars for more than a century. Much of the earliest work provides case studies or uses data on small samples of firms (e.g., Ichniowski, Shaw, and Prennushi 1997). More recently, access to larger data sets and systematic measurement of practices are enabling more robust empirical analyses. The World Management Survey has been a key data source as the largest cross-country data set of organizations including manufacturing and retail firms as well as schools and hospitals dating back to 2002. It focuses on managerial structures (as opposed to talent) such as whether firms monitor operations, set targets, and provide worker incentives, scoring them between 1 ("weak practices," or not structured) to 5 ("best practices," or well structured).[16]

With these data in hand, the economics literature studying how management practices affect organizational performance has grown dramatically over the past 20 years or so. For example, there is now ample evidence that management practices are key determinants of productivity. Enormous and persistent differences in firm productivity, even within the same industries, have been documented extensively (Schmalensee 1985; Dunne, Roberts, and Samuelson 1989; Syverson 2004, 2011; Yang 2021).[17] Although this is quite puzzling from an economic theory perspective, because productivity differences should narrow as competition increases, researchers have long suspected and increasingly are showing that management quality and practices can explain a lot. A consensus is emerging around how they are positively related to outcomes such as productivity, operating profit, output growth, exports, and R&D expenditures in many sectors (Bloom and Van Reenen 2007; Bloom et al. 2013, 2019; Scur et al. 2021).[18]

At the same time, there are several knowledge gaps that are important to fill for understanding which strategies and practices lead to better innovation outcomes. Relatively little is known about the effects on innovation broadly, let alone the direction of innovation.[19] The types of management practices that foster innovation could be different than those enhancing a firm's performance, and understanding what matters for green innovation specifically requires knowing whether and how such practices are applied specifically to sustainability efforts. For example, firms can set targets and provide worker incentives with a variety of objectives in mind—such as increasing sales or output—that might not align with the types of targets and incentives required for improving environmental performance (e.g., reducing emissions). The empirical evidence of whether corporate social responsibility (CSR)-style efforts enhance or dampen firm performance is limited and mixed, and firms traditionally seek to maximize private value as opposed to social value.

B.   Challenges with Using ESG Indicators

Investors and researchers often rely upon ESG indicators to assess a company's environmental performance as well as performance on other social and governance criteria, which are composite ratings constructed from responses to hundreds of questions in each category. These measures come with several weaknesses that make it difficult to tease out what types of environmental management practices and firm strategies can actually help foster innovation. There are also challenges that are less frequently discussed but important to address if managers and investors want to use the information to understand what management practices help foster green innovation.Taken together, the challenges can be broadly categorized as being related to (1) inconsistencies across indicators, (2) aggregation masking important details and conflating inputs with outcomes, and (3) difficulties with measuring and comparing environmental performance.

Inconsistencies across Indicators

There are numerous providers of ESG ratings, each with their own sets of (often proprietary) evaluation criteria and methodologies. They aggregate information from responses to hundreds of questions and assign weights to categories and subcategories to produce a weighted average as the overall score. The questions asked can be different across providers and what constitutes a good or bad score can be subjective. The weight choices also vary across providers, and the reasoning behind the ways in which they are determined is not always transparent.[20]

Unsurprisingly, this leads to significant divergence in ESG ratings across providers with little known about what might be "correct." By studying data from six of the most prominent rating providers, Berg, Koelbel, and Rigobon (2022) document this lack of agreement, finding that the correlations between them range from 0.38 to 0.71. They show that 56% of the divergence can be explained by measurement, 38% by scope, and 6%

by weights. Chatterji et al. (2016) also find significant lack of consistency across ratings and point to the choice of what ESG raters measure and whether it is measured consistently as two key explanations.

The divergence between indicators across providers raises questions around not only which one most accurately reflects the degree to which a firm is socially responsible but also the validity of all of them. This can ultimately reduce welfare if investors and firms use them to inform their capital decision-making (Chatterji et al. 2016). That is, in the traditional divestment and impact investing context, relying on ESG metrics will not direct capital as intended. Likewise, if investors are aiming to target dirty firms that are currently performing poorly so that they can invest in them and exert influence, they will also be misled.

Aggregation Masks (and Sometimes Conflates) Important Details

One particularly important limitation to using ESG indicators is that they mask the details required for understanding the management practices, governance, and strategies that can improve outcomes. There are several ways in which common aggregation approaches limit their usefulness, but two are particularly important for understanding "what works" when it comes to improving environmental performance.

First, the E of ESG conflate inputs into improving environmental outcomes (i.e., firm strategies and management practices) with outcomes (i.e., measures of actual environmental performance). For example, in many cases, the E component includes both reported pollution levels and resource use (i.e., outcomes) as well as information on how the company manages its environmental risks and opportunities, such as whether the company has a policy to improve emissions reductions, sets emissions reduction targets, and has a management team specifically responsible for carrying out the firm's environmental strategy (i.e., the inputs).[21] Understanding the strategies and practices that improve environmental performance therefore requires decomposing these indicators to a much more granular level.

Second, some questions related to environmental management practices, governance, and strategy are often included in the G and S components rather than the E. For example, the G component of some indicators includes whether the firm has a CSR committee and whether ESG-related performance is incorporated into compensation policies for executives. But the aggregated G is not necessarily a good proxy for environmental management practices, governance, and strategy, because it also incorporates many practices that may not necessarily be related to environmental management.[22]

Measuring and Comparing Environmental Performance

A final important limitation is that, even if one did decompose the indicators entirely, the information still would not enable a comparison of firms' emissions and other pollution-related information across sectors. Doing so is important if investors are interested in directing capital toward firms in any industry such that they have the greatest impact. Production across industries generates different types of pollution, which is measured using different units. Improving environmental performance also entails different types of activities and investments across industries. Standardization in environmental performance measurement is needed for cross-industry comparisons.

In fact, evaluating environmental performance even within industries with these measures can be misleading, since what constitutes "good" environmental performance can be subjective. Tracking specific firms' or industries' progress is straightforward if outcomes are measured consistently over time, but what is the threshold for, say, the emissions level that determines whether a firm is environmentally responsible? Some may argue that this is a normative question, but it need not be given the scientific evidence of how pollution contributes to climate change and the known reductions required to address it. More evidence-based methods for defining good environmental performance could help firms understand how to set their own emissions reduction targets and to determine whether they are aligned with the pathways laid out by the Paris Agreement. I discuss this further in the next subsection.

C. *Empirical Analysis Using a New Approach to Analyze Management Quality and Environmental Performance*

In this subsection, I turn to data to explore the correlations between environmental performance and specific management practices and strategies to demonstrate how, with the right data and methods, investors and managers seeking to foster green innovation in polluting industries might be able to improve their decision-making. Although ESG indicators come with many challenges, they are packed with information that could prove useful when decomposed and complemented with other sources and methods. I use information on responses to individual questions that go into the creation of ESG indicators with a particular focus on environment-specific management practices and strategies along with new methods for assessing environmental performance that are being developed in the literature. Using the results from this exercise, I then construct a new best practices measure that is highly correlated with environmental performance.

Measuring Environmental Performance and Management Quality

Rather than using aggregated ESG indicators to measure environmental performance, economists often zero in on pollution levels and intensity, and such data are increasingly accessible at various degrees of granularity.[23] Such information can be extremely valuable. That said, in its raw form, it comes with some of the same challenges associated with using ESG indicators. It is still difficult to compare firms across industries when the type of pollution and its units differ, and although changes over time can be tracked within-firm and firms can be compared relative to others in their own industries, definitions of what constitutes good performance could still vary.

Instead, I use a new measure of "carbon performance" developed by TPI, a global, asset-owner-led initiative that captures whether companies are on track for reducing their pollution levels relative to levels that must be achieved to meet international greenhouse gas emissions targets. Their approach entails translating the targets set by the Paris Agreement into sector-specific benchmarks, and then firms' current and (expected) future emissions intensities can be compared with the benchmark (Dietz et al. 2019).[24] Good environmental performance can then be defined as being aligned with the Paris Agreement pathways, which is not only guided by scientific evidence but also allows for comparisons between firms in any industry.

To develop a better understanding of which specific management practices and strategies are associated with better carbon performance, I use detailed responses to questions that are specifically related to environmental protection and frequently used as inputs into the creation of ESG indicators. I also gather these data from TPI, which extracts responses to 19 of the relevant questions.[25] To evaluate a firm's (environmental) management quality, TPI assesses the strength of each specific question on a scale from 0 (weakest) to 4 (strongest), as companies tend to follow a staged progression when implementing carbon management systems. For example, a first step is often publicly acknowledging that climate change is relevant for their business and developing some type of high-level policy. This might be followed by setting short-term pollution reduction targets and then by perhaps defining more precise, longer-term, quantitative targets. Each question is also mapped into being associated with three distinct categories: measurement and target-setting, governance, and strategy.

TPI then creates a composite company-level management quality score that also ranges from 0 to 4. Once companies answer "yes" to all questions in one level, they advance to the next. Level 0 reflects complete unawareness of climate change as a business issue. Level 1 is associated with acknowledging climate change as presenting risks and opportunities to the business, and level 2 indicates that the company is in a capacity-building stage (i.e., it is starting to develop management systems and report on practices and performance). Once a company is taking a more integrated approach, such as improving its operational practices and assigning specific board responsibilities for improving environmental performance, it moves up to level 3. Finally, if it reaches the point of developing a comprehensive understanding of risks and opportunities, and this is reflected in their expenditure decisions and business strategies, the company is assigned a 4. See Dietz et al. (2019) for more detail.

Sample Construction and Graphical Analysis

I gather data from TPI's two public databases on management quality and carbon performance, which cover the largest public companies by market value in the most pollution-intensive sectors. As of the end of 2021, the database included assessments of 401 companies representing 16% of global market value across four clusters of sectors (energy, industrial and materials, transport, and consumer goods and services) (Dietz et al. 2021).[26] TPI applies its environmental performance methodology described above to indicate whether the firm is on track for the Paris Agreement's 1.5°C scenario (strongest carbon performance), the 2°C scenario, or the national pledges scenario (the weakest). The management practice database contains both TPI's composite company-year level management quality score as described in the previous subsection as well as the answers to each specific question.

Table 1 contains the full list of questions that I use in my analysis categorized as being associated with measurement, targets, and reporting, governance, or strategy, along with the values assigned to capture each management practice's on a scale from 0 to 4.[27] One observation is that

Table 1
Categorization of Metrics, Governance, and Strategy Questions

	MQ Level
Measurement, targets, and reporting ("metrics"):	
Has the company set greenhouse gas emission reduction targets?	2
Has the company published information on its Scope 1 and 2 GHGs?	2
Has the company set quantitative targets for reducing its GHGs?	3
Does the company report on Scope 3 emissions?	3
Has the company had its operational (Scope 1 and/or 2) GHGs data verified?	3
Has the company set long-term quantitative targets for reducing its GHGs?	4
Governance:	
Does the company acknowledge climate change as a significant issue for the business?	0
Does the company explicitly recognize climate change as a relevant risk and/or opportunity to the business?	1
Does the company have a policy (or equivalent) commitment to action on climate change?	1
Has the company nominated a board member or board committee with explicit responsibility for oversight of the climate change policy?	3
Has the company incorporated environmental, social and governance issues into executive remuneration?	4
Does the company incorporate climate change risks and opportunities in their strategy?	4
Strategy:	
Does the company support domestic and international efforts to mitigate climate change?	3
Does the company undertake climate scenario planning?	4
Does the company have an internal price of carbon?	4

Note: Table contains the questions associated with the management practices and strategies studied in this paper. MQ level is their management quality strength as evaluated by the Transition Pathway Initiative, which I describe in Subsection V.C. GHG = greenhouse gas.

there is variation in management practice strength both within and across the three categories. For example, whether the company has broadly set greenhouse gas emissions targets is assigned a 2, whereas setting long-term quantitative targets is assigned a 4. Within the governance category, acknowledging that climate change is an issue for the business is assigned a 0, whether the company has nominated a board member or committee with explicit responsibility for oversight of climate change policy is assigned a 3, and whether the company incorporates ESG issues into its executive remuneration policies is assigned a 4. The strategy-related questions (e.g., setting an internal price of carbon) are all scored as either 3s or 4s, as they reflect integration of climate change risks into operational decision-making and strategy development.

After merging the management quality and carbon performance databases and dropping duplicates, the resulting unbalanced panel includes

1,780 observations across 492 firms between 2017 and 2022. However, not all firms are included in each set of evaluations, so the sample size decreases significantly when keeping only firm-year observations that match and dropping firms without suitable data for assessing carbon performance. The final data set that I use throughout the correlation analysis contains 545 observations across 258 firms from 2017 through 2021.[28] Most notably, the main difference in the characteristics of these firms relative to those in the full data set is that they score higher on the various management practices, which is unsurprising given how those that were dropped were those without suitable disclosed pollution data (disclosure is one of the management practices).[29]

Graphical Analysis. Before turning to a more formal correlation analysis, I start by visually exploring the raw data using TPI's composite company-level management quality scores and carbon performance assessments. Figure 3 illustrates the percentage of firms within each management quality level that is on track for meeting either the Paris Agreement 2°C pathway requirements or the national pledges pathway, as opposed to not being aligned with either or not disclosing enough information to be accurately assessed. There appears to be a positive relationship

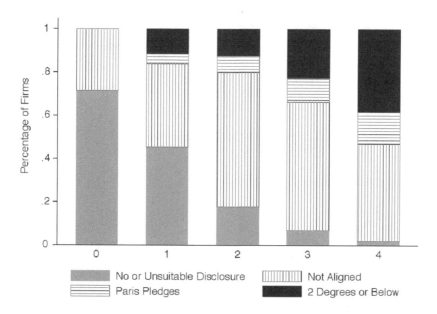

Fig. 3. Paris Agreement alignment by management quality level. Color version available as an online enhancement.

between management quality and whether firms are on track. All of those with a management quality score of zero are either not aligned with any target or pledge or do not disclose suitable emissions data to assess them. When moving from the lowest management quality level to the highest, though, the proportions of firms that disclose such information increases and the proportions meeting either the national pledge or 2°C targets increases. Of those with the highest management quality score of 4, only 2% do not disclose suitable emissions information, 38% are aligned with 2°C or below, and 15% are aligned with the pledges. At the same time, 45% are still not aligned with any of the targets or pledges.

In figure 4, I provide the breakdown of firms that fall within each environmental performance category by industry, which demonstrates the vast amount of heterogeneity. The oil and gas sector performs extremely poorly. More than 90% do report enough information on their emissions to assess their performance; however, less than 10% of those that do report are on track for any of the Paris Agreement targets. On the other hand, electric utilities are performing quite well relative to the others in this set of heavily polluting industries. Nearly 60% are on track for either the strongest or weaker Paris Agreement targets.

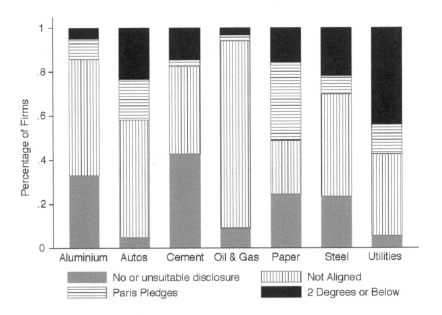

Fig. 4. Paris Agreement alignment by industry. Color version available as an online enhancement.

Another observation to consider is that the proportions of firms that are aligned in many of the other industries are quite low. For example, less than 20% of firms are aligned with either the strongest or weaker targets in the aluminum and cement industries. This highlights the importance of applying socially conscious investment standards beyond the fossil fuel industry itself, as these other industries are also heavy polluters.

Management quality also varies across industries, but perhaps surprisingly, there is less heterogeneity relative to the heterogeneity in environmental performance (see fig. 5). For example, a more than 20% of firms fall within the management quality level 4 for all industries except utilities. There are also very few firms that fall within the lowest management quality score, and there is a bit more variation for the categories in between. The key takeaway is that, even when limiting management practices to only those that are environment related and categorizing them into five different quality levels, there does not appear to be a strong correlation with environmental performance.

There are several potential explanations for this. The lack of (at least visual) correlation could indicate that the information extracted from the ESG indicators is not accurate or that management just does not matter for environmental performance. The importance of managerial ability

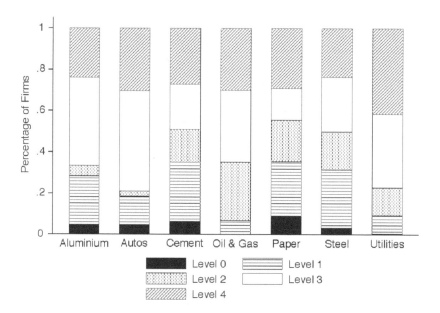

Fig. 5. Management quality level by industry. Color version available as an online enhancement.

also tends to vary across industries. It also could indicate that aggregating management practice quality at this level is still too coarse to provide meaningful information on what works. I explore this further in the next subsection.

Correlation Analysis

I now turn to examining the correlations between management quality and carbon performance more formally and with increasingly less coarseness in the management quality proxy. First, rather than using TPI's company-year level assessments (henceforth MQ Level), which are determined based on firms to responding "yes" to each question that TPI includes in each level before advancing to the next, I construct an additional measure that accounts for the possibility that firms engage in practices with higher ratings without indicating that they also employ practices at lower levels.[30] Instead, I calculate the proportion of total possible "points" that a firm earns, MQ Score, by summing the strength values associated with each question across all questions to find the total possible points and just those that the firm indicates that it implements for the points earned. For example, MQ Score is equal to 0.5 if a firm earns half of the total possible points when summing TPI's strength scores across all questions.

Then, to develop a better understanding of whether practices related to measurement and target-setting, governance, or strategy seem to be most important for improving carbon performance, I create three separate analogous measures for each of the broad categories (Metrics Score, Governance Score, and Strategy Score, respectively). In this case, the number of points earned and total number of points are only for those in each category. Last, I entirely decompose these aggregated measures to examine the correlations between carbon performance and each specific practice using indicators equal to one if the firm answers "yes" to a question and zero otherwise. This not only allows me to develop a better understanding of which specific practices seem to matter most but also avoids assuming how strong each practice is ex ante. Instead, the data can reveal which ones are most highly correlated with carbon performance.

I proceed by estimating various forms of the following model:

$$CP_{it} = MQ_{it} + \gamma_{st} + \epsilon_{it}, \tag{1}$$

where CP_{it} is the carbon performance of firm i in year t, which is an indicator equal to one if the firm is on track to meet different Paris Agreement targets and zero otherwise. Management quality, MQ_{it}, is either the firm's overall score that I construct, the set of scores for the three broad categories, or a set of indicators for individual questions depending on the specification. When examining each individual question, I estimate three separate models that include indicators only for the questions that fall within each of the broad categories. In all cases, sector-year fixed effects, γ_{st}, are included to control for how macroeconomic shocks might affect sectors differentially over time, and I cluster the standard errors by country.

Results

To be clear up front, it is important to keep in mind that the coefficient estimates presented in this section should not be interpreted as causal effects. Rather, they are correlations within sector-year, and I leave causal inference approaches for future work.

Management Quality Level and Scores. I start by exploring how management quality as proxied by the more aggregate measures is correlated with carbon performance and present the results in table 2. For comparison purposes, I first examine the relationship between TPI's company-year management quality level assignment and whether the firm is aligned with the Paris Agreement pathways for limiting global warming to ≤2°C (col. 1). The coefficient estimate of 0.08 is statistically significant at the 1% level, suggesting that moving from one level to the next is associated with an 8% increase in the probability of being aligned. Although this begins to demonstrate the importance of implementing stronger management practices, it does not provide a sense of whether there are different effects depending on a firm's initial management quality, making it difficult to understand the importance of basic management practices versus taking a more integrated, strategic approach and how much it pays off to reach the highest level.

In column 2, I estimate the model using the proportion of total possible points earned (MQ Score). Although this still does not differentiate between effects across the initial management quality distribution, it allows for the assessment of going from the lowest possible score of zero (or doing nothing) to the highest (doing everything), and it removes the assumption that firms do not implement stronger practices if they have not yet implemented weaker ones based on strength ratings that were determined ex ante. I find that this measure's correlation with ≤2°C pathway

Table 2
Correlation between Management Quality and Environmental Performance

Dependent Variable	≤2°C (1)	≤2°C (2)	≤2°C (3)	<2°C (4)	No Alignment (5)
MQ level	.080*** (.015)				
MQ score		.289*** (.047)			
Metrics score			.041 (.066)	.048 (.045)	−.099 (.082)
Governance score			.123 (.074)	.123* (.072)	−.043 (.085)
Strategy score			.126* (.065)	.117* (.063)	−.234*** (.082)
Observations	545	545	545	545	545
Mean dependent variable	.264	.264	.264	.207	.583

Note: Dependent variables are indicators equal to one if the firm's pollution levels are aligned with the Paris Alignment ≤2°C target in columns 1–3 and the <2°C target in column 4. In column 5, the dependent variable is equal to one if the firm is not aligned with any target or pledge. Independent variables are the firm's management quality level assigned by the Transition Pathway Initiative (col. 1), an overall score that I construct, (col. 2), and category-specific scores that I construct (cols. 3–5) as described in Subsection V.C., subsection Correlation Analysis. Sector-year fixed effects are included in all regressions. Standard errors are clustered by country. Asterisks denote *$p < .10$, **$p < .05$, ***$p < .01$.

alignment is 0.29 and statistically significant at the 1% level. In other words, when firms go from doing nothing to indicating that they implement all 15 practices listed in table 1, the probability of aligning increases by 29%, which is a 100% increase over the sample's mean probability. This finding begins to suggest that taking a fully integrated, strategic approach is particularly valuable.

Next, I explore whether the MQ Score effect appears to be driven by measurement, target-setting, and reporting; governance-related practices; or strategy (Strategy Score), measuring each as described in Subsection V.C., subsection Correlation Analysis. There is variation in practice strength within each category, so these measures still mask important details, but with some of the most commonly discussed practices mostly being related to those in the metrics category (i.e., public disclosure of pollution information and setting reduction targets), it can provide a sense of whether this is sufficient.

When considering alignment with the ≤2°C pathway (col. 3 of table 2), the strategy score's coefficient of 0.126 is the only one that is statistically significant (at the 10% level). It suggests that going from engaging in none of the practices in the strategy category to all of them increases the probability of alignment by 12.6%. The magnitude of the coefficient for governance is about the same but just barely not statistically significant. When using the stronger <2°C pathway alignment as the dependent variable instead (col. 4), both the governance and strategy scores are statistically significant at the 10% level and have similar magnitudes. On the other hand, the coefficient for the metrics score is about a third of what it is for governance and strategy and statistically insignificant in both cases. Last, when examining the correlations with not being aligned with any Paris Agreement pathways, including the weakest one associated with pledges only, there is a correlation only with the strategy score (col. 5).

Specific Management Practices and Strategies.   Still, the category-level scores mask potential heterogeneity in the specific practices, especially in the metrics and governance contexts given how they each include six different practices with varying degrees of strength. I now decompose them into their individual questions and estimate the model of equation (1) using indicators equal to one if the firm answered "yes" to the question.

The results for the questions included in the metrics category are presented in table 3. For the two main Paris Agreement scenarios (cols. 1 and 2), two of the practices are in fact correlated with alignment at the 1% statistical significance level: having operational (Scope 1 and/or 2) greenhouse gas emissions data verified and setting long-term quantitative targets for reducing greenhouse gas emissions. The latter is the only question in the metrics category rated as being in level 4 for management practice strength by TPI, and it is also the only one correlated with reducing the probability of not being aligned with any Paris Agreement pledge or pathway. When considering the small and statistically insignificant coefficients associated with the weaker metrics questions—such as having any quantitative emissions target without long-term objectives or publishing Scope 1 and Scope 2 emissions—the findings highlight the importance of having emissions data verified and of being forward looking.

A similar pattern emerges for the governance-related practices (see table 4). The one practice that is correlated with carbon performance as measured by alignment with the ≤2°C pathway is incorporating ESG and climate change performance into executive remuneration policies, one of the two strongest governance practices (col. 1). Implementing this practice is associated with a 15% increase in the probability of alignment.

Table 3
Correlation between Metrics Practices and Environmental Performance

	≤2°C	<2°C	No Alignment
Dependent Variable	(1)	(2)	(3)
Has GHG targets	−.017	.022	−.025
	(.106)	(.105)	(.101)
Publishes Scope 1 and 2	.074	.066	−.027
	(.055)	(.041)	(.059)
Quantitative GHG targets	−.135	−.126	.063
	(.119)	(.094)	(.148)
Scope 3 emissions reported	.042	.053	−.076
	(.047)	(.040)	(.051)
Verifies emissions data	.124***	.120***	−.035
	(.039)	(.037)	(.043)
Long-term quantitative GHG targets	.132***	.088**	−.185**
	(.039)	(.039)	(.081)
Observations	545	545	545
Mean dependent variable	.264	.207	.583

Note: Dependent variables are indicators equal to one if the firm's pollution levels are aligned with the Paris Alignment ≤2°C target in column 1 and the <2°C target in column 2. In column 3, the dependent variable is equal to one if the firm is not aligned with any target or pledge. Independent variables are the specific practices related to measuring and reporting greenhouse gases (GHGs) that I use to construct the metrics management score. Sector-year fixed effects are included in all regressions. Standard errors are clustered by country. Asterisks denote *$p < .10$, **$p < .05$, ***$p < .01$.

It is also associated with being aligned with the <2°C pathway and reduces the chance of no alignment with any pledge or target, maintaining statistical significance at the 1% level.[31]

Last, two of the three practices in the strategy category, both of which can be considered strong practices as they reflect the most integrated approaches (and are rated as being either a 3 or 4 by TPI), are associated with better carbon performance (see table 5). When considering the ≤2°C case (col. 2), supporting domestic and international efforts to mitigate climate change and setting an internal price of carbon are associated with an 8.3% and 10.7% increase in the probability of alignment, respectively. They are both also associated with reduced probability of no alignment with any pledge or target.

A New Proxy for Best Practices. The results presented in tables 3–5 point to a set of specific practices that are correlated with better carbon performance spanning all three categories. They tend to be those that are "strongest" in the sense that they are either more advanced versions of basic practices (e.g., setting long-term quantitative objectives rather

Table 4
Correlation between Governance Practices and Environmental Performance

Dependent Variable	≤2°C (1)	<2°C (2)	No Alignment (3)
Acknowledges CC	.183	−.099	−.252
	(.179)	(.076)	(.164)
Acknowledges CC as a risk	.061	.021	−.089
	(.071)	(.058)	(.095)
Has policy to act	−.211	.067*	.017
	(.172)	(.034)	(.188)
Board member responsible for CC	.047	.025	−.066
	(.064)	(.069)	(.062)
Exec remuneration incorporates CC perf	.154***	.122***	−.160***
	(.028)	(.027)	(.037)
CC risks and opps in strategy	.005	.047*	.013
	(.029)	(.025)	(.031)
Observations	545	545	545
Mean dependent variable	.264	.207	.583

Note: Dependent variables are indicators equal to one if the firm's pollution levels are aligned with the Paris Alignment ≤2°C target in column 1 and the <2°C target in column 2. In column 3, the dependent variable is equal to one if the firm is not aligned with any target or pledge. Independent variables are the specific practices related to firm governance that I use to construct the governance management score. Sector-year fixed effects are included in all regressions. Standard errors are clustered by country. CC = climate change. Asterisks denote *$p < .10$, **$p < .05$, ***$p < .01$.

Table 5
Correlation between Strategy and Environmental Performance

Dependent Variable	≤2°C (1)	<2°C (2)	No Alignment (3)
Supports domestic and int'l efforts	.045	.083***	−.118***
	(.033)	(.027)	(.042)
Undertakes scenario planning	.047	.022	−.068
	(.042)	(.034)	(.047)
Sets internal price of carbon	.123***	.107***	−.128**
	(.045)	(.040)	(.052)
Observations	545	545	545
Mean dependent variable	.264	.207	.583

Note: Dependent variables are indicators equal to one if the firm's pollution levels are aligned with the Paris Alignment ≤2°C target in column 1 and the <2°C target in column 2. In column 3, the dependent variable is equal to one if the firm is not aligned with any target or pledge. Independent variables are the specific practices related to the firm's strategy that I use to construct the strategy management score. Sector-year fixed effects are included in all regressions. Standard errors are clustered by country. Asterisks denote *$p < .10$, **$p < .05$, ***$p < .01$.

than any general pollution target) or those that involve the most integration into operational decision-making; for example, providing incentives to executives to implement objectives (and thus engage with lower-level management to do so) by tying environmental performance to their compensation. Although the weaker practices may be correlated with some other measures of environmental performance that I do not study, being on track for meeting the Paris Agreement targets overall is critical for avoiding the most detrimental consequences of climate change, so firms and investors may wish to think of good environmental performance as being in line with the pathways for meeting those targets.

With this in mind, I interpret the correlations that are statistically significant at least at the 5% level as potential best practices for improving environmental performance, at least for this set of firms and the practices considered, and construct a new proxy for management quality. I use the <2°C pathway alignment results—the strongest case—and create a "best practices score" as the proportion of total best practices points earned (i.e., the sum of the points associated with best practices that the firm implements as a proportion of the total number of potential points associated with all best practices). Although this is an aggregate measure and still masks details associated with each individual practice, it is arguably a better reflection of a firm's environmental management quality overall than other aggregated measures that incorporate many practices not correlated with better environmental performance.

I examine the relationship between this best practices score and carbon performance, and I find that the correlation is much higher than any of the other aggregated measures that I study as well as each of the individual questions (table 6). Going from implementing none of the best practices to all of them is associated with a 60% increase in the probability of being aligned with the ≤2°C pathway in comparison with a 29% correlation for the overall MQ Score shown in table 2.

Discussion

Although the results of these analyses do not allow for causal interpretation, and they should not be applied to other settings without further research given the small sample size and select set of industries studied here, the exercise provides three insights that might be of interest to investors and managers.

First, developing an understanding of how firms can improve their environmental performance requires decomposing aggregated measures such as ESG indicators. They tend to combine information on both management practices and actual environmental footprint even within the E of ESG,

Table 6
Correlation between Best Practices Score and Environmental Performance

	≤2°C	<2°C	No Alignment
Dependent Variable	(1)	(2)	(3)
Best Practices Score	.603***	.585***	−.780***
	(.096)	(.083)	(.146)
Observations	545	545	545
Mean dependent variable	.264	.207	.583

Note: Dependent variables are indicators equal to one if the firm's pollution levels are aligned with the Paris Alignment ≤2°C target in column 1 and the <2°C target in column 2. In column 3, the dependent variable is equal to one if the firm is not aligned with any target or pledge. "Best Practices Score" is the proportion of total points earned associated with the practices that I find are correlated with Paris Agreement alignment, which I detail in Subsection V.C. Asterisks denote $*p < .10, **p < .05, ***p < .01$.

conflating inputs with outcomes. Management practices are the inputs that can improve environmental performance, whereas emissions and resource reductions are the realized environmental performance improvements.

Relatedly, it is also important to decompose different categories of practices to capture how some forms of the same practice might be more effective than others. For example, simply setting emissions reduction targets and disclosing pollution levels does not appear to be associated with better environmental performance for the sample of firms that I study unless such targets are long term and quantitative. This highlights how the strength of the practice has implications for whether a firm might improve its environmental performance moving forward, and assessing this requires detailed information on the ways in which firms carry out practices.

Third, if constructing and using an aggregated management quality measure to inform decision-making is of interest, analyzing which specific practices and strategies are most effective (i.e., the best practices) might be one way to effectively determine the weights assigned to different practices and strategies. This comes with caveats, though. There is likely heterogeneity in what strategies and practices are most effective across industries and firm characteristics, which future research could explore. Whether aggregated indicators constructed on the basis of such analyses are better predictors of environmental performance than alternatives also should be explored. The best practices approach that I applied in this paper suggests that it offers such potential, but because my results might lack external validity, others may wish to test this when or if they construct similar measures in other settings.

VI. Conclusion

The objective of this chapter was to explore whether divestment might be an effective tool for inducing green innovation. Evidence from the literature so far suggests it may only have very small effects on the cost of capital for dirty firms. Although further research is needed to draw concrete conclusions, it seems unlikely that this will sufficiently reduce their investment opportunities.

Instead, I argue that investing in dirty industries might be an effective tool for promoting green innovation conditional on shareholders being socially conscious and actively governing through voice. Effectively guiding managers to do so, though, requires knowing which practices and strategies actually foster green innovation. I conduct an empirical exercise that, albeit descriptive, demonstrates how leveraging both existing data and new methods for measuring environmental performance can improve management and investment decision-making. A key takeaway is that it requires decomposing the commonly used aggregate proxies for environmental performance, such as ESG indicators. It is also important to develop and use standardized measures of environmental performance so that firms can be compared across industries.

There are many pathways for future research. Whether there are effects of specific environmental management practices and strategies on innovation rather than just environmental performance, for example, remains an open question. Although the ultimate goal of developing pollution-reducing technologies and processes is to improve environmental performance, and finding improvements in environmental performance suggests that innovation might be at play, studying innovation inputs and actual outcomes directly can shed more light on the underlying mechanisms. One could also consider heterogeneity across industries and firm characteristics because there is likely to be significant variation in "what works." Last, and perhaps most important, future work should examine these questions such that the results can be interpreted as causal, including those explored descriptively in this chapter.

Endnotes

Author email address: Pless (jpless@mit.edu). I thank Ben Jones, Josh Lerner, and participants of the 2022 NBER Entrepreneurship and Innovation Policy Conference for helpful comments and suggestions. For acknowledgments, sources of research support, and disclosure of the author's material financial relationships, if any, please see https://www.nber.org/books-and-chapters/entrepreneurship-and-innovation-policy-and-economy-volume

-2/starve-or-stoke-understanding-whether-divestment-versus-investment-can-steer-green-innovation.

1. For example, IPCC (2018) found that global net CO_2 emissions must decline by about 45% from 2010 levels by 2030 and reach net zero around 2050 to limit warming to below 1.5°C.

2. The president also recently signed the CHIPS and Science Act into law, providing $50.3 billion to the US Department of Energy's Office of Science for R&D.

3. This could be offset by firms needing to invest in R&D to absorb the ideas produced by the original innovator and to build upon them, though (Cohen and Levinthal 1989). Business-stealing can also lead to overinvestment (Aghion and Howitt 1998).

4. For example, Bloom, Griffith, and Van Reenen (2002), Rao (2016), Guceri and Liu (2019), Dechezleprêtre et al. (forthcoming), and Agrawal, Rosell, and Simcoe (2020) find that tax incentives increase R&D, and Bronzini and Piselli (2016), Howell (2017), Azoulay et al. (2019), and Myers and Lanahan (2022) find that grants have positive effects on patenting. Pless (2022) also finds that the two instruments have complementary effects on R&D for small firms.

5. Pless and Srivastav (2022) also examine the interaction of carbon pricing and R&D tax credits on energy and environmental innovation, but the R&D policy is not energy specific.

6. These calculations are made by PESP (2021) using data from Pitchbook.

7. They also show that the present value of global financial assets is an expected 0.2% higher when limiting warming to no more than 2°C even when including mitigation costs.

8. On the other hand, if dirty firms would have otherwise allocated the divested capital toward efforts that reduce their environmental impact, such as by increasing the efficiency of their operations, divestment could dampen their own green innovation investments.

9. It can sometimes take a decade before an initial idea developed through research is translated into a patented innovation in the energy sector (e.g., Popp 2016), let alone the time it takes to bring these technologies to market.

10. Their derivation applies the common assumptions behind the standard Capital Asset Pricing Model.

11. The coefficient estimating the effect on the instantaneous price appreciation is 0.24% and it is statistically not distinguishable from zero.

12. The specific Goldman Sachs (2020) values were extracted from Quinson (2021).

13. There is also a wider literature on how uncertainty affects investment decision-making that focuses on the irreversibility channel as opposed to the cost of capital channel (e.g., Bernanke 1983; Bloom, Bond, and Van Reenen 2007).

14. Their focus is more on firm exit and composition of industries as opposed to innovation.

15. For example, Dimson et al. (2015) find that firms with weak governance and those that are large, mature, performing poorly, and concerned about their reputation are more likely to engage.

16. See Scur et al. (2021) for a more comprehensive overview of the methodology and data. Although defining what makes a practice "good" can be subjective, their selection of practices ex ante was informed by discussions with industry experts and focused on those that have been shown empirically in the literature to be important factors.

17. For example, Syverson (2004) finds that US manufacturing plants at the 90th percentile of the productivity distribution transform the same inputs into almost twice as much output as firms in the bottom decile, and the dispersion is even larger in China and India (Hsieh and Klenow 2009).

18. See Quinn and Scur (2021) and Scur et al. (2021) for a more comprehensive overview of the literature. Also, the focus of this section is on management practices, but there is a broader literature studying how other factors, such as competition, organizational structures, and human capital, contribute to productivity differences.

19. One exception is Bloom, Van Reenen, and Williams (2019), who find positive effects on R&D and patents but do not study green innovation specifically.

20. For example, the description used by one major provider states "we have applied an automated, factual logic," and it is difficult to find a more detailed explanation.

21. They also break down the E into three subcategories, but these examples are all still included in the emissions subcategory.

22. They also provide a subcategory within G that focuses on CSR strategy, but questions in the other subcategories (management and shareholders) might be relevant as well.

23. For example, the US Environmental Protection Agency's National Emissions Inventory publicly provides facility-level information on various pollutants.
24. They follow what is known as the Sectoral Decarbonization Approach. See Dietz et al. (2019) for more detail.
25. FTSE Russell provides TPI with these data.
26. Specific industries include airlines, aluminum, autos, cement, diversified mining, electric utilities, oil and gas, paper, shipping, and steel.
27. I drop those that are not included over the entire sample period.
28. The data I use to construct the figures in the next subsection, however, include 619 observations across 290 firms. Additional observations fall out when running the regressions because of other missing data.
29. I discuss how my findings turn out to be upper bounds because of this.
30. Although most companies presumably do follow a progression toward stronger practices, there is always the chance of real exceptions or errors in the data. For example, a firm might incorporate climate change risks and opportunities in their strategy (which is rated as a 4) without having set any form of quantitative target for reducing emissions (which is rated as a 3).
31. For the <2°C pathway case, two other practices—having a policy to act and the incorporation of climate change risks and opportunities into the firm's strategy—are also correlated but only at the 10% statistical significance level.

References

Aghion, P., A. Dechezleprêtre, D. Hemous, R. Martin, and J. Van Reenen. 2016. "Carbon Taxes, Path Dependency and Directed Technical Change: Evidence from the Auto Industry." *Journal of Political Economy* 124 (1): 1–51.
Aghion, P., and P. Howitt. 1992. "A Model of Growth Through Creative Destruction." *Econometrica* 60 (2): 323–51.
———. 1998. *Endogenous Growth Theory*. Cambridge, MA: MIT Press.
Aghion, J., P. Van Reenen, and L. Zingales. 2013. "Innovation and Institutional Ownership." *American Economic Review* 103 (1): 277–304.
Agrawal, A., C. Rosell, and T. Simcoe. 2020. "Tax Credits and Small Firm R&D Spending." *American Economic Journal: Economic Policy* 12 (2): 1–21.
Ambrose, Jillian. 2021. "ExxonMobil and Chevron Suffer Shareholder Rebellions over Climate." *Guardian*, May 26.
Arrow, K. 1951. *Social Choice and Individual Values*. New York: Wiley.
Arrow, K. J. 1962. "The Economic Implications of Learning by Doing." *Review of Economic Studies* 29:155–73.
Azar, J., M. Duro, I. Kadach, and G. Ormazabal. 2021. "The Big Three and Corporate Carbon Emissions around the World." *Journal of Financial Economics* 142 (2): 674–96.
Azoulay, P., J. S. Graff Zivin, D. Li, and B. N. Sampat. 2019. "Public R&D Investments and Private-Sector Patenting: Evidence from NIH Funding Rules." *Review of Economic Studies* 86 (1): 117–52.
Berg, F., J. F. Koelbel, and R. Rigobon. 2022. "Aggregate Confusion: The Divergence of ESG Ratings." *Review of Finance* 26 (6): 1315–44.
Berk, J., and J. van Binsbergen. 2021. "The Impact of Impact Investing." Working Paper no. 3981. https://www.gsb.stanford.edu/faculty-research/working-papers/impact-impact-investing.
Bernanke, B. 1983. "Irreversibility, Uncertainty, and Cyclical Investment." *Quarterly Journal of Economics* 98 (1): 85–106.

Bloom, N., S. Bond, and J. Van Reenen. 2007. "Uncertainty and Investment Dynamics." *Review of Economic Studies* 74 (2): 391–415.

Bloom, N., E. Brynjolfsson, L. Foster, R. Jarmin, M. Patnaik, I. Saporta-Eksten, and J. Van Reenen. 2019. "What Drives Differences in Management Practices?" *American Economic Review* 109 (5): 1648–83.

Bloom, N., R. Griffith, and J. Van Reenen. 2002. "Do R&D Tax Credits Work? Evidence from a Panel of Countries 1979–1997." *Journal of Public Economics* 85 (1): 1–31.

Bloom, N., E. A. Mahajan, D. McKenzie, and J. Roberts. 2013. "Does Management Matter? Evidence from India." *Quarterly Journal of Economics* 128 (1): 1–51.

Bloom, N., and J. Van Reenen. 2007. "Measuring and Explaining Management Practices across Firms and Countries." *Quarterly Journal of Economics* 122 (4): 1351–408.

Bloom, N., J. Van Reenen, and H. Williams. 2019. "A Toolkit of Policies to Promote Innovation." *Journal of Economic Perspectives* 33 (3): 163–84.

Broccardo, E., O. Hart, and L. Zingales. 2022. "Exit vs. Voice." *Journal of Political Economy* 130 (12). https://doi.org/10.1086/720516.

Bronzini, R., and P. Piselli. 2016. "The Impact of R&D Subsidies on Firm Innovation." *Research Policy* 45 (2): 442–57.

Bushee, B. 1998. "The Influence of Institutional Investors on Myopic R&D Investment Behavior." *Accounting Review* 73 (3): 305–33.

Calel, R. 2020. "Adopt or Innovate: Understanding Technological Responses to Cap-and-Trade." *American Economic Journal: Economic Policy* 12 (3): 170–201.

Calel, R., and A. Dechezleprêtre. 2016. "Environmental Policy and Directed Technological Change: Evidence from the European Carbon Market." *Review of Economics and Statistics* 98 (1): 173–91.

Chatterji, A., R. Durand, D. Levine, and S. Touboul. 2016. "Do Ratings of Firms Converge? Implications for Managers, Investors, and Strategy Researchers." *Strategic Management Journal* 37 (8): 1–14.

Cohen, W. M., and D. A. Levinthal. 1989. "Innovation and Learning: The Two Faces of R&D." *Economic Journal* 99:569–96.

Crowley, Kevin. 2021. "DuPont Loses Plastic Pollution Vote with Record 81% Rebellion." *Bloomberg News*, May 3.

Dechezleprêtre, A., E. Einiö, R. Martin, K.-T. Nguyen, and J. Van Reenen. Forthcoming. "Do Tax Incentives Increase Firm Innovation? An RD Design for R&D, Patents, and Spillovers." *American Economic Journal: Economic Policy*.

Deloitte. 2021. "2021 Climate Check: Business' Views on Environmental Sustainability." https://www2.deloitte.com/content/dam/Deloitte/au/Documents/risk/deloitte-au-about-2021-climate-check-business-views-on-environmental-sustainability-300321.pdf.

Dietz, S., B. Bienkowska, D. Gardiner, N. Hastreiter, V. Jahn, V. Komar, A. Scheer, et al. 2021. "TPI State of Transition Report 2021." Transition Pathway Initiative, London.

Dietz, S., A. Bowen, C. Dixon, and P. Gradwell. 2016. "'Climate Value at Risk' of Global Financial Assets." *Nature Climate Change* 6:676–79.

Dietz, S., V. Jahn, M. Nachmany, J. Noels, and R. Sullivan. 2019. "Methodology and Indicators Report, Version 3.0." Transition Pathway Initiative, London.

Dimson, E., O. Karakas, and X. Li. 2015. "Active Ownership." *Review of Financial Studies* 28 (12): 3225–68.

Dunne, T., M. Roberts, and L. Samuelson. 1989. "The Growth and Failure of US Manufacturing Plants." *Quarterly Journal of Economics* 104 (4): 671–98.

Dyck, A., K. V. Lins, L. Roth, and H. F. Wagner. 2019. "Do Institutional Investors Drive Corporate Social Responsibility? International Evidence." *Journal of Financial Economics* 131 (3): 693–714.

Goldman Sachs. 2020. "Carbonomics: The Green Engine of Economic Recovery." https://www.goldmansachs.com/insights/pages/gs-research/carbonomics -green-engine-of-economic-recovery-f/report.pdf.

Guceri, I., and L. Liu. 2019. "Effectiveness of Fiscal Incentives for R&D: Quasi-experimental Evidence." *American Economic Journal: Economic Policy* 11 (1): 266–91.

Hall, B. G., and J. Lerner. 2010. "The Financing of R&D and Innovation." In *Handbook of the Economics of Innovation*, ed. B. G. Hall and N. Rosenberg. Amsterdam: Elsevier.

Howell, S. 2017. "Financing Innovation: Evidence from R&D Grants." *American Economic Review* 107 (4): 1136–64.

Hsieh, C., and P. Klenow. 2009. "Misallocation and Manufacturing TFP in China and India." *Quarterly Journal of Economics* 124 (4): 1403–48.

Ichniowski, C., K. Shaw, and G. Prennushi. 1997. "The Effects of Human Resource Management Practices on Productivity: A Study of Steel Finishing Lines." *American Economic Review* 87 (3): 291–313.

IEA (International Energy Agency). 2021. "The Cost of Capital in Clean Energy Transitions." https://www.iea.org/articles/the-cost-of-capital-in-clean-en ergy-transitions.

Invest-Divest. 2021. "Invest-Divest 2021: A Decade of Progress towards a Just Climate Future." https://www.divestinvest.org/wp-content/uploads/2021 /10/Divest-Invest-Program-FINAL10-26_B.pdf.

IPCC (Intergovernmental Panel on Climate Change). 2018. "Global Warming of 1.5° C." IPCC, Geneva.

Jaffe, A., R. Newell, and R. Stavins. 2005. "A Tale of Two Market Failures: Technology and Environmental Policy." *Ecological Economics* 54:164–74.

Kerr, W., and R. Nanda. 2015. "Financing Innovation." *Annual Review of Financial Economics* 7:445–462.

Martin, R., L. De Preux, and U. Wagner. 2014. "The Impact of a Carbon Tax on Manufacturing: Evidence from Microdata." *Journal of Public Economics* 117:1–14.

Myers, K., and L. Lanahan. 2022. "Estimating Spillovers from Publicly Funded R&D: Evidence from the US Department of Energy." *American Economic Review* 112 (7): 2393–423.

Nelson, R. R. 1959. "The Simple Economics of Basic Scientific Research." *Journal of Political Economy* 67 (3): 297–306.

PESP (Private Equity Stakeholder Project). 2021. "Private Equity Propels the Climate Crisis: The Risks of a Shadowy Industry's Massive Exposure to Oil, Gas and Coal." Private Equity Stakeholder Project, Chicago, IL.

Pless, J. 2022. "Are Complementary Policies Substitutes? Evidence from R&D Subsidies in the UK." Working Paper, MIT, Cambridge, MA.

Pless, J., and S. Srivastav. 2022. "Unintended Consequences of Tech-Neutrality: Evidence from Environmental and Innovation Policy Interactions." Working Paper.

Popp, D. 2002. "Induced Innovation and Energy Prices." *American Economic Review* 92 (1): 160–80.

———. 2016. "Economic Analysis of Scientific Publications and Implications for Energy Research and Development." *Nature Energy* 1 (4): 1–8.

Quinn, S., and D. Scur. 2021. *Management Practices*. Vol. 37. Oxford: Oxford Review of Economic Policy.

Quinson, Tim. 2021. "Cost of Capital Spikes for Fossil Fuel Producers." *Bloomberg News*, November 9.

Rao, N. 2016. "Do Tax Credits Stimulate R&D Spending? The Effect of the R&D Tax Credit in Its First Decade." *Journal of Public Economics* 140:1–12.

Romer, P. 1990. "Endogenous Technological Change." *Journal of Political Economy* 98: 1–12.

Schmalensee, R. 1985. "Do Markets Differ Much?" *American Economic Review* 75 (3): 341–51.

Scur, D., R. Sadun, J. Van Reenen, R. Lemos, and N. Bloom. 2021. "The World Management Survey at 18: Lessons and the Way Forward." *Oxford Review of Economic Policy* 37 (2): 231–58.

Shleifer, A., and R. Vishny. 1986. "Large Shareholders and Corporate Control." *Journal of Political Economy* 94 (3): 461–88.

Syverson, C. 2004. "Product Substitutability and Productivity Dispersion." *Review of Economics and Statistics* 86 (2): 534–50.

———. 2011. "What Determines Productivity?" *Journal of Economic Literature* 49 (2): 326–65.

Xu, Z. 2020. "Economic Policy Uncertainty, Cost of Capital, and Corporate Innovation." *Journal of Banking and Finance* 111:105698.

Yang, M.-J. 2021. "The Interdependence Imperative: Business Strategy, Complementarities, and Economic Policy." *Oxford Review of Economic Policy* 37 (2): 392–415.

Racial Differences in Access to Capital for Innovative Start-Ups

Robert Fairlie, *University of California, Santa Cruz, and NBER,* United States of America

David T. Robinson, *Duke University and NBER,* United States of America

Abstract

This paper uses data from the Current Population Survey and the Kauffman Firm Survey to examine racial differences in the prevalence of innovative business ownership and in the amount of financing that innovation-intensive firms obtain. We find clear evidence that the racial differences in access to capital among start-ups found more broadly in Fairlie, Robb, and Robinson (2022) are also visible among innovation-intensive firms. Part of the disparity arises because Black founders are much more likely than white founders with similar credit scores to anticipate that banks will reject their loan applications, and thus not apply for credit at all. Policies aimed at addressing funding disparities must confront these challenges.

JEL Codes: L26, J15

Keywords: entrepreneurship, racial inequality, Kauffman Firm Survey, financing, innovation, startups, Black startups

I. Introduction

A large body of economic research points to the importance of self-employment and business ownership as channels for wealth accumulation. Not only is wealth disproportionately concentrated in the hands of entrepreneurs, but entrepreneurs are also more likely to experience greater upward mobility in wealth over their lifetimes (Quadrini 1999). Entrepreneurship is thus often viewed as a mechanism for promoting

Entrepreneurship and Innovation Policy and the Economy, volume 2, 2023.
 https://doi.org/10.1086/723238

economic mobility, wealth accumulation, and job creation in minority communities, representing a potential tool for alleviating racial disparities (Boston 1999, 2006; Stoll, Raphael, and Holzer 2001; Bradford 2003, 2014; Fairlie and Robb 2008).

Recent research finds large disparities between Black- and white-owned start-ups in access to financing, both in the initial year of founding and in subsequent years (Fairlie, Robb, and Robinson 2022). Black-owned businesses not only start smaller but also do not converge to the size of white-owned businesses: financial injections in later years do not make up for the initial racial difference. Robb and Robinson (2014) show that bank financing is the most common source of capital for new businesses; indeed, reduced reliance on bank financing among Black founders is a major driver of the overall differences in total financial capital identified by Fairlie et al. (2022).

The differential access to bank financing has its roots in both supply-side and demand-side considerations. On the demand side, across the distribution of credit scores, Black entrepreneurs are more likely to report fear of denial as reason they did not seek a loan. They thus "self-screen" out of the debt market, not applying for loans when a white entrepreneur with a similar credit rating otherwise would. Their reluctance is perhaps understandable: on the supply side, areas with stronger local banks support greater small business lending but not for Black borrowers. Reliance on "soft information," often thought to favor lending to small, new, opaque businesses, exacerbates rather than attenuates racial differences in bank debt for start-ups.

The findings of Fairlie et al. (2022) are based on a broad cross section of entrepreneurs, representing businesses ranging from unincorporated businesses operating out of the home of the founder with no additional employees to venture-backed firms with employees and patents in the year of their founding. Although their results control for industry and location, entrepreneurship comes in a wide range of flavors. Many policy discussions treat self-employment and entrepreneurship as though they are one and the same, yet self-employed individuals and entrepreneurs differ on a number of important dimensions (Levine and Rubinstein 2018). Nonemployer businesses make up the vast majority of firms in the United States (Davis et al. 2007). Most of these firms have low capital requirements, only very modest growth ambitions, and are primarily driven by nonpecuniary motivations (Hurst and Pugsley 2011). On the other hand, a small number of new firms born every year grow dramatically, create jobs, and consume financial resources in the process (Haltiwanger, Jarmin, and Miranda 2013).

Given what we know about the pronounced racial wealth disparities in the United States (US Census Bureau 2016), the stark differences in human and financial capital across the self-employment/entrepreneurship spectrum raise an important question. Are the racial differences in financing that we observe an artifact of sorting into self-employment with relatively low capital requirements, or do racial differences in financing exist even among high-growth-potential start-ups?

The policy implications of this question are important. If the racial differences in access to capital for start-ups in the cross section primarily reflect differential sorting of Black founders into less capital-intensive, lower-growth-potential businesses, then this places the onus on policies to rectify racial disparities in access to education and training that aim to boost representation in innovation fields, as identified in Cook, Gerson, and Kuan (2021). If, on the other hand, racial disparities persist even among innovation-intensive businesses, then policies that address the supply-side and demand-side causes for racial disparities in access to funding are likely to be important for boosting rates of minority representation in high-tech innovation.

We take up this question by analyzing microdata from both the Current Population Survey (CPS) and the Kauffman Firm Survey (KFS). The CPS data allow us to explore racial inequality in rates of business ownership for innovation-intensive businesses and in representation in the labor force in those industries. The CPS data do not allow us to examine the sources of financing for innovation-intensive businesses. For that we turn to the KFS.

To preview our key results: the CPS data show that Blacks are underrepresented in innovation-intensive business ownership. This is consistent with recent work by Cook, Gerson, and Kuan (2021), who illustrate racial disparities in the education and training that leads to many careers in innovation, and by Atkins and Burrage (2022), who show that minorities are less likely to be self-employed in tech industries than whites. When we examine data from the KFS, we find that the gap between Black-owned and white-owned innovation-intensive businesses is at least as large, if not larger, than what we observe when we look at the broader cross section of self-employment and entrepreneurship. Thus, although the CPS data support the idea that there is sorting into lower capital self-employment along racial lines, we still find large racial differences in access to bank financing among incorporated, employer businesses with intellectual property.

The remainder of the paper is organized as follows. In Section II, we describe the CPS and KFS data sets. Section III presents business ownership patterns by race using the CPS. Section IV presents our results on racial inequality in financing using the KFS. Section V concludes.

II.   Data

A.   Current Population Survey

We measure self-employed business ownership at the individual owner level using microdata from the basic monthly files of the CPS. The CPS, conducted monthly by the US Bureau of the Census and the US Bureau of Labor Statistics, is representative of the entire US population and contains observations for more than 130,000 people. The CPS has been conducted monthly since 1940 and is the underlying source of official government statistics on employment and unemployment. Data are collected by personal interviews. The data cover all persons in the civilian noninstitutionalized population of the United States living in households. To estimate business ownership in the CPS data, we identify all individuals who own a business as their main job in the survey month (based on the class of worker question and monthly labor force recode). The main job is defined as the one with the most hours worked during the survey week. Thus, individuals who start side businesses will not be counted if they are working more hours on a wage and salary job. The CPS captures the current work activity of the business owner and whether that business owner is currently operating the business. Only individuals aged 18–65 who are in the labor force are included to focus on business ownership patterns among the working-age population. The measure of business ownership in the CPS captures all business owners including those who own incorporated or unincorporated businesses, and those who are employers or nonemployers. In addition to providing information on business ownership and current activity, the CPS data include detailed demographic information such as the race and ethnicity of the owner. The data also include information on the industry and incorporation status of the business. The CPS data have been used in previous research to study self-employment, business ownership, and entrepreneurship (e.g., see Fairlie and Chatterji 2013; Chatterji, Chay, and Fairlie 2014; Hipple and Hammond 2016; Levine and Rubenstein 2016; Fairlie and Fossen 2017; Wang 2019).

B.   Kauffman Firm Survey

We use the confidential, restricted-access version of the KFS to study how start-ups access capital markets. The KFS is a longitudinal survey of new businesses in the United States, collecting annual information for a sample of 4,928 firms that began operations in 2004. The underlying sample frame for the KFS is Dun and Bradstreet (D&B) data.

The KFS data contain unprecedented detail on the financing patterns of start-ups, as well as detailed information on both the firm itself and up to 10 business owners of the firm. In addition to the 2004 baseline year data, we use the 7 years of follow-up data covering calendar years 2005 through 2011. Detailed information on the owners includes race, gender, age, education, previous start-up experience, and previous work experience. Detailed information on the firm includes industry, physical location, employment, sales, intellectual property, and financial capital used at start-up and over time. The detailed financing information in the KFS allows us to examine the relative importance of each source of financing at start-up and over time. The confidential, restricted-access version of the KFS includes credit scores, continuous measures of key variables, such as financing, and more detail on industries and geographic locations than the publicly available KFS. The KFS was also designed using sample weights to be representative of all new businesses in the US economy and not restricted to a narrow set of industries or business types. We also have administrative data on credit scores from D&B matched to all firms in the KFS. Credit scores are not available on most surveys, perhaps because most entrepreneurs do not readily know what their scores are. Although the KFS contains unprecedented detail on the business formation process, the availability of business credit scores allows us to control for many differences in firm characteristics that would be observable by bank lending personnel but typically unobservable to the econometrician.

The KFS is the only large, nationally representative, longitudinal data set providing detailed information on new firms and their financing activities. Most previous research on the use of financial capital among small businesses has relied on cross-sectional data on existing businesses (e.g., the Survey of Business Owners and Survey of Small Business Finances). Another advantage of the KFS is that fundraising levels are measured annually and are thus less prone to recall bias than cross-sectional data sets asking for retrospective information.

We restrict our attention to the set of firms that either survived over the sample period or that have been verified as going out of business over the sample period. In most analyses, we condition on survival in that year, but previous work finds that results are robust to alternative approaches to addressing survival (Fairlie et al. 2022). We also specifically focus on firms that have a white or Black primary owner.

To do this, we assign owner demographics at the firm level based on the primary owner. For firms with multiple owners (35% of the sample), the primary owner is designated by having the largest equity share in the business. In cases where two or more owners owned equal shares, hours worked and a series of other variables are used to create a rank ordering of owners to define a primary owner following the algorithm proposed by Ballou et al. (2008). We include businesses with owners of all races in the regression analysis but focus our comparisons on Black- and white-owned businesses. Following standard conventions in the literature, the white category includes only non-Hispanic whites. Using these definitions, we find that 9.1% of the KFS sample of start-ups is Black-owned. The percentage of Black-owned start-ups does not notably change over time, indicating similar survival rates. In the seventh year after start-up, we find that 8.4% of the KFS sample is Black-owned.

C.   Identifying Innovative Businesses

The CPS and KFS are very different surveys, and they require us to take a slightly different approach to identifying innovative businesses. For the CPS, we focus on the individual-level industries that have the highest growth and innovation potential. These are Information, Financial activities, and Professional and Business Services.

For the KFS data, we offer both an industry-based definition and a firm-based definition of whether a start-up is innovation intensive. For the firm-based measure, we flag firms that are incorporated, have employees in addition to the founder, and have some kind of intellectual property—either a patent or trademark.[1] This is no doubt a restrictive definition, one that many innovation-intensive firms do not meet in the year of their founding, but this nevertheless leaves us with a set of firms that have a high likelihood of pursuing innovation. By imposing a strict criterion for whether a business is innovation intensive, we presumably make it more difficult to detect racial differences because we screen out many more firms that lack sufficient amounts of initial capital regardless of whether a firm operates in North American Industry Classification system (NAICS) codes 31 (manufacturing) or 71 (arts, entertainment, and recreation). These are industries that have high rates of employer businesses and business incorporation in the KFS.

III.   Racial Differences in the Rate of Business Ownership

A.   Overall Business Ownership Patterns

We start at the broadest level of examining differences in business own-ership patterns by race using the CPS microdata. Analyzing business ownership patterns allows us to examine the extensive margin of partic-ipation in innovative start-up activity by Black and white founders be-fore turning to the intensive margin of financing differences. Figure 1 displays business ownership rates for Blacks and whites (non-Latinx) from 1996 to 2021.

Over the entire time period, Blacks have lower levels of business own-ership than whites, and the disparity is large. Blacks have an average business ownership over the time period of 4.4% compared with 10.1% for whites. The trends show some evidence of convergence over time in rates but this is because of a decline in white rates as much as an increase in Black rates. There are also some large changes in 2020 and 2021 that are likely due to COVID-19 disruptions (Fairlie 2020).[2] We do not focus on those here. Overall, Blacks are much less likely to own businesses than

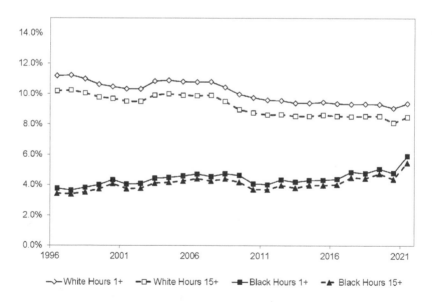

Fig. 1.   Racial differences in business ownership in the Current Population Survey. Color version available as an online enhancement.

are whites. The gap has narrowed over the past 2.5 decades but remains large in recent years. Just prior to the economic disruptions of COVID-19, Black business ownership rate was 5.1% compared with 9.3% for whites. This is the starting point for racial inequality in business ownership before turning to innovative businesses.

B. Innovative Business Ownership

We turn next to examining differences by race in the ownership of innovative businesses. Figure 2 displays the ownership of innovative businesses by race. Blacks have much lower levels of ownership of innovative businesses than do whites. In the early 2000s, around 1.1% of Blacks own innovative businesses. In comparison, more than 3% of whites were owners of innovative businesses in the early 2000s. Although the rate of Black innovative business ownership has trended upward slightly since then, innovative business ownership is about twice as prevalent among whites as among Blacks.

There are two underlying reasons why Blacks are less likely to own innovative businesses: (i) Blacks are less likely to work in innovative

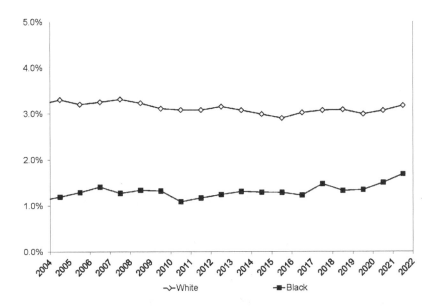

Fig. 2. Racial differences in business ownership for high-growth firms in the Current Population Survey. Color version available as an online enhancement.

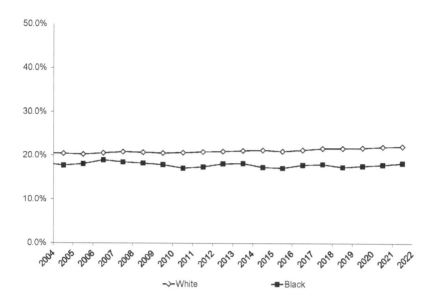

Fig. 3.   Racial differences in labor force representation for high-growth industries. Color version available as an online enhancement.

industries, and (ii) Blacks are less likely to own businesses conditioning on working in innovative industries. To explore this question, figure 3 displays the percentage of the labor force in innovative industries by race, and figure 4 displays the business ownership rate among the labor force in innovative industries.

Figure 3 shows that Blacks are slightly less likely to work in innovative industries. An average of around 18% of Blacks work in innovative industries compared with around 22% of whites. Conditioning on working in an innovative industry, Blacks are substantially less likely to own a business than are whites in these innovative industries. As figure 4 shows, the number of Blacks working in innovative industries who own a business has grown from around 6% in 2004 to around 9% today, whereas the rate for whites working in innovative industries who own a business has dropped from around 16% to around 14%.

Thus, to conclude, the evidence from the CPS shows that Blacks are underrepresented among owners of innovative businesses. This is a combination of underrepresentation in the innovative labor force and being less likely to own businesses conditional on being in the innovative labor

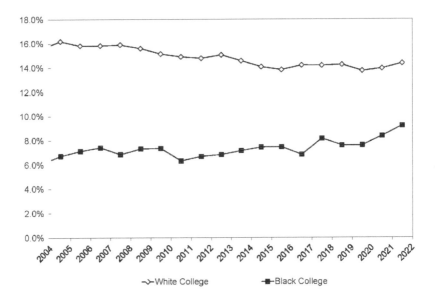

Fig. 4. Racial differences in business ownership in high-growth industries. Color version available as an online enhancement.

force. In the next section, we move from the extensive margin of firm entry to the intensive margin of firm size conditional on entry.

IV.   Racial Differences in Funding for New Businesses

Next, we focus on the set of entrepreneurs operating innovation-intensive businesses with data from the KFS to examine racial differences in access to capital for innovation-intensive start-ups.

Figure 5 illustrates that indeed, innovation-intensive start-ups are, on average, also capital-intensive start-ups, at least relative to the prototypical firm in the KFS.

The figure compares firms that meet our firm-level innovation-intensive definition (incorporated, employer firms with patents or trademarks) to those that do not. Innovation-intensive firms are around three times larger at inception, on average, with around $250,000 of start-up capital in 2004 compared with around $75,000 for nonintensive firms. Although low-innovation-intensive firms certainly grow during the sample period of the KFS, increasing from about $75,000 at birth to around $300,000 at the end of the sample, the growth among innovation-intensive businesses

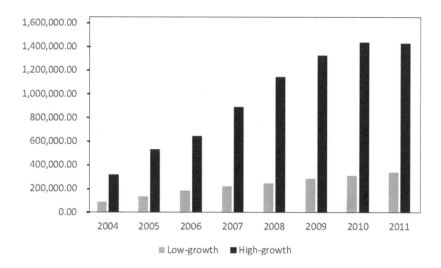

Fig. 5. High-growth businesses have high capital requirements. Color version available as an online enhancement.

is dramatically larger. By 2010, the average (surviving) innovation-intensive firm has raised more than $1.4 million in total capital.

Given that innovation-intensive firms are so much larger and grow so much more, the immediate question becomes whether we see racial differences in access to capital among these firms. Figure 6 takes up this question by comparing the amount of business debt at inception. The overall difference reported in the left two columns is at least as pronounced when we focused on innovative-intensive firms, as defined either by their industry or by their firm characteristics.

To put the scale of this difference in perspective, we computed the average amount of total capital in 2004, including not just business debt but debt from all sources, for Black- and white-owned innovative businesses. The 278 white-owned innovation-intensive businesses reported an average total capital in 2004 of around $340,000; for the 21 Black-owned businesses, the number was $41,487.

These differences in initial firm size could wash away over time if Black-owned businesses raised more outside capital in subsequent years to make up for their lower initial funding amounts. This time-series pattern of initial differences narrowing over time would naturally arise in a setting where initial borrowing conditions were heavily influenced by perceptions of racial differences in creditworthiness in the absence of information about the firm itself but became less important over time as the start-up became less opaque as it matured. We do not find this pattern

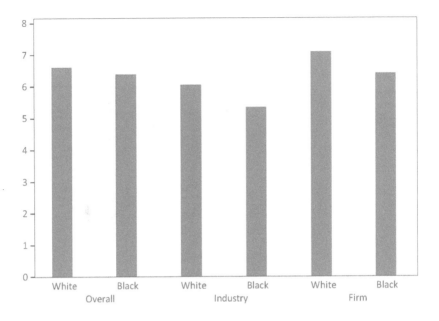

Fig. 6. Racial differences in business loans at inception

in the outside debt-raising of Black-owned firms in the later years of the survey, as figure 7 shows.

Figure 7 compares the overall difference between Black-owned and white-owned firms in the logarithm of new business debt raised in 2008–11 with the difference observed in innovation-intensive businesses. Using an industry-based definition of innovation intensity, the average amounts of outside debt are essentially equal, and when we focus on a firm-based measure of innovation intensity, we find that Black-owned businesses continue to rely on less outside debt than white-owned businesses.

This culminates in what we might term a "Black Start-up Capital Deficit," which can be seen in figure 8. To generate this figure, we regressed the total outside financial capital raised as of 2011 on firm, owner, and industry characteristics and reported the coefficient on the variable for founder race. The interpretation of the figure is that it captures the incremental difference attributable to the race of the founder, controlling for other confounding characteristics.

As the figure shows, Black-owned businesses lag behind white-owned businesses more in innovation-intensive settings, not less. Overall, we find that Black-owned businesses are around $90,000 smaller than white-owned businesses by the end of the sample. But controlling for business and owner characteristics, Black-owned businesses in innovation-intensive

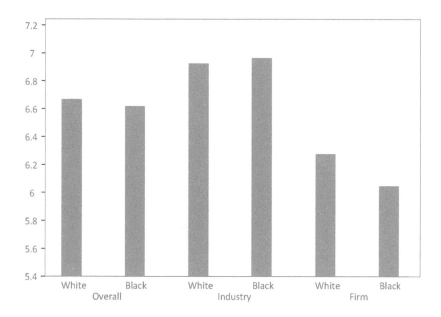

Fig. 7. New debt for business in later survey years

industries are around $650,000 smaller than white-owned businesses. If we use a firm-based definition of innovation intensity, Black-owned businesses are around $250,000 smaller than similar white-owned innovation-intensive businesses.

Why does this occur? Evidence from Fairlie et al. (2022) shows that an important factor is the fact that Black entrepreneurs have worse expectations of banking outcomes than white entrepreneurs with similar credit scores. Consider entrepreneurs whose credit scores place them above the 75th percentile of the distribution of entrepreneurs in the KFS. In this group, the authors report that 32% of Black entrepreneurs report that they did not apply for a loan for fear of being denied credit. The corresponding figure for white entrepreneurs in this group is 15%, less than half the amount. This indicates that Black entrepreneurs expect rejection to a far greater degree than white entrepreneurs and screen themselves out of the market for business loans based on these expectations. Similarly, more than 70% of high-credit-score white entrepreneurs report that they are always approved for loans, whereas only around 25% of high-credit-score Black entrepreneurs report always being approved.

Figure 9 explores whether these same factors are at play among innovation-intensive businesses. The first set of columns reports the difference between Black and white entrepreneurs in reporting that they did

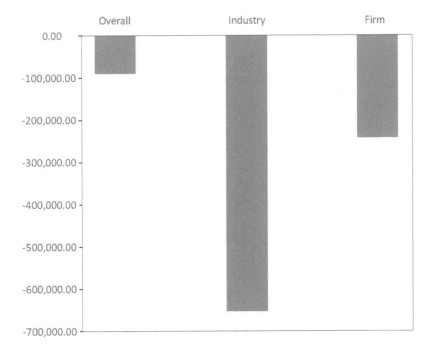

Fig. 8. Black-owned innovative businesses are smaller

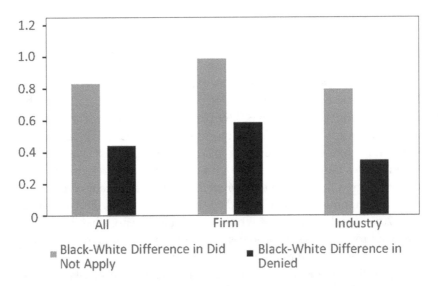

Fig. 9. Fear of denial shapes borrowing behavior. Color version available as an online enhancement.

not apply for fear of being rejected and are obtained from regressions in which an indicator variable flagging "did not apply for fear of rejection" is regressed on owner race, other owner demographics, business, and other characteristics. On the left, the point estimate obtained from the full sample is reported, and the remaining two columns report the value for innovation-intensive start-ups, defined either by industry or firm characteristics. The point estimates indicate that Black entrepreneurs are about twice as likely to report that they did not apply for fear of denial in the innovation-intensive sample.

The second set of columns reports the difference between Black and white entrepreneurs in the probability that they are actually denied credit, conditional on borrowing. Here we see a different story than that found in the work of Fairlie et al. (2022). Although in the full sample, the rate of denial is considerably higher among Black entrepreneurs, the statistical significance of the difference among innovation-intensive firms vanishes. In short, there is no statistically discernible difference in reported loan denial rates between white and Black entrepreneurs operating innovation-intensive businesses. We might be underpowered, however, to detect differences here.

V. Conclusion

Racial inequality in access to financing contributes to broader inequality in business success, growth, and job creation. This paper builds on recent work that demonstrates pronounced racial differences in the amount of start-up capital associated with new firms.

Using data from the KFS, Fairlie et al. (2022) show that Black-owned start-ups receive significantly lower amounts of bank debt than similar white-owned start-ups, both in the initial year of founding and in later years. Instead of focusing on the entirety of firms covered by the KFS, this paper zeroes in on firms that have high growth potential either because they possess characteristics at founding that are correlated with high growth potential or because they operate in high-growth industries.

A priori, it is unclear whether we should expect racial differences in start-up characteristics found in the broader cross section to also be present in the subsample of innovative firms. One reason we may see racial differences in average funding is because we see sorting based on racial lines; indeed, our examination of data from the CPS shows that Black founders are underrepresented in innovative industries. The primary driver of differences in the broader cross section could thus be sorting of Black founders into settings with low capital requirements, a reflection of lack of equal representation in innovative industries and settings. On the other hand, many innovative start-ups have large capital requirements, and thus racial differences in access to capital may be exacerbated in these settings because the demand for capital is relatively large.

Our findings show that the racial differences in access to capital for start-ups found in the broader cross section are at least as large, if not larger, among innovative start-ups. Innovation-intensive businesses founded by Black entrepreneurs start with less capital in their year of founding. Over time, they do not make up for this initial gap with greater funding; if anything, the funding gap in follow-on capital exacerbates the differences in initial conditions. As a result, we observe a "racial capital deficit" in innovation-intensive businesses after controlling for founder demographics, business characteristics, and other factors that is at least as large as the overall racial capital deficit in start-ups more broadly. Racial differences in access to capital for start-ups thus are not primarily explained by sorting of Black founders into settings with low capital requirements.

Endnotes

Author email addresses: Fairlie (rfairlie@ucsc.edu), Robinson (davidr@duke.edu). We thank participants at the NBER EIPE workshop and New York University Racial Equity in Technology Entrepreneurship Workshop for comments and suggestions. For acknowledgments, sources of research support, and disclosure of the authors' material financial relationships, if any, please see https://www.nber.org/books-and-chapters/entrepreneurship-and-innovation-policy-and-economy-volume-2/racial-inequality-capital-access-innovative-firms.

1. See Fairlie and Miranda (2016) for evidence linking incorporation status and employment to growth orientation.

2. See Couch, Fairlie, and Xu (2020) for COVID-19 disruptions to unemployment rates by race.

References

Atkins, Rachel, and April Burrage. 2022. "Measuring Racial and Ethnic Representation in 21st Century High Tech Self-employment." Working paper, New York University.

Ballou, J., T. Barton, D. DesRoches, F. Potter, E. J. Reedy, Alicia Robb, Scott Shane, and Z. Zhao. 2008. "Kauffman Firm Survey: Results from the Baseline and First Follow-Up Surveys." Research Report, Kauffman Foundation, Kansas City, MO.

Boston, T. D. 1999. "Generating Jobs through African American Business Development." In *Readings in Black Political Economy*, ed. J. Whitehead and C. Harris, 211–32. Dubuque, IA: Kendall-Hunt.

Boston, T. D. 2006. "Black Patronage of Black-Owned Start-Ups and Black Employment." In *African Americans in the U.S. Economy*, ed. C. A. Conrad,

J. Whitehead, P. Mason, and J. Stewart, 373–77. Lanham, MD: Rowman & Littlefield.

Bradford, William D. 2003. "The Wealth Dynamics of Entrepreneurship for Black and White Families in the U.S." *Review of Income and Wealth* 49 (1): 89–116.

———. 2014. "The 'Myth' That Black Entrepreneurship Can Reduce the Gap in Wealth between Black and White Families." *Economic Development Quarterly* 28 (3): 254–69.

Chatterji, Ronnie, Kenneth Chay, and Robert W. Fairlie. 2014. "The Impact of City Contracting Set-Asides on Black Self-Employment and Employment." *Journal of Labor Economics* 32 (3): 507–61.

Cook, Lisa, Janet Gerson, and Jennifer Kuan. 2021. "Closing the Innovation Gap in Pink and Black." In *Entrepreneurship and Innovation Policy and the Economy*, Vol. 1, ed. Josh Lerner and Scott Stern. Chicago: University of Chicago Press.

Couch, Kenneth, Robert Fairlie, and Huanan Xu. 2020. "Early Evidence of the Impacts of COVID-19 on Minority Unemployment." *Journal of Public Economics* 192:1–11.

Davis, Steven J., John Haltiwanger, Ron Jarmin, C. J. Krizan, Javier Miranda, Al Nucci, and Kristen Sandusky. 2007. "Measuring the Dynamics of Young and Small Businesses: Integrating the Employer and Nonemployer Universes." Working Paper no. 13226, NBER, Cambridge, MA.

Fairlie, Robert. 2020. "The Impact of COVID-19 on Small Business Owners: Evidence from the First Three Months after Widespread Social-Distancing Restrictions." *Journal of Economics and Management Strategy* 29 (4): 727–40.

Fairlie, Robert W., and Ronnie Chatterji. 2013. "High Tech Entrepreneurship in Silicon Valley: Opportunities and Opportunity Costs." *Journal of Economics and Management Strategy* 22 (2): 365–89.

Fairlie, Robert W., and Frank M. Fossen. 2017. "The Two Components of Business Creation: Opportunity versus Necessity Entrepreneurship." Working Paper no. w26377, NBER, Cambridge, MA.

Fairlie, Robert W., and Javier Miranda. 2016. "Taking the Leap: The Determinants of Entrepreneurs Hiring Their First Employee." https://ssrn.com/abstract=2748848.

Fairlie, Robert W., and Alicia M. Robb. 2008. *Race and Entrepreneurial Success: Black-, Asian-, and White-Owned Businesses in the United States*. Cambridge, MA: MIT Press.

Fairlie, Robert W., Alicia Robb, and David T. Robinson. 2022. "Black and White: Access to Capital among Minority Owned Startups." *Management Science* 68 (4): 2377–400.

Haltiwanger, John C., Ron S. Jarmin, and Javier Miranda. 2013. "Who Creates Jobs? Small vs. Large vs. Young." *Review of Economics and Statistics* 95 (2): 347–61.

Hipple, Stephen F., and Laurel Hammond. 2016. "Self-Employment in the United States." Spotlight on Statistics Report, US Bureau of Labor Statistics, Washington, DC.

Hurst, Erik, and Benjamin Pugsley. 2011. "What Do Small Businesses Do?" Papers on Economic Activity, Brookings Institution, Washington, DC.

Levine, Ross, and Yona Rubinstein. 2016. "Smart and Illicit: Who Becomes an Entrepreneur and Do They Earn More?" *Quarterly Journal of Economics* 132 (2): 963–1018.

———. 2018. "Selection into Entrepreneurship and Self-Employment." Working Paper no. 25350, NBER, Cambridge, MA.

Quadrini, Vincenzo. 1999. "The Importance of Entrepreneurship for Wealth Concentration and Mobility." *Review of Income and Wealth* 45 (1): 1–19.
Robb, Alicia, and David T. Robinson. 2014. "The Capital Structure Decisions of New Firms." *Review of Financial Studies* 27 (1): 153–79.
Stoll, Michael A., Steven Raphael, and Harry J. Holzer. 2001. "Why Are Black Employers More Likely than White Employers to Hire Blacks?" Working paper, Institute for Research on Poverty, University of Wisconsin, Madison.
US Census Bureau. 2016. "Income and Poverty in the United States: 2015." https://www.census.gov/library/publications/2017/demo/p60-259.html.
Wang, Chunbei. 2019. "Tightened Immigration Policies and the Self-Employment Dynamics of Mexican Immigrants." *Journal of Policy Analysis and Management* 38 (4): 944–77.

Place-Based Productivity and Costs in Science

Jonathan Gruber, *Massachusetts Institute of Technology and NBER,*
United States of America

Simon Johnson, *Massachusetts Institute of Technology and NBER,*
United States of America

Enrico Moretti, *University of California, Berkeley, and NBER,* United States
of America

Abstract

Cities with a larger concentration of scientists have been shown to be more productive places for additional scientists to do research and development (R&D).
At the same time, these urban areas tend to be associated with higher costs of
doing research, in terms of both wages and land. Although the literature on the
benefits of agglomeration economies is extensive, it offers no direct evidence of
how productivity gains from agglomeration compare with higher costs of production. This paper aims to shed light on the balance between local productivity and
local costs in science. Using a novel data set, we estimate place-based costs of carrying out R&D in each US metro area and assess how these place-based costs vary
with the density of scientists in each area. We then compare these costs with estimates of the corresponding productivity benefits of more scientist density from
Moretti (2021). Adding more scientists to a city increases both productivity and
production costs, but the rise in productivity is larger than the rise in production
costs. In particular, each 10% rise in the stock of scientists is associated with a
0.11% rise in costs and a 0.67% rise in productivity. This implies that firms moving
from cities with a small agglomeration of scientists to cities with a large agglomeration of scientists experience productivity gains that are six times larger than the
increase in production costs. This finding is consistent with the increased concentration of R&D activity observed over the past 30 years. However, although the
productivity estimate has only modest nonlinearities, the cost estimates suggest
much larger nonlinearities as the concentration of scientists increases. For the most
concentrated R&D cities, the difference between productivity gains and cost increases is close to zero.

Entrepreneurship and Innovation Policy and the Economy, volume 2, 2023.

JEL Codes: J24, R32, R52

Keywords: productivity, scientific research, place-based policies

I.   Introduction

In recent decades, the United States has experienced increased concentration in the location of innovation (Moretti 2012). Cities that have come to dominate the information technology and biotech sectors, primarily on the east and west coasts, have increasingly pulled away from the rest of the country, including other large urban areas. Such so-called superstar cities have become the predominant loci of innovation in the United States, to a degree not previously experienced (Atkinson, Muro, and Whiton 2019). For example, the top 10 cities in the fields of "computer science," "semiconductors," and "biology and chemistry" account for 70%, 79%, and 59% of all US inventors in 2009, respectively (Moretti 2021). At the same time, restrictive zoning policies in these cities keep housing prices high and limit the inflow of population. As a result, these places and the firms located there are unable to take full advantage of the implied agglomeration economies, depressing overall US growth below what would otherwise have been achievable (Hsieh and Moretti 2019).

The agglomeration of innovative activity raises important questions about the economic geography of the innovation sector. Why does private research and development (R&D) activity tend to be so geographically concentrated, despite the higher costs? Firms deciding where to locate their R&D activities presumably consider both costs and benefits offered by each location.

On the one hand, large technology clusters have been shown to increase individual and firm productivity, as working in large clusters tends to make scientists and engineers more creative and innovative—thanks to localized agglomeration economies. Marshallian spillovers stemming from human capital externalities and labor pooling have long been thought to be an important determinant of productivity and innovation, especially in the high-tech sector (Henderson, Jaffe, and Trajtenberg 1993). Moretti (2021), for example, estimates the productivity advantages of large clusters relative to small clusters and finds that scientists located in areas with a 10% larger stock of scientists in their specific research field produce 0.5%–0.9% more patents per year. This effect appears to be causal, rather than driven by selection of the best scientists into the largest clusters.

On the other hand, it has become notoriously expensive to live and operate a business in the existing coastal superstar cities. Labor and real estate costs in places such as the San Francisco Bay Area, Boston, and New York City are among the highest in the nation, by a considerable margin.

Thus, there appears to be a clear trade-off between productivity and production costs, with large, established high-tech clusters offering high productivity and high production costs and smaller clusters offering lower productivity along with more affordable costs. From the point of view of an innovation-oriented firm deciding where to locate its operations—or the federal government deciding where to pursue place-based science policies—what matters is how productivity in a location compares to costs in that location. If an area with 10% higher output per scientist is 20% more expensive as a location to carry out R&D, then it is an inefficient location for a new lab, whether private or public.

This paper aims to shed light on the balance between local productivity and local costs in science. We assemble a novel data set on cross-area costs of doing R&D, and we use this to measure place-based costs of carrying out R&D in each US metro area and to assess how place-based costs vary with the density of scientists in each area. We compare these costs with estimates of the corresponding productivity benefits of higher scientist density from Moretti (2021).

Although the literature on the benefits of agglomeration economies is extensive, it offers no direct evidence of how productivity gains from agglomeration compare with higher costs of production in science. It is often assumed that, in the long-run equilibrium, localized productivity gains from agglomeration are exactly offset by higher local costs. But actual empirical evidence on the costs of the R&D-intense "innovation sector" is scarce. Moreover, it is not obvious even in theory that localized industry-specific productivity advantages need to be exactly offset by higher costs in each industry and city, if cities contain multiple industries.[1]

The exact nature of the trade-off between productivity and costs matters for our understanding of the drivers of agglomeration of innovative private-sector firms. But understanding this trade-off is not just an academic question: it also has important implications for the efficiency of a new set of proposed place-based initiatives designed to boost federal spending on science and innovation. For example, Gruber and Johnson (2019) and Atkinson et al. (2019) propose ambitious agendas for "place-based science," with the aim of creating new technology hubs around the country that can complement the existing coastal superstar cities. By late 2021, the idea had been picked up in multiple legislative proposals, including the bipartisan Endless Frontiers Act, which would commit $10 billion over the next 5 years for grants to create 10–12 new technology hubs; the Innovation Centers Acceleration Act, which would provide $80 billion over 10 years for a competition for cities to become technology centers; and the Federal Institute of Technology Act, which would invest nearly $1 trillion in public R&D over 10 years and would target a significant share of those funds to new technology centers.[2] Shifting additional publicly supported R&D activity from being centered in established technology clusters toward other places likely creates efficiency trade-offs.[3] Properly evaluating the efficiency of such place-based polices requires measuring both costs and benefits.

To quantify local costs of R&D, we gather data from a variety of sources on the place-based costs of conducting scientific research. Using data from the Bureau of Economic Analysis (BEA 2019) and the National Science Foundation (NSF) Business R&D Survey, we decompose the costs of R&D into components that vary by location (wages and building costs) from those that do not (machines). We use data from Glassdoor—the largest privately available source of information on wages in the R&D sector—to estimate wage costs for scientific personnel by city. For land values and rents, we use CoStar, one of the largest and most comprehensive databases of commercial real estate in the United States, and the American Community Survey (ACS).

Combining these sources of data, we estimate the area-specific costs of carrying out R&D for a sample of 133 US cities. We match this information to data on the stock of scientists by city to estimate how costs vary with the stock of scientists, and then compare these costs with Moretti's (2021) estimates of how productivity varies with the stock of scientists.

Using linear models, we find that adding more scientists to a city increases both productivity and production costs, but the rise in productivity is larger than the rise in production costs. In particular, we uncover statistically significant but economically modest effects of cluster size on costs. Each 10% rise in the number of scientists in a city is associated with a 0.105% rise in costs, mostly due to higher wage costs. This is well below Moretti's estimate of productivity gains as the stock of scientists increases (also confirmed in our sample).

Thus, larger and more established clusters offer productivity advantages that more than offset increased costs at the margin. Our estimates imply that firms moving from cities with a small agglomeration of scientists to cities with a large agglomeration of scientists experience productivity gains that are six times larger than the increase in production costs. This finding is consistent with the significant increase in the spatial concentration of innovative activity observed since the 1970s.

Although Moretti's estimate of increased output has only very modest nonlinearities, our estimates for costs have much larger nonlinearities—meaning that costs increase a great deal when there are already many scientists in an area. Estimates from our nonlinear models suggest that the relationship between productivity gains and cost increases varies significantly across areas. Using a spline regression specification, we find that although productivity gains remain larger than cost increases in cities with a sizable presence of scientists, the difference between productivity gains and cost increases is closer to zero for the most R&D-intensive cities.

The remainder of the paper is structured as follows. Section II describes the data. Section III presents our empirical findings. Section IV concludes.

II.   Data: Measuring the Area-Specific Costs of R&D

We measure area-specific R&D costs as a weighted average of the costs of the various factors needed in the R&D process, with weights reflecting the relative importance of each factor in the production function of R&D. We proceed in two steps. The first is to measure the factor weights in the R&D production function (i.e., the relative importance of various factors of production). The second is to measure the area-specific costs of the two spatially varying components of R&D costs, wages and building/land costs.

A.   Weights

To measure factor weights, we rely on Robbins et al. (2012), who use NSF Business R&D Survey Data to calculate the average share of expenditures in R&D activities for five basic spending categories: wages for scientists and engineers, wages for support personnel, materials and supplies, current cost depreciation, and other R&D costs. To identify the real estate share, we combine the Robbins et al. (2012) shares with data from the Input-Output tables to estimate the share of intermediate inputs, defined as materials, supplies, and other R&D costs, spent on real estate and other leasing services. Specifically, we use BEA industry input-output data for the industry "miscellaneous professional, scientific, and technical services industry," which includes scientific R&D. We assume that the cost of physical capital does not vary across cities, once installed. It appears plausible that the market for machines and other forms of physical capital is national in scope.

We find that labor accounts for 38% of the costs of R&D, office space accounts for 5.1%, and physical capital (e.g., machines and equipment of all kinds) and other non–area-specific costs (e.g., raw materials for laboratories) account for the remaining 56.9%. We note that our factor weights do not vary by location. It is possible that firms adjust their inputs based on local prices, so that shares vary geographically, but our data preclude estimates of area-specific cost shares.

B.   Costs for Factors of Production

To measure labor costs of R&D personnel by location, we use two sources: Glassdoor for 2020, and the ACS for 2015–20. Although the ACS is more representative, Glassdoor has information on salaries at a much finer occupational level. For example, the Glassdoor data categorize workers as "scientists and engineers" separately from "support personnel."

In Glassdoor, we focus on 33 occupations in the biology, chemistry and materials, and computer and information research industries. Glassdoor annual salary averages per occupation are calculated cumulatively using all available entries, which means our data span 2010–20. In the ACS, we focus on data from 2014–18 for 11 occupations in the following industries: computer and mathematical; architecture and engineering; and life, physical, and social science. In some cases, certain occupations are missing information; in those cases, we average data for the available occupations. Our baseline estimates are based on Glassdoor labor costs. We also show estimates based on ACS data.

To measure area differences in real estate costs, we combine ACS data on housing prices with real estate data from CoStar to estimate the average sale price per square foot for R&D labs. The CoStar data are based on industrial and commercial land properties using public record comparable sales from 2017 to 2020. The ACS data were sampled for household values in metropolitan statistical areas (MSA) in 2018. We use the CoStar R&D category specifications with the least amount of missing data: Class B commercial real estate and an area of 20,000–50,000 square feet. We calculate a weighted average sale price of $137.54 per square foot for R&D facilities. The CoStar data for R&D space costs are available for only 253 MSAs. In the 253 cities for which we do have CoStar commercial prices, the average CoStar commercial prices for all commercial properties are highly correlated with average ACS house prices. A regression of CoStar commercial prices on ACS mean house prices yields a coefficient of 0.154 (standard error of 0.008) and an R^2 of 0.5966.

To construct land costs, we find the ratio of the average sale price per square foot of R&D facilities from CoStar data to the average house value from ACS data. We then scale the average house values in each city by this ratio of average R&D sale price to average house value. Land costs are therefore at the level of R&D real estate costs, shifted relatively across MSAs according to variation in house values from the ACS.

C. Geographical Differences in Total Costs

Finally, we combine wage costs, land costs, and other costs to create overall area-specific costs of R&D. We also restrict the analysis to the 133 BEA Economic Areas, because this is the level at which the stock of scientists is measured. In most cases, "economic areas" are similar to an MSA. For large areas such as the San Francisco Bay Area, Boston, or New York City, they tend to be larger than the corresponding MSAs, because they include the entire economic region. For example, the economic area for the San Francisco Bay Area includes the entire area between Santa Rosa to the north and San Jose to the south. In the rest of the paper, we will refer to economic areas as "cities."

Geographical variation in total area-specific costs of R&D is mainly driven by differences in wage costs, as they account for more than one-third of total costs. Land costs do vary across locations and contribute to spatial variation in overall costs, but their share is only 5.1%—about one-seventh of the labor share.

Table 1 reports summary statistics of annual wages for scientists and engineers, annual wages for support personnel, land costs, and a cost index with a mean value of 100 (which uses the input factor weights described above). That is, for the index, we first normalize the value in each

Table 1
Summary Statistics of City Costs

	Mean	Std. Dev.	Median	N
Cost variable:				
Annual wages for scientists/engineers ($)	61,839.34	8,792.77	62,677.19	133
Annual wages for support personnel ($)	32,170.34	3,368.66	32,012.29	133
Land costs (sale price in $/sq. ft)	52.407	22.817	45.912	133
Overall cost index	100	5.870	99.882	133

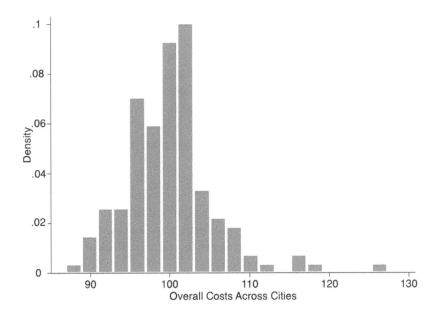

Fig. 1. Distribution of overall costs. Color version available as an online enhancement. Note: Histogram of the distribution of the overall costs constructed from our data.

category of costs relative to the national average, and then we take a weighted average of these normalized indices using input factor weights.

Figure 1 shows the roughly normal distribution of overall costs for the 133 cities in our full sample. Most cities have an overall cost that is within 10% of the average (mean) city—namely between 90 and 110—but there is an important right tail of significantly more expensive cities.

Table 2 lists the 10 most expensive cities, the median city (Clarksburg-Morgantown, West Virginia), and the 10 least expensive cities (all "cities" are actually MSAs). The top 10 cities have systematically higher costs in all categories. San Jose–San Francisco–Oakland, CA; Honolulu, HI; and Boston-Worcester-Manchester, MA-NH, are the metro areas where the production of R&D is the most expensive. By contrast, Dayton-Springfield-Greenville, OH; Milwaukee-Racine-Waukesha, WI; and Grand Rapids–Muskegon-Holland, MI, are the metro areas where the production of R&D is the least expensive.

Costs in the metro area at the top of the distribution—San Jose–San Francisco–Oakland, CA—are 38% higher than costs in the metro area at the bottom—Grand Rapids–Muskegon-Holland, MI. Although these

Table 2

Costs of 10 Least Expensive Cities, Median City, and 10 Most Expensive Cities

	Overall Cost Index	Annual Wages for Scientists and Engineers ($)	Annual Wages for Support Personnel ($)	Land Costs (Sale Price in $/sq. ft)
	(1)	(2)	(3)	(4)
Ten most expensive cities:				
San Jose–San Francisco–Oakland, CA	127.27	96,786.74	39,810.49	151.59
Honolulu, HI	119.13	77,912.53	36,557.43	162.44
Boston-Worcester-Manchester, MA-NH	116.12	71,873.22	55,434.76	86.59
San Diego–Carlsbad–San Marcos, CA	115.56	74,253.94	35,605.35	145.20
Anchorage, AK	113.04	85,182.56	37,201.02	65.61
New York–Newark-Bridgeport, NY-NJ-CT-PA	110.81	74,256.59	36,957.06	91.28
Portland-Vancouver-Beaverton, OR-WA	110.68	75,790.26	34,563.31	92.22
Bend-Prineville, OR	109.00	70,822.55	34,394.40	97.34
Sacramento-Arden-Arcade-Truckee, CA-NV	108.68	72,759.07	36,529.79	77.48
Washington-Baltimore–N Virginia, DC-MD-VA-WV	108.40	69,137.43	36,233.01	91.58
Median city:				
Clarksburg-Morgantown, WV	99.88	63,419.17	30,750.27	49.53
Ten least expensive cities:				
Joplin, MO	86.85	40,015.67	26,275.52	34.46
Evansville, IN-KY	89.05	45,680.54	25,866.85	33.89
Raleigh-Durham-Cary, NC	89.94	44,649.64	28,295.99	38.42
Greensboro–Winston-Salem–High Point, NC	90.44	42,384.03	32,198.56	38.69
Huntsville-Decatur, AL	90.50	44,463.75	30,742.14	35.68
Kennewick-Richland-Pasco, WA	91.14	44,646.15	29,288.61	47.01
Harrisburg-Carlisle-Lebanon, PA	91.26	46,155.57	27,903.62	46.87
Dayton-Springfield-Greenville, OH	91.67	47,296.16	31,950.61	30.83
Milwaukee-Racine-Waukesha, WI	92.12	44,240.18	32,714.46	45.91
Grand Rapids–Muskegon-Holland, MI	92.49	47,767.18	31,424.06	39.24

spatial differences are large, they are somewhat smaller in magnitude than the differences in the consumer cost of living indexes for high-income households and significantly smaller in magnitude than the differences in the consumer cost of living indexes for low-income households. In particular, Diamond and Moretti (2023) estimate that the overall cost of living in the commuting zone that is the most expensive for high-income households is 49% higher than the overall cost of living in the commuting zone that is the least expensive for high-income households. The corresponding difference for low-income households is 99%. The range of prices that low-income families are exposed to is much wider than the range of prices that high-income families are exposed to, because low-income households put a higher weight on housing expenditure, which is the item in the consumption basket whose price varies the most across cities.

III.   Comparing Costs and Productivity in R&D

Empirically determining the productivity advantage of Silicon Valley–style clusters is difficult, because location is endogenous. Comparing the productivity of inventors in large clusters to the productivity of inventors in small clusters may yield biased estimates of agglomeration effects if particularly productive inventors select into large clusters.

In a recent paper, Moretti (2021) uses longitudinal data on inventors to identify the productivity benefits for inventors who locate in Silicon Valley–style clusters. He defines a cluster as city × research field and estimates how inventors' productivity—defined as number of patents produced in a year—varies with the size of the relevant cluster, measured by the number of other inventors in the same city and field, excluding the focal inventor.

He first studies the experience of inventors in Rochester, NY, where the high-tech cluster declined due to the demise of its main employer, Kodak. Kodak was the market leader in films for cameras and one of the most prolific patenters in the United States. But due to the diffusion of digital photography and the decline of physical film, Kodak employment collapsed after 1996. Essentially, demand for Kodak's main product evaporated due to a global technology shock. By 2007, the number of Kodak inventors in Rochester had declined by 84%. Moretti (2021) shows that Kodak's decline had a profound effect on the broader Rochester high-tech cluster. Measured by the number of inventors in all fields, its size declined by 49.2% relative to other cities, dragged down by Kodak's downsizing. The shock was large and arguably exogenous, as it was caused by the advent of digital photography and not factors specific to Rochester's local economy. The experience of Rochester therefore offers an interesting case study for testing the hypothesis that high-tech cluster size affects inventor productivity. Moretti (2021) focuses on non-Kodak inventors outside the photography sector. He finds that, following the decline in the Rochester high-tech cluster, non-Kodak inventors in Rochester experienced large productivity losses relative to non-Kodak inventors in other cities. The within-inventor estimates indicate that the log productivity of non-Kodak inventors in Rochester declined by 0.206 (0.077) relative to other cities. This is consistent with the existence of important productivity spillovers in the high-tech sector stemming from geographical agglomeration.

Next, Moretti (2021) uses data for all US clusters and presents estimates based on 109,846 inventors observed between 1971 and 2007, located in 895 clusters (179 cities × 5 research fields). He regresses the patents held by a particular scientist on the field and city-specific stock of scientists. His approach uses moves to identify the effects of each scientist.

In his richest specification, he finds that a scientist in a city-field with 10% more scientists produces 0.67 more patents. This indicates that a 10% increase in cluster size is associated with a 0.67% increase the number of patents produced by a scientist in a year.

To get a sense of the magnitude implied, consider an inventor in computer science who moves from the median cluster to the cluster at the 75th percentile of the size distribution. Moretti's (2021) estimate suggests that the scientist would experience a 12.0% increase in the number of patents produced in a year, holding constant the inventor and the firm. In biology and chemistry, a move from the median cluster to the 75th percentile cluster would be associated with a productivity gain of 8.4%, holding constant the inventor and the firm.

Of course, that scientist (or the firm that employs her) would also face a higher cost of carrying out research in areas that have the most scientific expertise. To see how R&D costs vary across cities as a function of the size of the local R&D sector, we regress our estimate of costs on the number of scientists who are active in the relevant metropolitan area. The stock of active scientists in a metropolitan area is from Moretti (2021) and is measured as the ratio of the number of inventors who file for a patent in any research field in a year over the number of all active inventors in the United States in that year. These estimates are based on data on the universe of US patents filed between 1971 and 2007 from the COMETS (Connecting Outcome Measures in Entrepreneurship, Technology, and Science) patent database.

Ideally, we would measure field- and city-specific costs, but our cost data are not ideal in this respect. Although we can measure wage costs for a broad set of fields by cities, we cannot create field-specific land costs. However, there is no specific reason to expect that the cost of land or office space varies significantly within a city for different research fields. Thus, in our baseline estimates, we consider only city-specific costs. In an extension, we present additional analyses for city- and field-specific labor costs, which allow us to include city fixed effects.

The results of our baseline regressions are shown in table 3. Columns 1–3 show regressions of the log of total area costs on the stock of scientists, for different specifications. Columns 4–6 show the regressions for equivalent specifications using productivity data from Moretti (2021); the dependent variable is the log number of patents produced in a given year by an inventor. The level of observation is an inventor-year pair.

We begin in column 1 with a log-linear regression of log area-specific costs on the log of the stock of scientists. We find an elasticity of 0.0105, indicating that each 10% rise in the stock of scientists is associated with a 0.105% rise in total area costs. Column 4 reports the estimate for productivity using the same log-linear specification. A comparison of columns 1 and 4 suggests that the increase in cost associated with a larger cluster size is about one-sixth of the Moretti (2021) estimate for the increase in productivity. This specification suggests that the higher productivity enjoyed by

Table 3
Regressions of Log Total Area Costs on Log Stock of Scientists

Dependent Variable	Log Total Area Costs			Log Inventor Productivity		
	(1)	(2)	(3)	(4)	(5)	(6)
Log (stock)	.0105	.0654		.0676	.2876	
	(.0038)	(.0251)		(.0139)	(.0346)	
Log (stock)^2		.0046			.0236	
		(.0020)			(.0031)	
1st spline			.0373			.0636
			(.0156)			(.0132)
2nd spline			−.0095			.0721
			(.0051)			(.0142)
3rd spline			.0525			.0772
			(.0125)			(.0148)
N	133	133	133	823,375	823,375	823,375

Note: Columns 1–3 show regressions from our data of the log of total area costs on the stock of scientists from Moretti (2021). Columns 4–6 show regressions using data from Moretti (2021). Columns 1 and 4 show linear specification; 2 and 5 show quadratic specification; 3 and 6 show three-piece spline. Standard errors are in parentheses.

scientists in larger innovation clusters is only partially offset by the higher costs of carrying out research in those larger clusters.

Taken at face value, this specification indicates that by moving to bigger innovation clusters, firms will experience productivity gains that are significantly larger than the increase in production costs—a result that is broadly consistent with the increase in concentration of innovative activity that we have seen over the past 30 years. For example, Moretti (2021) reports that the share of inventors in computer science, semiconductors, biology, and chemistry in the top 10 largest clusters is larger today than it was in the 1970s.

Figure 2 shows a graph of the relationship between cluster size and costs. The upward slope in the data is apparent, but what is more striking is the apparent nonlinearity for the cities with the largest numbers of scientists (i.e., the superstar cities). To illustrate this, we show fitted regression lines for a log-linear regression, a regression that is quadratic in logs, and a three-piece spline with cutoffs of log(stock) of −8 and −5. The latter cutoffs were chosen to model the trends in the Lowess smoother and the Local-Linear Kernel Regression. The value of −8 is at the 13th percentile of the log(stock) distribution, and −5 is at the 76th percentile. Visually, these

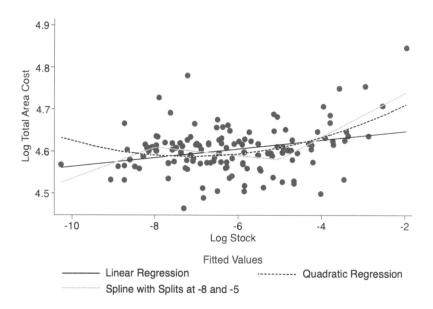

Fig. 2. Total area costs versus area stock. Color version available as an online enhancement.
Note: X-axis is log stock of scientists, and Y-axis is log total area costs. Fitted lines from linear, quadratic, and spline regressions are included.

nonlinear models fit the data much better, reflecting the fact that wages and real estate costs—and therefore total costs—are much higher in a handful of cities than even in other relatively dynamic (and high-productivity) cities.

The second and third columns of table 3 present regression results from these nonlinear specifications. The quadratic log specification (col. 2) suggests a rapidly rising cost for the places with the largest stock of scientists. For example, it implies that for a place at the 80th percentile in the scientist stock distribution, adding 10% more scientists raises costs by 0.46%, about four times the estimate from the linear specification.

The spline specification is even more interesting. It shows that for places with relatively few scientists, adding 10% more scientists raises costs by 0.37%. For places in the typical range of our sample, the relationship between cost and stock of scientists is negative and marginally significant, albeit quite small. For places with the most scientists, in contrast, the effect is large, with each additional 10% of scientists raising costs by 0.53%.

For an apples-to-apples comparison, columns 5 and 6 of the table replicate the Moretti (2021) productivity regressions for the same nonlinear specifications, using his richest model of covariates. As noted earlier, the Moretti linear coefficient is much larger (about six times) than the associated linear cost coefficient. But the Moretti productivity relationship is more linear (in a log-log model) than what appears on the cost side. In the quadratic specification in column 5, the quadratic term is statistically significant. But the implied curvature (i.e., increasing returns to more scientists) is limited. The estimated coefficients imply that adding 10% more scientists in a city at the 80th percentile of the distribution (i.e., Kansas City), raises productivity by 0.74%, not too far from the linear specification. The spline specification in column 6 suggests that for scientists in the largest clusters, each 10% rise in the stock of scientists raises productivity by 0.77%. The productivity increase is still above the corresponding cost increase in column 3, which is 0.52%, but the difference between the productivity and cost increases is now quantitatively smaller and not statistically significant (using the 95% confidence interval).

Overall, our nonlinear specifications suggest that the relationship between productivity gains and costs increases varies significantly across areas. Productivity gains from adding scientists are much larger than cost increases in cities that have a limited presence of scientists. At the same time, productivity gains remain larger than cost increases but not by very much in cities with a sizable presence of scientists.

Table 4
Regressions of Log Area Labor Costs on Log Stock of Scientists with Field
Fixed Effects

	Log Area Labor Costs		
Dependent Variable	(1)	(2)	(3)
Log (stock)	.0030	.0576	
	(.0037)	(.0245)	
Log (stock)^2		.0045	
		(.0020)	
1st line			−.0401
			(.0153)
2nd line			−.0187
			(.0064)
3rd line			.0460
			(.0131)
N	399	399	399

Note: Regressions from our data on the log of labor costs by city and field on the
stock of scientists in that city and field from Moretti (2021). Regressions include
field fixed effects. Column 1 shows linear specification; 2 shows quadratic specification; 3 shows three-piece spline. Standard errors are in parentheses.

As noted above, for labor costs, we can go further and analyze field-
specific estimates. We do so in table 4, reestimating our models at the
city*field level for the three fields for which we are able to measure labor
costs: biology, chemistry and materials, and computer and information
research. We create these three fields by assigning the 38 Glassdoor occupations to each category, which allowed us to fully populate each of
our 133 cities.

Our linear regression in table 4 gives a weaker result than for the overall costs in table 3, suggesting that the linear impact of scientist stock on
costs in table 2 is driven by land (real estate) and other physical plant costs.
When we move to nonlinear specifications, we see a more extreme version
of our earlier finding, with a strong positive effect on labor costs from
adding scientists at the top and bottom of the distribution, and no relationship in the middle.

Table 5 assesses the robustness of our results to the source of labor-
cost data. We show our base results using Glassdoor data (cols. 1 and 2),
as well as the estimates that instead use data from the ACS, which provides
large samples but less precise worker classifications (cols. 3 through 6). For
the ACS, we show the results using both unconditional values (cols. 3
and 4) and values conditional on worker age, sex, marital status, race,
and education level (cols. 5 and 6). Using the ACS data reduces the sample

Table 5
Robustness Table for Varying Wage Data Sources for Regressions of Total Area Costs
on Log Stock of Scientists

Wage Source	Glassdoor Wage Data		Unconditional ACS Wage Data		Conditional[a] ACS Wage Data	
	(1)	(2)	(3)	(4)	(5)	(6)
Log (stock)	.0105	.0654	.0195	.1003	.0194	.0999
	(.0038)	(.0251)	(.0052)	(.0243)	(.0052)	(.0244)
Log (stock)^2		.0046		.0068		.0068
		(.0020)		(.0020)		(.0020)
N	133	133	98	98	98	98

Note: Columns 1 and 2 show regressions from our data with Glassdoor wage data of the
log of total area costs on the stock of scientists from Moretti (2021). Columns 3 and 4 instead
use unconditional ACS data for similar occupations and industries. Columns 5 and 6 use
ACS data for similar occupations and industries conditional on observable characteristics.
Columns 1, 3, and 5 show linear specification; 2, 4, and 6 show quadratic specification. Standard errors are in parentheses.
[a]Conditional on age, sex, marital status, race, and education level.

size slightly (from 133 to 98), but we still find results that are consistent
with Glassdoor data.

IV.   Conclusions

Scientists located in areas with a larger stock of related scientists tend to
be more productive (Moretti 2021). This is likely to be an important factor
in explaining the geographical concentration of innovative activity in the
United States and in other developed countries (Kerr and Robert-Nicoud
2020).

Our findings suggest that, on average across US cities, the productivity
gains stemming from agglomeration exceed the higher research costs that
characterize larger clusters. However, the ratio of productivity gains and
costs increases varies significantly across areas. For areas that currently
have a small cluster, the productivity gains of adding an additional scientist are much larger than the corresponding cost increases. For the largest
innovation clusters (i.e., those with most scientists), the productivity gains
of adding an additional scientist are still larger than the corresponding
cost increases, but not by much.

A natural question is whether there is a case for place-based government
technology policy, even in the absence of costs that offset productivity differentials. A first issue to consider in this respect is equity. In a world of imperfect mobility and imperfect information on underlying needs, place has

a role in redistribution (e.g., Gaubert, Kline, and Yagan 2021). Redistributing by place allows a tool for targeting needy individuals that are missed by other redistributive systems. This is particularly important given the findings of Bell et al. (2019) on the intergenerational correlation of patenting.

A second argument in favor of these policies is robustness to geographic shocks—particularly in a nation as large as the United States. Catastrophes, man-made or natural, would have an outsized effect on the United States if they happen to occur in the very few most-agglomerated locations. A broader portfolio of technology centers provides a form of insurance against geographically focused shocks.

A third, and by far the most speculative argument, relates to politics. Gruber and Johnson (2019) point out that one of the reasons for the weak public support in the United States for public investment in R&D is the geographical concentration of such investment. In a nation where voting is related to population and geography, not income or productivity, investments that concentrate their benefits in small geographic (even if densely populated) places may suffer from a lack of political support. Gruber and Johnson (2019) argue that even if there is some efficiency loss from redistributing R&D, the rate of return to more R&D is high enough that more geographic dispersion may lead to more overall efficiency by raising the level of support for public science spending.

Endnotes

Author email addresses: Gruber (gruberj@mit.edu), Johnson (sjohnson@mit.edu), Moretti (moretti@econ.berkeley.edu). We are grateful to Ben Jones, Josh Lerner, and participants at the NBER conference Entrepreneurship and Innovation Policy and the Economy for helpful comments. Lauren Rice provided excellent research assistance. For acknowledgments, sources of research support, and disclosure of the authors' material financial relationships, if any, please see https://www.nber.org/books-and-chapters/entrepreneurship-and -innovation-policy-and-economy-volume-2/place-based-productivity-and-costs-science.

1. In equilibrium, labor and land costs are determined at the city level based on demand and supply forces in all sectors, and productivity may vary across sectors within a city as a function of sector-specific local factors (e.g., the size of that sector's particular cluster). In the case of multiple sectors within a city, the spatial equilibrium should be such that marginal worker and the marginal firm are indifferent between cities. Different sectors may have a different ratio of productivity to costs.

2. Endless Frontiers Act: https://www.young.senate.gov/newsroom/press-releases /young-schumer-unveil-endless-front-act-to-bolster-us-tech-leadership-and-combat -china. Innovation Centers Acceleration Act: https://www.coons.senate.gov/news /press-releases/sens-coons-durbin-announce-legislation-to-expand-federal-randd-extend -tech-economy-to-more-cities-across-america. Federal Institute of Technology Act: https:// khanna.house.gov/media/in-the-news/lawmaker-proposes-federal-institute-technology -and-new-contracting-set-aside.

3. In the presence of large agglomeration externalities, federal place-based policies aimed at shifting additional R&D jobs toward new technology hubs could be costly in terms of overall innovation produced in the United States. Indeed, Moretti (2021) estimates

that in an extreme scenario where the quality of US inventors is held constant and their geographical location is changed so that all cities have the same number of inventors in each field, the overall number and quality of patents produced in the US in a year would drop significantly.

References

Atkinson, Robert D., Mark Muro, and Jacob Whiton. 2019. "The Case for Growth Centers: How to Spread Tech Innovation across America." Report (December). Brookings Institution, Washington, DC. https://www.brookings.edu/wp-content/uploads/2019/12/Full-Report-Growth-Centers_PDF_BrookingsMetro-BassCenter-ITIF.pdf.
Bell, Alex, Raj Chetty, Xavier Jaravel, Neviana Petkova, and John van Reenen. 2019. "Who Becomes an Inventor in America? The Importance of Exposure to Innovation." *Quarterly Journal of Economics* 134 (2): 647–713.
Bureau of Economic Analysis. 2019. "Industry Economic Accounts Data: Input-Output, the Use of Commodities by Industries." US Department of Commerce, Washington, DC. https://apps.bea.gov/iTable/iTable.cfm?reqid=52&step=102&isuri=1&table_list=4&aggregation=sum.
Diamond, Rebecca, and Enrico Moretti. 2023. "Where Is Standard of Living the Highest? Local Prices and the Geography of Consumption." Working paper (July), Stanford University and University of California, Berkeley. https://eml.berkeley.edu/~moretti/consumption.pdf.
Gaubert, Cecile, Patrick Kline, and Danny Yagan. 2021. "Place Based Redistribution." Working Paper no. 28337, NBER, Cambridge, MA.
Gruber, Jonathan, and Simon Johnson. 2019. *Jump-Starting America: How Breakthrough Science Can Revive Economic Growth and the American Dream.* New York: Public Affairs.
Henderson, Rebecca M., Adam Jaffe, and Manuel Trajtenberg. 1993. "Geographic Localization of Knowledge Spillovers as Evidenced by Patent Citations." *Quarterly Journal of Economics* 108 (3): 578–98.
Hsieh, Chang-Tai, and Enrico Moretti. 2019. "Housing Constraints and Spatial Misallocation." *American Economic Journal: Macroeconomics* 11 (2): 1–39.
Kerr, William, and Frederic Robert-Nicoud. 2020. "Tech Clusters." Working Paper no. 27421, NBER, Cambridge, MA.
Moretti, Enrico. 2012. *The New Geography of Jobs.* Boston: Houghton Mifflin Harcourt.
Moretti, Enrico. 2021. "The Effect of High-Tech Clusters on the Productivity of Top Inventors." *American Economic Review* 111 (10): 3328–75.
Robbins, Carol, Olympia Belay, Matthew Donahoe, and Jennifer Lee. 2012. "Industry-Level Output Price Indexes for R&D: An Input-Cost Approach with R&D Productivity Adjustment." Working Papers 0090, Bureau of Economic Analysis, Washington, DC.